ENTEBBE

The Jonathan Netanyahu Story

A Defining Moment in the War on Terrorism

IDDO NETANYAHU

Balfour Books

First printing: June 2003

ISBN: 0-89221-553-4
Library of Congress Number: 2003106315

Originally published in Hebrew by Maariv Book Guild, Tel Aviv, and in English by Gefen Publishing, Jerusalem. Translated from the Hebrew by Yoram Hazoni.

Printed in the United States of America

Please visit our website for other great titles:
www.newleafpress.net

The present work is based on numerous taped interviews, mostly with participants of the raid at Entebbe. I further examined the written reports of the squad leaders from the Unit, describing various phases of the action. Of assistance also were materials from a few broadcasts and published accounts, which helped me complete the overall picture. Unless otherwise indicated, the quotes included are from taped interviews.

CONTENTS

INTRODUCTION

A few minutes past midnight on July 4, 1976, a band of Israeli commandos drove along the silent runways of Entebbe Airport in Uganda. The Hercules transport plane that had brought them receded from view, and before them stretched dark asphalt, hedged on either side by tall African grass. The lead car of the tiny convoy was a black Mercedes waving a Ugandan flag. Close behind it were two Land Rover jeeps. All three cars bore "Ugandan" license plates made of cardboard and drove with their lights on to add to their innocent appearance.

Their target — the old terminal building at the east end of the airfield — was drawing closer. In less than a minute, the men in the three cars would carry out one of the most spectacular and successful commando missions in military annals — the rescue of 105 hostages, held there at gunpoint for nearly a week by both the terrorists who had hijacked their plane and the Ugandan army.

Thirty-odd soldiers comprised the assault force. All belonged to the General Staff Reconnaissance Unit of the Israeli army (known as the "Unit" or *Sayeret Matkal*). Their commander, who rode in the front seat of the Mercedes and who, like his soldiers, wore Ugandan camouflage fatigues, was my brother, Lt. Col. Jonathan (Yoni) Netanyahu. At 30, he was the oldest man in the group.

Several hours later, a phone call from an officer I knew from my own service in the same unit woke me up in my home in Jerusalem. I was still assigned to the Unit as a member of the army reserves, and wondered what it was that he wanted from me at that early hour of the morning. "For the time being, stay at home," he said. "Once all this is over, you can go back to your usual routine." Only half awake, I vaguely remembered a phone call earlier in the week from the Unit, following the hijacking of the Air France plane to Uganda, telling me that I should be ready for call-up at any moment if I was needed. "By the way, can you give me Bibi's phone number in Boston?" added the officer who had woken me up, referring to my other brother, Benjamin Netanyahu, who was then studying in the United States.

I gave him Bibi's number and put the phone down. I had no inkling that a rescue mission had taken place, and even less that anything had gone awry. But along with the rest of the country, I soon found out about the operation, once the first report was broadcast on the radio and everyone in Israel began phoning one another to pass on the news. It didn't take long before I got a call from Bibi. He was overjoyed at the news of the raid and its success, and asked if I'd heard yet from Yoni — there was no question, of course, that Yoni and his Unit were at the center of the action.

Not long after that, I was called at home and informed of Yoni's death. He was the only Israeli soldier who died in the battle.

To the general public, Yoni was virtually unknown during his lifetime because of the secret nature of his work in the army. In less than 24 hours after the safe landing of the hostages and soldiers in Israel, Yoni's name would become a household word throughout the country; his life and person would take their hold on the imagination of countless Israelis.

What hasn't been said about the raid on Entebbe since then? It occurred two and a half decades ago, yet evokes images of legends from the distant, heroic past. An "operation with no precedent in military history," it was called by Drew Middleton, military analyst of the *New York Times*. But it was outstanding not only in military terms. Refusing to knuckle under to blackmail and terror, a beleaguered nation of only three million people sent its finest men thousands of miles away to a hostile land, on a mission fraught with risks. In a world grown almost indifferent to brutality, in which purported disagreement over right and wrong is often merely a cover for moral feebleness and cowardice, the raid on Entebbe touched the souls of men and women across the globe in the most fundamental way possible. For it proved that at least once, even against inconceivable odds, justice could be done and right could win.

No wonder, then, that the raid took on mythic proportions almost overnight. The story was told and retold in countless newspaper and magazine articles, and four different movies, as well as songs and poems. In many different ways, people strove to record this incredible event and reflect on its meaning.

Yet in spite of the plethora of accounts, the true story of Entebbe was not told. For its essential part — the feat of the men from the Unit who planned and prepared the heart of the mission, the rescue itself, who fought to have it approved, and who eventually carried it out — was not portrayed.

Part of the reason for this was that the activities of the Unit my brother headed were closely guarded secrets of the Israel Defense Forces (IDF). The very name of the Unit — General Staff Reconnaissance Unit — was classified information until a few years ago. Even now, a thick veil of secrecy surrounds the Unit and its activities. So reporters and researchers in the early years after Entebbe lacked any ready access to the men who actually fought the terrorists and the Ugandan army. Moreover, even if someone had been able to identify these men and gain access to them, he would have soon found that he was still up against a wall of silence, for the men would certainly have hesitated to speak candidly, if at all, to an outsider.

Perhaps too young to be concerned about what would be recorded for posterity, the soldiers remained content to keep the truth about their role in the raid to themselves. Thus, the official secrecy surrounding the Unit and the strong self-discipline of its soldiers combined to keep key data about the operation hidden from the public eye.

What's more, even the Israeli army never made an effort to record, thoroughly and accurately, the role played by the Unit in the raid. The reasons are manifold and complex, and I will only touch on some of them. One was that Yoni, the Unit's commander, was killed in the operation. Left leaderless, the Unit conducted only a short and inadequate debriefing, which was not recorded. After that session, the officers quickly moved on to reorganize and shoulder the enormous work load the Unit had at the time. By the following day, they had put

Entebbe behind them. Nor was much done by anyone else in the IDF to preserve the details of the Unit's involvement. With one exception, the Military History Division, in compiling its own account of the mission, failed to use information from the actual personnel of the Unit. And the limited information they received was on the whole unreliable and inaccurate.

The result was that the role played by the main fighting force in the Entebbe operation went essentially undocumented. Virtually all that was left of the Unit's part in the raid, and the part of its fallen commander, was the personal recollections of the soldiers. These memories were never recorded and collected, never organized and analyzed. And as the years went by, they were slowly fading away.

It was this situation that I and other members of my family set out to remedy when we began conducting recorded interviews with the soldiers and officers who had participated in the Entebbe operation. The first few interviews were conducted by my brother Benjamin and my father, Prof. Benzion Netanyahu. I continued with the bulk of the task.

Since I was both Yoni's brother and a veteran of the Unit, the members of the Unit were willing to speak to me freely and frankly. Indeed, many were only too happy to be able to give me their side of the story before a microphone. The information was thus gathered piece by piece, one man's account after another, and what emerged was a tale of enormous strength. Such a tale, combining the drama of Entebbe and the tragedy of Yoni's last days, could not, of course, remain in the archives. Thus, this account began taking shape.

Having been a member of the Unit helped me to write this book also beyond the collection of data. My firsthand experience with the workings of the Unit, its way of thinking, and the manner in which it prepared and executed its missions, enabled me to give an insider's account of how such a singular operation as the Entebbe rescue could be put together and successfully carried out. And the "inside" aspect of the story goes further: Yoni, besides being my brother, was also, in one way or another, my commander during most of my years of military service. Such an intimate knowledge of the man who led the rescue force could not but bring an added, critical dimension to the work. Only by acquaintance with the personal side of the major decisions and actions, including the motives that determined them, can one understand how such events could come about.

This book is being published at a time when the world's attention is focused on the issue which was at the heart of the Entebbe operation — the issue of terrorism. In 1976, when the rescue took place, terrorism was often presented as Israel's problem alone. Pundits and experts not only downplayed its threat to Israel (and most certainly to the world), but also belittled the very notion of terrorism, claiming that one man's "terrorist" is merely another man's "freedom fighter." Since then, we've all seen how terrorism has unmistakably emerged as a real and imminent danger to free nations. We now find very few commentators who would categorize acts of wholesale slaughter and indiscriminate murder, directed against citizens of countries such as the United States, as actions of "freedom fighters."

The example of Entebbe and the rationale behind it — of courage in facing cruel killers and defiance in the face of murderous extortion, despite the risks such an unyielding stand entails — have often been disregarded in the intervening years. Indeed, Israel itself abandoned its long-standing policy of non-negotiation and for a time implemented an opposite policy, that of wholesale appeasement to terrorist organizations.

It would not be erroneous to say that the considerable political gains achieved by the terrorists over the years, whether extorted from Israel or from other countries, succeeded merely in upping the terrorists' demands and exponentially boldening them in their actions. In many ways, 9/11 is a logical outcome of this trend.

But the attacks on New York and Washington have finally caused a turning in the world's attitude toward terrorism. Thus, Israel's traditional view of terrorism as being an existential threat and its policy of uncompromising confrontation with it, have been adopted by the world's foremost power, the United States, and some of its allies. Since the World Trade Center bombing, the West has embarked on a long and arduous war against those who wish to destroy it by terrorist means. Will it have the will to persist for the long haul in this struggle and show, over and over again, the kind of courage that was exhibited by Yoni and his men at Entebbe? One does not know for certain, but for the future of our civilization, let us hope that it does.

A feat like the Entebbe rescue requires unique individuals, or those who at the critical moment can rise above themselves to uncommon heights. Without such people, the raid on Entebbe (renamed "Operation Jonathan" by Israel's government in memory of Yoni) would simply have been impossible.

"The Israeli army concentrates within it . . . a type of person who is to my taste," wrote Yoni, not long after he returned to the army as a junior officer in the Unit. "People with initiative and drive, willing to break with convention when necessary, people who do not stick to one solution but are constantly seeking new ways and new answers."

This is the way that Yoni viewed the men with whom he served in the Unit. Not many years after he wrote these lines, he led them to Entebbe. This is their story, and the story of their commander.

— Iddo Netanyahu

Jonathan Netanyahu reading the names of the fallen from Sayeret Matkal, 1976.

CHAPTER I

First the barren expanses of the Sinai Desert, then the green orchards and fields of the Gaza Strip and of Lachish's farming villages further inland, and at last the white stripe of waves breaking on the shore, the city blocks sprawling across the coastal lowlands, and the bare hills rising above them to the east: This was the landscape Yoni watched pass below him on Thursday, July 1, 1976, as he flew into Tel Aviv, in the center of the country. Next to him sat Captain Avi Livneh, the Unit's intelligence officer, who had spent the last several days with him. Over the past year, the two had put in long hours together, working through a day and a night and on through the next. Often their overloaded weekdays would stretch into Saturdays spent in Yoni's apartment over cups of coffee, maps and aerial photographs spread out before them as they drafted plans to the last detail. It was a work relationship, but with time a level of warmth and mutual respect had been added.

Now, on the plane, Yoni exchanged a few words with Avi and, as he looked at the land below, let his mind wander. He may have tried to doze a little too, knowing he wouldn't find time for that when he got back to the Unit. He had just put a sleepless, event-packed week of work behind him, and ahead of him already lay the possibility of a new mission. Though the chances of it actually taking place were close to zero, the idea alone was enough to set his imagination on fire. And what imagination suggested — even if reason did not dwell on it — was that if only constraints were cast aside, if only courage were given a chance, a deed might be done that would be remembered for generations.

* * *

The hijacking of an Air France airliner had been a concern for Yoni all week. Until Thursday, though, it was not his main one; he was caught up in other important operational activities, which are still classified and can't be recounted here.

On Sunday, June 27, several hours after the airliner was hijacked by a Palestinian terror group, a detachment of the Unit was put on routine alert, standard for such circumstances. Not much was known — only that the airliner had been hijacked over Europe, en route from Tel Aviv to Paris, and that about a third of the passengers were Israelis. The plane had been hijacked in the afternoon, following a stopover in Athens.

Yoni, who was busy that day with one of the Unit's operations, was kept informed about what was happening by the Operations Branch of the General Staff. Based on that information, he gave directives by phone to Maj. Muki Betser, the Unit's duty commander that day, and thus the officer responsible for the detachment on alert. Yoni went over various points with him, making sure that certain key officers, men, and materiel were on the base.

"Listen," he told Muki at the end of one conversation, "get everything you can ready now, before it's too late."

At around midnight, Muki arrived with the Unit's contingency force at Lod Airport (now Ben-Gurion Airport), outside Tel Aviv, where they prepared for the possible return of the airliner to Israel. The plane, which had landed in Libya, had taken off from there. But the airliner was now heading south, and the detachment was sent back to the base. Yoni, who was at the Sinai Desert for the Unit's operation, called Muki again for a quick report on what had happened.

"How does it look now?" Yoni asked.

"We're still on alert and waiting to see if the terrorists decide to come here. We've been called back to Lod again."

Yoni gave an order that Yiftah Reicher, the Unit's second-in-command, go to Lod with the detachment, and said that he himself would meet them there, flying in from the Sinai early Monday morning.

As it turned out, the hijacked airliner landed that morning at Entebbe Airport in Uganda. After meeting with his men at Lod, Yoni went back to the base and met with Muki, Yiftah, and other officers. He made a few changes in the plans for storming the airliner, if it did return to Israel, and in the make-up of the force assigned to the task. After the meeting, he resumed his other operational duties. Activity on the base went on as usual, except that the alert remained in force, since no one could know whether the plane would stay in Uganda or for how long.

At this point, on Monday, June 28, the demands of the hijackers, from Wadi'a Haddad's Revolutionary Front for the Liberation of Palestine, had not yet been announced. It was clear, though, that they would soon be issued. The 241 hostages were held inside the Air France jet for about 12 hours after the plane put down at Entebbe. On Monday afternoon they were moved from the plane to the main passenger lounge in the airport's old terminal. That building had once served those entering or leaving Uganda by air, including the Israelis who served in that country in the late 1960s and early 1970s. Since 1972, when the Israeli military and economic advisers had been expelled from Uganda after strongman Idi Amin suddenly tilted toward the Arabs, the airport had been expanded, a new and longer runway added, and a new terminal and control tower built at the west end of the field on a long, low hill over a mile from the old terminal. The old terminal, unused and deserted, provided the terrorists a convenient place to hold their hostages.

The four hijackers — the German man who had led the operation, a German woman, and two young Arabs — were joined in Uganda by three or more Arab terrorists. Among them was the Arab who from then on would be commander of the entire group. In contrast to the tension among the four hijackers while they were on board the plane, the terrorists now appeared relaxed. The difficult and dangerous part of their mission, the hijacking itself, had been a success, and here in Uganda they felt far from any threat.

"The terrorists felt sure of themselves," recounts Sarah Davidson, one of the hostages. "We were trapped in their hands, like a mouse in a cat's paws." Whatever the final outcome of the hijacking — Israeli capitulation or liquidating the hostages — the work before them could be carried out without any real interference.

That day almost nothing was done within the Israeli military to examine options for freeing the hostages, though Lt. Col. Joshua (Shiki) Shani, commander of the Israel Air Force's squadron of Hercules C-130 transport planes, did call a meeting of his staff on his own initiative to discuss the hijacking. He assumed that if any action were taken, his squadron would be involved, since the Hercules were the only military aircraft Israel had that could reach Entebbe. The meeting in the squadron HQ was brief. Shani and his officers mainly discussed flight ranges and possible routes. Given the distance from Israel to Uganda, about 2,200 miles, it was clear that only the squadron's two tanker planes, intended for in-flight refueling, could make the round trip to Uganda on their own fuel supply. A regular Hercules could make it to Uganda, but after taking off again would have only enough fuel for an hour-and-a-half flight.

The next day, Tuesday, June 29, Prime Minister Yitzhak Rabin called a late afternoon meeting of the senior cabinet ministers with whom he consulted on important matters of state. The terrorists had already announced their demands. They included the release of 40 terrorists who were held in Israeli prisons, including Kozo Okamoto, a Japanese enlisted by the PLO, who killed 24 people at Lod Airport in 1972, and the release of a number of other Arab and German terrorists imprisoned in other countries.* The terrorists set Thursday, July 1, at 2:00 p.m., as the deadline for meeting their demands. If the prisoners on their list were not freed by then, they threatened, as was their wont, to execute the hostages. This time, it seemed, Israel had no choice but to submit to the demands of terrorists — the hostages were in a hostile country thousands of miles from Israel, in the hands of Arab and German killers, and subject to the whims of a ruthless African despot.

Nevertheless, Rabin did summon the army's chief of staff, Lt. Gen. Mordechai (Motta) Gur, to the meeting. He intended to ask him whether there was any chance, however slim, of a military solution. Gur received Rabin's message minutes before he was due to fly to the Sinai to observe a divisional exercise. He realized immediately why Rabin had summoned him. With Gur was his adjutant, Lt. Col. Hagai Regev, and Gur told him to contact the Kiryah, the sprawling Tel Aviv headquarters of the Israel Defense Forces.** Stopping the car at a public phone booth on the road to Jerusalem, Regev called the Operations

---

* The terrorists' official list of demands reached Israel only on Wednesday morning. They included the release of 53 imprisoned terrorists by Israel, West Germany, Kenya, France, and Switzerland. Among those on the list were several members of Germany's Baader-Meinhof Gang.

** The official name of the Israeli military, including ground forces, air force, and navy.

Branch commander, Maj. Gen. Yekutiel Adam, and passed on Gur's orders to begin examining options for military action. At the cabinet meeting, in response to Rabin's question, the chief of staff said that the army had not yet looked into ways to free the hostages — but that in principle such an operation was feasible. Gur even made a few suggestions about how it might be done.

The meeting of the ministers ended without reaching a decision. At the time, the Israeli government considered France duty-bound to help find a solution, as the plane was French and most of the passengers were non-Israelis. Apart from this, since the terrorists had made demands involving various other countries, any negotiated resolution to the crisis would necessarily relate to those countries as well.

At 9:00 p.m., Chief of Staff Gur called a preliminary meeting concerning the hijacking, prior to a conference with Defense Minister Peres. About a day and a half had passed since the hijacked plane had landed at Entebbe. Among those at the meetings were Operations Branch chief Adam and Air Force Commander Maj. Gen. Benny Peled. Before the meetings, Peled asked his men to provide him with basic data on the air force's capability to reach Entebbe. "We've got four fully operational Hercules air crews suitable for this kind of operation," he was told by Maj. Iddo Embar, an air force section commander. In principle, Iddo added, it was possible to send a larger number of Hercules planes, as well as Boeing 707s. Peled also decided to speak directly with Shani, the commander of the Hercules squadron, and discussed with him on the phone a number of technical questions, mostly dealing with navigation to Entebbe and the range of the plane with different payloads on board.

Armed with this information, Peled went into the meetings with the chief of staff and the defense minister and spoke strongly against giving in to the terrorists under any circumstances.

"What do you suggest?" he was asked.

"We're capable of putting down a force of over 1,000 men at the airport and taking control of it," said Peled, speaking of a major operation lasting several days. "From our perspective, I don't think there will be a problem with Ugandan air defenses. A problem would only come up if the runway at Entebbe is blocked for some reason — if, for instance, some drunken driver has parked his truck right in the middle." Peled added that a more limited operation was also an option, making use of only four Hercules planes, for which operational flight crews were available.[1]

The idea still lacked form. What, for instance, would be done with the hostages once they were freed? How would the force be brought home? Yet, in light of later events, it is clearly significant that the air force had stated it could reach Uganda, and that it took seriously the possibility of a "soft" landing at Entebbe — i.e., without cover from combat aircraft.

Chief of Staff Gur was extremely doubtful about an operation of that type; Adam, the Operations Branch chief, said the proposal was worth examining further. Besides landing planes at the airport, other ideas for possible action were raised at the meeting with the defense minister.[2]

That same evening, before the meeting with Peres, Adam had assigned responsibility for checking possible military options to Col. Ehud Barak, then on loan to the Operations Branch. Ehud had been commander of the Unit in the early 1970s, when Yoni was second in command, and had extensive experience in planning and carrying out special operations. As commander of the Unit, he'd done much to develop its special operations role, and had personally commanded several such actions, including the storming of a hijacked Sabena 707 at Lod Airport in May 1972, and a nighttime raid inside Beirut in April 1973, in which several top PLO commanders were killed.

Ehud had been given a room at the Operations Branch, where a number of men gathered late Tuesday night, including Muki and Yiftah, who had been delegated by Yoni to attend. It was natural for the Unit to be represented, since it was fairly clear that it would play the central role in any mission of this kind. Also present were representatives from the marine commandos, the air force, and military intelligence. Before dawn, Lt. Col. Haim Oren arrived to represent the head of the Infantry and Paratroops Command, Brig. Gen. Dan Shomron. With him was Lt. Col. Amnon Biran, the Infantry and Paratroops intelligence officer. Biran had been the Unit's intelligence officer some years earlier, and was personally familiar with its intelligence needs for a special operation.

The group had virtually no information on Entebbe. Maj. Embar of the air force, who would play a key part throughout the week in preparing the aerial component of the operation and in coordinating between the air force and the ground forces, came to the meeting with a Jeppesen, the civil aviation guide to the world's airports. The book gave the group extremely limited but vital information. It had a sketch showing the locations of the runways at Entebbe and their lengths, and the location of the old terminal. Muki, who had served for a short time in Uganda in an Israeli military mission, also remembered the building. The field was on the shore of Lake Victoria, the inland sea that is the main source of the Nile and lies between southern Uganda and the western tip of Kenya.

Ehud was convinced that a military action had to be attempted, if at all feasible. Various options were raised; naturally, each man suggested a mode of operation best suited to his own unit. The marine commando representative suggested reaching Entebbe via Lake Victoria by dinghy; Lt. Col. Oren, of the Infantry and Paratroops, proposed parachuting forces into the area; and Muki suggested the ruse of landing a civilian aircraft carrying the rescue force. The proposals, of course, were extremely general; no one could go into details, since almost nothing was known about the target. There was no real certainty that the hostages were in the old terminal, nor was there any information on the terminal itself beyond the small rectangle representing it on the diagram in the guide.

A full-scale assault using the C-130 Hercules transport planes was also mentioned. But the idea was given little attention, since the underlying assumption in the discussion was that Ugandan strongman Idi Amin and his army were not cooperating with the terrorists, but had simply fallen into the role of "hosts," which they would be happy to get rid of. The officers at the meeting therefore thought that only a minimal force, capable of eliminating the terrorists, would be needed. With that accomplished, they assumed, Amin would allow the hostages and their rescuers to leave his country peacefully.

At the end of the meeting, which extended into Wednesday morning, it was decided that the preferred plan was parachuting onto the lake. At this stage, Chief of Staff Gur preferred that option as well, though Peled, the air force commander, was skeptical. The idea was for the air force to drop soldiers of the Unit and the marine commandos, along with rubber dinghies, onto Lake Victoria. After a trip of several hours, the men would secretly land at the airport and attack the terrorists.

Throughout the day, Muki returned periodically to the Unit, at one point instructing the commander of one of the squads that was on the base that week to get five men ready who knew how to swim. "We're leaving tonight," he said, half seriously. "Get ready for a sortie that includes a flight, a drop, and swimming freestyle among alligators." The officer ran around preparing equipment and notifying his men, but after a few hours word came that the mission had been postponed.

Meanwhile, Rabin dismissed the proposals that were presented to him out of hand. "It will be Israel's Bay of Pigs," he said.[3]

Yoni was kept constantly apprised of various ideas being raised. He spoke over the phone with Ehud a number of times, if only to ensure that the operation, if it took place, would be assigned to the Unit. Perhaps he was worried that his absence from the Kiryah would allow another unit to get the prize. On Wednesday, Yoni flew to the Sinai. From there, he spoke with Muki and others to receive reports and to try to get a sense of how seriously a military option was being taken at the Kiryah.

"Listen, the chances of this going through are pretty slim," Muki told him on the phone.

"Is it worth my coming?" Yoni asked anyway, even though it was nearly impossible for him to do so at the time.

"I don't think so. Believe me, what you're doing now is much more important. The Unit's represented here, and outside of us sitting here and planning, there's absolutely nothing going on. In any case, I'm keeping you posted."

That answer must have put Yoni a bit more at ease, though he undoubtedly felt somewhat trapped, unable to get to the Kiryah and help personally to push the military option.

Meanwhile, the second in command of the Operation Branch's special operations division, Col. Shai Tamari, asked Yekutiel Adam to transfer authority for handling the Entebbe crisis from Ehud to him. Tamari had just been freed up by the end of a major exercise, and since standard procedure was for him or his immediate superior to coordinate planning in such matters, Adam granted the request. It was less than a day since Ehud had begun exploring ideas for an operation. That afternoon, Wednesday, June 30, Tamari called a meeting in his office and was briefed on the proposals raised the night before. He ordered each unit to continue its planning and told the team from the Infantry and Paratroops Command to work on developing a larger operation, involving landing transport planes at the airport itself and taking full control of it.[4] While leaving that option open, though, Shai focused mainly on the proposal for a smaller operation in which forces would parachute with rubber dinghies onto the lake and strike from there.

Yet from the air force's perspective, landing at Entebbe remained the most realistic option. Familiar with how airports functioned day to day, the air force's men figured no one would notice a plane landing at night without lights. Even if someone did pay attention, they conjectured, he wouldn't immediately realize what kind of plane it was or what it was doing there. By the time anyone started asking questions, the hostages could be freed. That afternoon, Defense Minister Peres called in Adam and Air Force Commander Peled and asked them how much stock they put in the idea of landing Hercules transports at Entebbe. Both answered that they believed in the idea.[5] With additional officers from the general staff taking part, a brief discussion was held at Peres's office on the size of the force that would be needed to seize control of the airport.[6]

That day, Shomron, the Infantry and Paratroops commander, was at the IDF's Staff College, interviewing newly graduated officers for his command. Whatever type of operation was finally decided on, it was clear that Shomron would command the ground forces since, by virtue of his position, he was to supervise all special operations of this kind. Toward evening, he met at the college with Oren and Biran, his representatives at the meetings at the Kiryah, to go over the different options. Shomron preferred a full-scale takeover of the airport to a limited operation. Throughout the day, the feeling had grown that Idi Amin was collaborating with the terrorists, and Shomron believed the rescue force would have to prevent intervention by Amin's troops during the operation and be able to return unassisted to Israel with the freed hostages. His thinking, in line with Peled's original proposal, was to use a large enough force to take the entire airport and to hold it if the Ugandan army counterattacked. That meant bringing a substantial quantity of troops and equipment to Entebbe, and one feasible way to do that was landing the Hercules planes.

"We sat for two hours . . . and put together an operational concept, an idea. I wouldn't even call it a plan," recalls Lt. Col. Biran. The essentials of the concept seem to have been as follows: The planes would land on the main runway, a considerable distance from the old terminal. The rescue force — made up of men from the Unit — would land first and move toward the old terminal to free the hostages. To avoid alerting the enemy too soon and spoiling the rescue, additional planes carrying reinforcements would land only after the assault on the terminal began. A second force would take the new terminal and control tower; no hostile forces were expected in that part of the airport, but the buildings there overlooked the main runway and the parking area where the planes would wait until the end of the operation. A third backup force would take up positions on the diagonal runway between the new terminal and the old.

The three men also discussed using vehicles of some sort to move the troops and possibly considered bringing in light armored personnel carriers for defensive purposes. In addition, Shomron wanted to find out how many people could be put on the air force tankers. If the released hostages could all be squeezed on board the planes, they could be taken to Israel; at least for them, the problem of getting out of Uganda would be solved. The option of refueling the other Hercules planes from Entebbe airport's underground tanks, suggested earlier by the air force, may also have been raised at this meeting.

In passing, it is worth noting the lack of agreement among various sources on who came up with this concept and how it developed. "It's a *Rashomon*. I'm not sure anyone will ever get to the absolute truth," said Gur, who several years later interviewed the men involved. "There's no way for me to reach a conclusion." Listing at least five different figures who claim credit, he added, "Each has his own version of the story. . . . But in the last analysis, that doesn't really interest me. What matters is that in the end an idea was developed."*

What's clear, though, is that various ideas were raised over the three days between Monday and Thursday, and that the first of these was perhaps the landing of a force at Entebbe by means of Hercules transports. It is also clear that this proposal was given some additional content in the meeting Shomron conducted at the staff college, where he laid down several principles for implementing the idea.

---

* The difficulty in determining the true story of this phase of preparations is due in large part to the death, subsequently, of Maj. Gen. Yekutiel Adam, who oversaw all IDF activities in the operation and who was the overall commander in the airborne command post during the mission itself. Adam was killed in June 1982, in the first week of the Lebanon War, without ever having given his version of events. In fact, the author's brother, Benjamin (Bibi) Netanyahu, had set a meeting with Adam in May 1982 in order to interview him, but was forced to postpone it. Days later the war broke out and Adam was killed.

Late that night, Lt. Col. Oren returned to the Kiryah and presented the conclusions of the meeting to Col. Tamari of Operations Branch. Tamari, dissatisfied, told him to go back to work. The Infantry and Paratroops Command's plan sounded vague and half-baked to him, and he wanted it to be elaborated on and presented to him again. Yet, until the more practical planning for the operation began a day later, on Thursday evening, the idea lacked operational substance. "Nothing was done during that time to treat the subject in depth, to broaden the background planning," says Biran, Shomron's intelligence officer.

Meanwhile, as Wednesday passed, Defense Minister Peres became more convinced that Israel would have to find a military solution to the hostage crisis, even though the IDF had not yet recommended a course of action or developed a real plan of operation. The former head of Israel's military delegation to Uganda, Baruch (Burkah) Bar-Lev, whom Idi Amin still considered a personal friend, had been phoning the Ugandan despot from the Defense Ministry, in the hope of gaining information and having a moderating influence. The contents of these conversations strengthened the defense minister's sense that Amin was cooperating with the terrorists and had no interest in helping secure the release of the hostages. What was more, the terrorists' demands for the release of prisoners in countries besides Israel were making it extremely hard to reach a deal with them. At his meeting Tuesday night with Adam and Peled, who had wholeheartedly supported a military solution, it had been agreed that the IDF would push ahead on the matter. By Wednesday night, the air force had already begun working on the aerial side of the operation in a more detailed way. If it couldn't get the rescue force to Entebbe and bring it home again with the freed hostages, an operation would obviously be out of the question.

Meanwhile, the Infantry and Paratroops Command conducted a trial run of the amphibious option on Wednesday night, with the marine commandos and a Hercules flight crew under Shani's command taking part. The trial revealed a number of difficulties, particularly in parachuting the rubber dinghies onto the water. A second attempt, at midday Thursday, would be more successful. Squadron leader Shani, like many others in the air force, including Peled, had, however, serious doubts about the amphibious plan, and was patiently waiting for the air force's preferred plan to be implemented: landing the Hercules planes at Entebbe and taking the airport.

At midnight Wednesday, Peres called another meeting at his office, and the various options were gone over again. The available intelligence was still so limited that it was virtually impossible to make real plans. That night, though, Yoni received calls from Muki, the Unit's representative at the Kiryah, and others, telling him that the army's top echelon was begin to tilt, at least ever so slightly, toward considering a military operation.

"Wednesday night the phone calls began to come in," says Avi, who was with Yoni, "saying a directive had been issued for the Unit to start planning. It's true that it still looked like the kind of situation where people say things without really being serious. But during the night there were quite a few calls . . . mostly from Muki, who was talking at that point about a paradrop onto Lake Victoria. Muki was pressing us to come, because they kept asking him, 'When can Yoni get here?' and because they were asking him to start planning. . . . With every phone call you said to yourself, 'Maybe there's a chance something will happen after all.' The pressure was pretty serious, and we understood that by the next day, first thing, we'd have to fly back."

So, before dawn, Yoni ordered one of the men responsible for logistics to get things organized as quickly as possible once that night's activities were completed. "Pack it up," he told him. "Something may move with the hijacked plane."

It's hard to know what went through Yoni's mind during the flight to the center of the country on Thursday morning. He'd just had a strenuous week; he was about to throw himself into a new mission of the utmost significance; and the flight offered him a brief rest, almost against his will. He couldn't begin to tackle planning of the operation, since he lacked the most basic information; even the role of the Unit had not yet been defined, although it was obvious that he and his men would be assigned the central task — freeing the hostages.

That week, perhaps during that flight or just before it, Yoni wrote his girlfriend, Bruria, a letter full of sad musings:

> I'm at a critical point in my life, facing a deep inner crisis that
> has been shaking up the way I see things for a while. . . . Most of what
> I've written ends with question marks. If I knew the answers, I wouldn't
> keep agonizing, going back and forth. It's tough; there have been only
> a few times in my life when it's been so tough. . . .

I have to stop and get off now, right away, or soon, and I'll do it, too — but not quite yet.

I remember the sad, crazy cry in a play I saw a long time ago — "Stop the world, I want to get off!"

But you can't keep this crazy world we're on from turning, and the law of gravity won't let us pull free of it. So, like it or not, alive or dead (alive, of course, and as long as possible), you're in.

Yoni hadn't let the men under him see his sadness, but it was there. And now he had reached the point of crisis. His mental state was tied up with his growing, unrelenting, physical fatigue. "I'm tired most of the time," he said in the same letter, "but that's only part of the problem."

For the short time he was in the air, he was free to contemplate where he was in life and where he was going. From the moment the plane touched ground, he would be forced to draw on immense physical and mental strength to overcome his exhaustion and inner tension.

In the next two days — nearly 48 hours of almost continuous work — he would have to plan the ground operation for his unit, coordinate it with his commanders and the other forces involved, and prepare the Unit's men for battle. Above all, he would have to infuse his men with faith in their own ability to meet the test, and to instill absolute confidence among the country's military and civilian leaders in his ability and that of the Unit to succeed in a mission where failure would mean a national catastrophe.

When those two days had passed, he and his small group of fighters would board the Hercules transport that would carry him to his last mission.

* * *

The same morning, Prime Minister Rabin called another meeting of the senior members of his cabinet. Chief of Staff Gur repeated what he had told them the day before: As things stood at the moment, he was unable to recommend any military operation to release the hostages. The IDF, he said, did not have a plan to solve the problem.[7] The terrorists' ultimatum would run out at 2:00 that afternoon. And so, at that Thursday morning meeting, the decision was made to free terrorists held by Israel in exchange for the release of the hostages at Entebbe. To implement the decision, Israel would begin indirect negotiations with the hijackers. "My intention was not a ruse or a tactical ploy to gain time," Rabin later wrote, "but serious negotiations, with Israel fulfilling whatever commitments it made."[8] The decision was approved by the full cabinet in the course of the morning; the opposition, led by Menachem Begin, also officially supported it. After the Israeli decision was made public, the terrorists announced at midday in Kampala, Uganda's capital, that they had extended their ultimatum until Sunday, July 4.[9]

By Thursday afternoon, it should be noted, the military still had taken almost no practical steps to prepare for a rescue mission. A second attempt to parachute rubber dinghies had gone better than the previous night's trial, and a count had been made of the number of people who could be placed aboard a tanker. But only two days before the rescue force actually left for Entebbe, the IDF had still made no real preparations for action: troops hadn't been put on a true combat alert, arms and equipment hadn't been readied, and a real operational plan hadn't been formulated. The military machine had simply not been put in gear.

At the same time, though, crucial information had begun to trickle in, for the first time creating a realistic chance of carrying out an operation. The reports came from several members of a group of hostages who had been released from Entebbe and had reached Paris. All those who had been freed were non-Israelis. In fact, as early as Tuesday the terrorists had shown that they distinguished between the Israeli and non-Israeli passengers.

First, they divided the hostages into two groups. The Israelis, along with several Orthodox Jews from other countries who could be identified by their skullcaps or kerchiefs, had been put in the smaller of the terminal's two passenger halls, while the other passengers had remained in the large hall. The terrorists had put a beam across the opening between the two halls, and they had forced the Israelis to stoop under the beam to get to their new quarters. Although some Jews remained in the large hall, it wasn't clear whether the terrorists were fully aware they were Jewish.

The implications had become clear to the hostages on Wednesday, when the gunmen began releasing some of the hostages from the large hall. Wednesday night the first group of 47 hostages, mainly children and the elderly, were freed and flown to France on a French-chartered plane. The rest, about 100, were freed and flown out on Thursday morning. At Entebbe remained 94 Jews, almost all Israelis, along with the 12 members of the Air France flight crew, including the captain, Michel Baccos. When Baccos had heard on Wednesday that some of the hostages were about to be released, he called the crew together and said he believed they should refuse to leave Entebbe until the last of the passengers was released. None of the crew members voiced objections, and Baccos informed the terrorists of their decision. There's no way of knowing whether the crew members would otherwise have been released.

For the 106 hostages who remained in that distant corner of the world, the prison walls seemed higher than ever. Four days had passed since the moment on the plane when they had become captives. The fates of a mother and her two small sons, of a high school girl traveling alone, of an elderly couple who had survived the concentration camp — all were now in the hands of the "freedom fighters" of the Palestinian revolution; the gunmen's leader, Wadi'a Haddad, would decide what use to make of this human merchandise. In the cramped, mildewed hall, the hostages sat on the floor or spread out on mattresses, and spoke to each other in whispers. The slow passing of the minutes seemed like torture — but at least they kept passing, instead of being cut short by some horror. All felt a confused mixture of hope, despair, and above all, fear. Would a dozen of them be taken out the next morning and shot as the opening gambit in negotiations, their bodies exhibited before the world? Maybe an hour from now? Wondering how they had ended up here, they must have shouted inside: But I didn't do anything to deserve this! And yet, it seems they had committed one ancient sin, from which there was no escape: They were Jews. Perhaps the Israelis among them who had grown up in their own country did not understand what their "crime" was. But to the Arabs and Germans standing guard over them, hands on their weapons, it was obvious, entirely self-evident.

When the released hostages reached Paris, some were debriefed, providing the first hard information on the situation in Entebbe. The hostages reported that the Ugandan army was in control of the building and helping guard the prisoners, and it was clear beyond any doubt that Idi Amin was cooperating fully with the terrorists. It was possible to find out now exactly where the hostages were being held inside the old terminal, or at least where they had been until Thursday morning, and to get some information about the terrorists themselves.

Though most of the intelligence would be passed on to Israel and processed only later, even the first bits made it possible to think of forming a more concrete plan to free the hostages.

Now that the degree of the Ugandan army's collaboration was clear, the IDF's top commanders believed any rescue operation would have to be on a big enough scale to include neutralizing the Ugandan forces and extricating the hostages and their rescuers from the country. "Thursday afternoon Yekutiel met with me and Ehud," says Col. Shai Tamari. "There was a reliable report then that Idi Amin was collaborating. We said that the only choice was an all-out military operation . . . it couldn't be a small group of men arriving, overpowering the terrorists, and then handing themselves over to the Ugandans. We'd have to take control of the airport."

Afterward, Yekutiel Adam called more officers into his office at Operations Branch, including Shomron, the Infantry and Paratroops commander. Adam reported to them on how serious the situation was in Uganda, and he told Shomron that a major operation, in which forces would land at Entebbe, had to be prepared. Shomron announced that he had a plan; Adam responded that it would be discussed at a meeting already scheduled to take place in the defense minister's office. Before the meeting with Peres, Shomron met with several officers at the Operations Branch and went over the various possible approaches. "This wasn't a serious discussion, just a sort of strategy jam session. . . . It still wasn't planning, just talking in generalities," Maj. Iddo Embar of the air force recalls. Shomron suggested bringing as many troops to Entebbe as could be carried in all the Hercules transports Israel had. The air force men continued to stress that it had only four fully operational Hercules flight crews. Muki, too, spoke in favor of a more limited operation.

The meeting with Peres took place later that afternoon. Among those present were Gur, Adam, Peled, and Shomron, as well as several mid-echelon officers, including Barak, Embar, and Brig. Gen. Avigdor (Yanosh) Ben-Gal, who was Adam's assistant. Peled again advocated landing aircraft and troops at Entebbe. Adam explained the basic idea of a night landing of a rescue force that would knock out the terrorists and evacuate the hostages to airplanes. Shomron, for his part, outlined to the defense minister the general plan for taking control of the entire airport that he had sketched out the night before at the staff college and discussed at the "strategy jam session." The air force men said it would be possible to refuel the planes at Entebbe itself, using a fuel pump that the force would bring with it, but added that they preferred to have an alternative refueling stop available, just in case. It was mentioned that the last possible time for the operation, before the terrorists' final ultimatum ran out, would be Saturday night — only two days away.[10]

Gur felt that the suggestions remained too vague and too risky to implement. He also said that without certain pieces of intelligence that were still lacking, he was not ready to approve an operation of any sort. Still, he continued, he would put off making a final judgment on what he had just heard. "The only one who had his feet firmly on the ground — for good reason, since he was chief of staff and bore all the responsibility — was Motta Gur. At that point the operation was resting on such foggy intelligence that no responsible person would have dared approve it," says Maj. Embar. However, with both Adam and Peres voicing intense support for a military solution, it was agreed to begin preparing for a rescue, and Shomron was appointed commander of the ground forces for the operation.

Almost all the officers left the defense minister's room, except for Gur, Adam, and Benny Peled, who remained with Peres. Gur now expressed his opinion more openly: The plan was wild and, most important, impractical, since it lacked the most basic intelligence information.[11] He also doubted the raid could be carried out before the ultimatum expired. "Here Yekutiel interrupted," Peres writes, "and suggested we begin work on a detailed plan, organize a force and train it, and stage a full dry run, on the assumption that the operation could be canceled at any time without any harm having been done. No one objected."[12]

Outside the defense minister's office, Yekutiel Adam ordered the officers involved to work non-stop on planning and preparing for the operation, without taking time out to get the usual clearances and approvals. They should push forward, he told them, unless there were an explicit order to stop.[13] Once again, Adam showed the sense of urgency that had characterized his efforts over the last two days to create a military option. From the moment on Tuesday when Gur asked him to begin checking the possibilities, Adam's interest in the matter hadn't let up. "The one who had pushed hard for the operation was Yekutiel," says Col. Tamari. "He was the one who tried, in spite of everything, to find solutions. Without a doubt, he was the driving force."

At 5:00 p.m., Prime Minister Rabin consulted in his office with Peres, Gur, army intelligence chief Maj. Gen. Shlomo Gazit, and the chief of the Mossad. Gur expressed his opinion that the plan, as formulated, was not realistic, and said he therefore could not endorse it. The mission, as one account would later put it, "looked like a distant dream."[14]

And yet Rabin said efforts to find a military solution should continue. "Bring me something we can implement," the prime minister said.[15] Only a few hours had passed since he and his cabinet had decided to capitulate to the terrorists. To conduct negotiations, with France acting as mediator, he had already sent his adviser on terrorism, Rehavam Ze'evi, to Paris. For the duration of the crisis, Rabin acted simultaneously on two fronts: negotiating in earnest and preparing to free the hostages by force. If he had a realistic option for a rescue, and if the expected casualties were tolerable, Rabin maintained, so much the better. If not, there would be no choice but to release imprisoned terrorists in exchange for the hostages. The Jewish heart, even a statesman's, isn't ruled by the dictates of statecraft. Rabin listened to the families of hostages who came to see him, and he knew he would be unable to sacrifice their loved ones. But he also knew his decision would mean the collapse of Israel's policy of not surrendering to terror — a policy it had taken years to build, at a formidable cost in innocent blood.

Yoni arrived at the Kiryah in the afternoon and was briefed at Operations Branch on how matters stood. "His uniform was still covered with dust," recalls Maj. Embar. "It was obvious he had just come back from several nights in the field. I remember he was very tired."* Yoni also met with Muki, who outlined the information gathered so far and the various proposals that had been made, and briefly met with Shomron. He then returned to the Unit's base and issued orders for some of his officers and men to return from exercises and furloughs. He didn't yet know how many men he would need for the mission, but he wanted to be ready for any eventuality.

---

* Embar says that if his memory is not mistaken, Yoni arrived in time to participate in the "strategy jam session" before the meeting with Peres. Avi remembers that Yoni met with Yekutiel Adam that afternoon.

Afterward, he drove to Paratroops House — a clubhouse for off-duty para-troopers in Ramat Gan, outside Tel Aviv — where Shomron had called an 8:00 p.m. briefing for the commanders of the participating units. Yoni took his intelligence officer, Avi, as well as his two top administrative officers — Yohai Brenner, his head of staff, and Rami Sherman, his operations officer. There they met with Muki and others from the Unit, who came directly from the Kiryah. Yoni sat with them for another brief update before they headed to the conference room.[16] Men from the Golani Brigade, an elite infantry unit, and the paratroops — both under Shomron's command — had been summoned to the meeting as well. But not all of them had come yet, so when Yoni and his companions arrived, they comprised most of those present.

Lt. Col. Biran, the Infantry and Paratroops Command's intelligence officer, was the first speaker. Pointing at a diagram of the airport, he told the assembled officers, "The hostages and terrorists are here, approximately, but we don't know exactly where — or what is going on."

"I didn't have much to convey to them," Biran remembers. "I only knew there were Ugandans outside, maybe two battalions, about 1,000 troops, but I couldn't say anything about the extent of their collaboration with the terrorists. We didn't know the exact location of the hostages, or how to get to them."

Next, Shomron laid out the concept of the mission: the IDF would land ground forces at Entebbe Airport, using Hercules transports, rescue the hostages, and fly them back to Israel. Though Shomron may not have explicitly said so, it was clear that the real fighting would be at the old terminal, where both the Ugandans and the terrorists were located.

Then he made a basic division of the forces and their roles. "We were told: 'The Unit's mission is the old terminal. Of course, there will be other forces guarding the planes . . . and securing the new terminal. . . . Your role will be to mount the assault on the old terminal, free the hostages, and bring them to the plane,' " Avi recalls.

The area of the Unit's operations, the eastern sector of the airport, was a separate complex; it bordered on a military base used by the Ugandan Air Force. The paratroops and Golani would take the new terminal and control tower in the airport's western sector, guard the plane for evacuating the hostages, and serve as the reserve force.

Shomron again spoke of landing as many Hercules planes as the air force could provide. His goal was to bring to Uganda a force so large that it would enjoy unquestioned superiority on the ground. But objections were raised once more. Yoni, Muki, and others expressed their opinion that such an operation would be too cumbersome and could end in disaster. In their view, only enough forces to carry out the assault and to secure the area against attack were needed. "They said Shomron's operation would be too big and unwieldy," says Avi, "and a more limited, compact way had to be found, one that would have a better chance of succeeding."

Shomron, Avi recalls, also presented the other ideas raised in previous planning sessions, such as parachuting forces and arriving by dinghy. "Everything is still wide open," Shomron said.[17]

"The instructions were extremely general," says Biran. "Yoni had logistical questions — how many troops to plan on, how many vehicles — for which we had no answers. Everything was still up in the air. We didn't go into specifics at all about who and how many, how and what. It was obvious that this thing would have to be studied and developed. As for the Unit's plan of action, Shomron didn't get involved. He said, 'These are men who know their job. There's no point for me to interfere.' "

At 7:00 the next morning, Shomron said, he would issue the formal battle orders at a base close to the Unit's camp. There the paratroops and Golani forces slated to participate in the mission would also assemble for the dry run later that day. With this, Shomron adjourned the meeting.

Yoni returned to his base by 10 p.m. Until now, the tension of the crisis had hardly touched the Unit; now, Yoni knew, he had very little time to get everything moving to prepare for the mission. Nearly all the tasks would have to be carried out simultaneously. He asked his secretary at the Unit's headquarters to make urgent calls to staff officers who were away from the base. "At some point I got a call from Yoni's office," says Tamir, the Unit's signal officer, who was at the General Staff at the time in connection with another of the Unit's operations. "I was simply told that he wanted me to get back to the Unit after my meeting, because there was something that had to be discussed."

Yoni then called Muki and Avi into his office, and the planning began. Avi had already managed to make it to an intelligence base and get an update on what was known. Lt. Col. Amiram Levine, a former officer of the Unit, flew to Paris Thursday morning and arrived there in the early afternoon. His task was to gather, through French intermediaries, information from the freed hostages on the status of the terminal, the hostages, the hijackers, and the Ugandan army — in short, the kind of information essential for planning a raid. By Thursday night, his reports started filtering back to Israel. Sometime after Avi had returned to the Unit's base with information, Ehud Barak arrived and stayed for part of the planning. Yiftah Reicher, Yoni's deputy, likewise participated in it. Both Barak and Muki already "knew" the airport from earlier planning sessions. And, as a member of the Israeli military delegation to Uganda in earlier years, Muki had arrived in and left the country via the old terminal.

In the previous discussions Ehud and Muki had attended, the concept had been that a small team of soldiers would slip into the building where the hostages were held and would eliminate the terrorists. Now that it was clear that the Ugandan army was working hand in hand with the terrorists, an entirely different approach was needed. The Unit would have to overcome the problems posed by the presence of the Ugandan forces, take control of the entire area around the old terminal, secure the airport against additional forces that might arrive during the operation, and get the hostages out.

With the limited intelligence obtained so far, key questions remained unsettled, such as which of the two halls the hostages were being held in, how many terrorists were guarding the hostages, did they have explosives, how large the Ugandan force was, and how it was deployed. Even a detailed sketch of the airport was lacking; the group in Yoni's office was still relying on the Jeppesen guide. The book showed the location of the main runways but not all the connecting strips between them, and the buildings were not drawn to scale or in any detail. The group also had a schematic (and inaccurate) sketch of the ground floor of the old terminal, drawn on the basis of what Israelis who had once served in Uganda could remember. Though additional material arrived during the meeting and was used in formulating the plan of action, the lack of requisite information kept them from filling in all the details at that meeting, and was the main reason for the changes and additions that Yoni made later, mostly by Friday afternoon. Certainly, the kind of precise and detailed intelligence the Unit was accustomed to use in preparing its operations was missing. Despite important information that was gathered, much remained unknown even when the forces set out for Entebbe.

The discussion was based on the common agreement that the forces would land directly at Entebbe in Hercules transports. The officers examined the diagram of the airport, and discussed ways to reach the objective after landing. At least at the start, the plane carrying the Unit's men could not be brought too close to the old terminal; the aircraft being large and noisy, it would attract unnecessary attention and be vulnerable to attack by Ugandan units deployed in the area. That meant that the rescue force would have to deplane on the main runway and advance along the diagonal runway to the old terminal. But the more time that passed between the first plane touching down and the actual rescue, the more chance there was that the Ugandans would realize the airport was under attack. The time spent crossing the large airport had to be cut to a minimum, to reduce the risk of the terrorists and Ugandan sentries at the terminal being alerted by the control tower — and to make sure that even if they were warned, they would not have time to understand exactly what was happening and respond. The rescue force, it appeared, would have to come equipped with some type of vehicles in which to drive across the field.

The intelligence Avi had received indicated that about 100 Ugandan soldiers were guarding the building, deployed as a security belt around it and on its roof and balconies. Yoni understood, says Avi, that the key problem would be how to prevent this security belt from effectively opening fire on the small Israeli force approaching the terminal. If the Ugandans delayed the rescue force for even a minute or two, it would give the terrorists enough time to realize that an operation was underway and to massacre their prisoners. It was obvious to Yoni that a standard, frontal assault, in which the force would hit the belt of Ugandans first and break through it, would alert the terrorists and might spark resistance that could keep the Unit from reaching the hostages in time. What's more, if the security belt were indeed so substantial, a frontal assault by the small Israeli force would be quite dangerous. Muki, who had worked with the Ugandan soldiers, voiced absolute scorn for their fighting ability. But Yoni couldn't disregard the difficulties they might create and the casualties they could inflict. Not that he expected the Ugandans to act like an organized fighting unit and return fire in a disciplined way when attacked. But a few panicked Ugandan soldiers shooting wildly would be enough to wreak havoc on the Unit's force and turn the operation into a fiasco.

"Yoni was adamant that we had to find some sort of solution to the problem of the Ugandan security belt," says Avi. So the idea was born of using a ruse to throw off the Ugandans for the crucial moments needed to get into the building. The rescue force, which would be arriving in vehicles under cover of darkness, would pose as a Ugandan army unit, it was decided. "There were enough Israelis who had been to Uganda, including Muki, who could give us specifics on what kinds of vehicles they had, what color they were, and so forth. . . . The question was even raised of the order the Ugandan vehicles would move in — what the procession would look like if, say, an important visitor arrived, like a colonel."[18] Variations on this were also considered, such as posing as Ugandan police. Avi was given the job of finding out how the Israeli force would have to look in either case.

The officers first thought of using three Land Rovers, but later they hit on a plan to improve the ruse: a military motorcade seemingly following Idi Amin in a civilian car. On Saturday night, it turned out, Amin was scheduled to fly back to Uganda from Mauritius, where he was chairing a summit meeting of the Organization of African Unity. There were reports that Amin had already visited the hostages several times, so why shouldn't he come to see them the night of his return?* At the least, the Ugandans might waver rather than open fire, and with a bit of luck, maybe they would let the "motorcade" pass without stopping. The cars would have their headlights on, to appear innocent, and the lights would also make it hard for someone standing in the darkness to tell who was in them. Photos that military intelligence gave to the Unit showed Amin occasionally riding in a Mercedes, and Muki said that all senior officers in Uganda drove such vehicles. That car produced a kind of automatic deference among the Ugandans, Muki said. So it seemed like a good idea to have the rescuers' motorcade headed by a Mercedes. The Unit's men would wear camouflage fatigues resembling Ugandan army uniforms to further confuse the Ugandan soldiers and the terrorists.

But the ruse could only be taken so far. The suggestion was made that the Israelis wear black-face, but since this would increase the chance that they would

---

* In fact, Amin did visit the hostages on his return, but this took place a few hours before the raid.

make mistakes in identifying one another, the idea was dropped the next day. Someone also pointed out that in Uganda, a former British colony, cars drive on the left side of the road, so their steering wheels are on the right. In Israel, though, there was virtually no chance of getting a car with the wheel on the right. "We knew it would be nighttime, and in the dark only someone close enough to talk to you would be able to see whether the wheel was on the right or the left . . . and if it got to that you'd be at the point of no return anyway, you'd have to open fire."[19]

In any case, the hope was that as the rescue force drove down the diagonal runway and then along the access road leading from it to the old terminal, it would appear innocent. Yoni and Muki would ride in a stretch Mercedes along with seven more men carrying light arms. Behind the Mercedes would come two Land Rover jeeps packed with troops, who would be equipped with machine guns and RPG shoulder-fired missiles. The heavy weapons could be used if the Ugandans did open fire while the force was en route, and would provide covering fire once the action began at the terminal. No more jeeps could be taken, since a Hercules could carry a maximum of three vehicles.

The first goal was to get as close as possible to the terminal and "delay opening of fire by the Ugandans as long as possible," explains Avi. If the Ugandans were completely taken in and let the rescue force through without trouble, so much the better. If they did suspect something and tried to hold up the Israelis, or if they appeared to realize that a hostile force was arriving, "the men would have to open fire" and to eliminate the Ugandan soldiers. The Ugandans couldn't be left at the rear, since they could start shooting from behind or sound the alert. If possible, the men in the Mercedes would take care of them, using handguns with silencers. In the worst case, if a noisy gun battle began with the Ugandans, the nine men in the Mercedes would leave the fighting to the men in the Land Rovers, speed to the terminal, jump out and storm the two main halls inside — even if there were not a single other Israeli behind them — to wipe out the terrorists before they could begin slaughtering the hostages.

Even as the discussion went on, Yoni used the intercom on his desk to issue instructions, and called in staff officers to give them orders. To each he briefly explained the outlines of the mission, and instructed him as to the preparations he was to make. Among them was Amitzur Kafri, the Unit's weaponry and special equipment officer, a farm boy from the Galilee. Yoni told him to check into the types of weapons with silencers that could be issued to the men in the Mercedes, ways to neutralize booby traps at the entrances to the terminal or inside, and options for vehicles to use. He also told him to prepare small charges for blowing open any barricaded doors and larger blasts for destroying the vehicles if they had to be left behind.

Meanwhile, the men in Yoni's office began discussing how to take control of the terminal and assigning teams of men to different parts of the building. As the night went on, more detailed intelligence arrived regarding the terrorists' routine of guarding the hostages, their weapons, the location of the Ugandan soldiers in the building, the lighting in the halls, and the layout of the terminal itself. The old terminal was a two-story building about thirty feet east of the old control tower. The main halls on the ground floor faced out toward a parking area for planes, and each had at least one entryway from the outside. At the west end of the building was what had been the passport control and customs hall for travelers entering Uganda. Next to that, in the center of the building, was the largest hall on the ground floor, with two entries from the outside. This had once been the departures hall, and as far as it was known the hostages, or at least some, were being kept here. Past the large hall was the smaller one — once the V.I.P. lounge — where the Israeli hostages had been put after the division of the passengers into two groups and where some might still be held. The old photos showed the building ending here, with an empty lot next to it; only the next day would it emerge that an extension had been built next to the small hall, with rest rooms and additional rooms that were now serving as the terrorists' living quarters.

Taking the large and small halls would be the focus of the attack on the building. A team or two was assigned to each of the three entrances leading into these halls. Other teams were assigned to the main entrances of the other rooms and to the second floor where the Ugandan soldiers had set up their living quarters. One more team, consisting of a commander and the drivers of the three vehicles, would remain on the jeeps outside the building. Its main objective would be to provide covering fire against the high points commanding the area — the control tower and roof of the terminal.

The chances of neutralizing the enemy forces on the roof and particularly in the control tower would be limited, especially at the beginning of the battle. If the rescue force began by laying down heavy covering fire against them and only then advanced into the building, it would give the terrorists time to kill the hostages.

"We knew the control tower presented a threat, and Yoni addressed himself to this. It was mentioned several times as a problem spot," says Avi. "But it was clear that we couldn't begin the action by storming or attacking the tower. Instead, we talked in terms of a force that would be ready to pin down anyone in the tower immediately, even as the building was being stormed, if there was fire from above. If we had started the other way and given the Ugandans and the terrorists warning by opening fire early, I think it would have caused serious damage. We made the decision without feeling good about it. We knew what it meant."

No attempt would be made to take the tower itself, since penetrating such a building would be likely to result in substantial casualties, and in any case the Unit would not have the men needed for it. Covering fire would have to be enough.

The number of men in the rescue force, including Yoni's command team, would be just over 30.[20]* That was the most that could be squeezed into a Mercedes and two jeeps, even once the interiors of the jeeps were altered. No more vehicles could be put on one plane, and Yoni knew — as did those above him who drew up the initial plans — that the rescue could not wait until more planes arrived with additional troops. If the Ugandans saw a number of planes landing, rather than just one, they might realize they were under attack, and the element of surprise on which the mission's success depended would be lost. Reinforcements from the Unit would arrive only after the initial force had carried out the main part of the mission. The Unit's 30-odd men would have to break through the Ugandan security belt, eliminate the terrorists, take control of the old terminal, and pin down any additional Ugandan troops who were likely to remain around it and in the control tower.

Now the planning group moved on to discussing the need for a peripheral security force at a greater distance from the old terminal, to be provided by the reinforcements. "It was obvious to us that taking the old terminal would not be

---

* By the time of the operation, Yoni's rescue party (including himself) had apparently been pared down to 29 men. (See page 49, endnote 20)

enough. We'd also need broader defenses, and we knew we'd be responsible for providing them."[21] To the east of the old terminal, no more than two hundred yards off, was the military base, where a squadron of Mig fighters was stationed. As far as it was known, a battalion or two of Ugandan troops was also on the base. To the north and west of the terminal were numerous smaller structures, some adjoining it and some further off. And to the northeast, just beyond a fence surrounding the terminal area, the outskirts of the town of Entebbe began. To cover the area and the surrounding buildings and to counter any possible threat from Ugandan reinforcements, it was decided that the Unit's reinforcements would need four more vehicles, preferably armored. One would be deployed in the parking area in front of the terminal itself to provide close defense and block any hostile forces coming from the direction of the new terminal; a second would guard the east flank, on the side of the military field; and two more would swing around the terminal and the dozens of small buildings adjacent to it on the north and secure the rear of the terminal.

To bring in the armored vehicles would require two more Hercules transports, each carrying two armored personnel carriers (APCs). Altogether then, the Unit's operational requirements alone called for three transport planes. If indeed only four Hercules were taken, with one designated for returning the freed hostages, almost no room would remain for combat vehicles for Golani and the paratroops. In fact, though, they would only have serious need for vehicles if a large-scale battle broke out and they had to intervene. Their main assignment, capturing the new terminal, was not expected to involve real fighting. What's more, the planes would bring them fairly close to their objective. For the Unit's purposes, then, only four Hercules transports were needed, which matched the air force's preferences.

Yoni now turned to choosing his troops for the operation, starting by putting Muki in command of the teams that would storm the halls. Effectively, he would also be the second-in-command for the Unit's contingent. Yoni had high regard for him as a fighter and an officer from the years they had spent together in the Unit, and especially from the Yom Kippur War, when Muki had served directly under him. Selection of the rest of the men was based as a rule on seniority in the Unit. For the teams that would storm the main hall, Yoni picked a group of men who had gone on a pre-discharge furlough only a few days earlier.

He told the secretaries to call the men and their officer, Amnon Peled, back to the Unit.

Capt. Yiftah Reicher, the Unit's new deputy commander, was put in charge of the force that would secure the second floor. Maj. Shaul Mofaz,* Yoni's previous No. 2, who had left the Unit for a different assignment in the army only a few weeks earlier, after working with Yoni for most of the past year, was put in command of the force that would land in the second and third planes and would be responsible for the peripheral defenses. Shaul had already been summoned back to the Unit at the beginning of the week by Yohai, the Unit's head of staff, and he had spent a day or two at Lod Airport with the Unit's detachment. He had considerably more combat experience than most of the Unit's officers, and though it had seemed to Yohai that Yoni had been angry for a moment that Shaul had been summoned without his knowledge, in the end Yoni was clearly pleased that Shaul was there.

After midnight, the four took a short break in their discussion. Yoni told the secretaries to phone everyone whom he had listed as taking part and who had not yet returned to the Unit. Meanwhile, he summoned the officers who were on the base for the first presentation of the mission. Before beginning the briefing, he crossed the base to where the tactical vehicles were kept, and spoke to Yisrael, who was responsible for them. He explained that a plan to free the hostages was taking shape, and that it required fixing the Land Rovers so that each could carry about a dozen men. Yoni ordered him to prepare six or eight vehicles — most apparently intended for the peripheral defense force if getting armored personnel carriers small enough to load on the planes proved impossible, or if using them turned out to be impractical. During the night, Yoni returned every once in a while to check how the work was progressing. "When I thought they were ready," recalls Yisrael, "I called him and he came back again, this time with two or three other people. They sat on the panels I'd put in, and we went for a drive. We made a sharp stop to see whether they were stable. Yoni asked me to reinforce them here and there, but he basically approved the alterations."

At 1:00 a.m. the officers gathered in the Unit's memorial room for the introductory briefing. A few still did not know an operation was being planned,

---

* Later, chief of staff of the IDF, minister of defense.

and they had been wondering why Yoni was keeping them on base when they were eager to go on home leave after the grueling week in the Sinai.

On the lawn outside this room, the Unit's men assemble every year to mark Israel's Memorial Day and listen as their commander reads the names of those who have fallen while serving in the Unit. The room itself was built by the Unit's men; on its western wall hang pictures of the fallen. The opposite wall is lined with bookshelves. Besides being a place where the soldiers can come to remember their comrades, it is also used by those staying on the base on weekend alert for reading and relaxation. And now and then, as on this night, it is used for meetings. When Yoni arrived, the officers were already gathered inside. Some sat on the carpet, others in armchairs.

Avi hung up a map of Africa. A smile appeared on some of the officers' faces when they noticed the huge scale of the map — a million to one. Avi pointed to a spot on the map, and said: "Here." It was over 2,000 miles away, in the heart of sub-Saharan Africa, in a strange land that not one of them, other than Muki, had set foot in. To the west, the intelligence officer showed them, Uganda bordered on Zaire, to the south Rwanda and Tanzania, to the north Sudan, and to the east Kenya — the only one of the countries that maintained any ties whatsoever with Israel.

Yoni outlined the purpose of the operation — freeing the hostages, most of them Israelis, the rest non-Israeli Jews and the members of the French airliner's flight crew. He explained the basics of the plan, pointing out the particular objectives, and then gave them a timetable for the following day. The officers asked a few questions, and the short meeting ended.

Most of the officers laughed under their breaths when they heard the idea of the mission. It looked too fantastic ever to be approved. They knew the routine: They would get ready, prepare equipment, practice, and, because of the crowded timetable, work non-stop — and in the end nothing would happen. Yoni could also see that enormous obstacles stood in the way of approval, but he spoke to them about it and the chance of getting a go-ahead with total seriousness. Beyond being their commander and not allowing himself to act differently, perhaps there was another, more compelling explanation for his tone. It was as if his attitude, the force of his will alone, would be enough to bring about the objective he so desired.

After the meeting, Yoni returned to his office and, together with Muki, Avi, Yiftah, and others, continued developing the plan. As he worked he was inundated with demands from various officers to include their men in the operation. There was not room for all of them, and he had no choice but to stick to his original list. Danny Arditi, one of the Unit's officers, recalls that only minutes before, when Yoni had been briefing them on the operation, he had thought it was "pie in the sky, the whole thing: illogical, impractical to implement, with zero chance of being approved." Now he came in to demand that all of his men be included, without exception, because he had heard that one would be left out for lack of space. "You'll have to tell one of your men that he can't take part," Yoni said, cutting the argument short. Danny left the office indignant, and as he came down the steps, he ran into Muki and angrily told him about Yoni's decision. Muki tried to calm him down, saying, "There's no choice, Danny, that's the way it is."

Muki entered Yoni's office and suggested that the staff officers get some sleep, since many of them were exhausted from the week's activities. Yoni agreed, and so most of them finally went to bed. Muki also went to his room to sleep. Yoni remained alone. He knew the plan was nearly completed. The next day's schedule had been set, the orders for the initial preparations had been given, and people had begun their work. Now he could go to sleep. His eyes, heavy, nearly shut of their own accord. His body demanded sleep with all its being. But rather than picking himself up from his chair and going to bed, virtually for the first time in several nights, he remained at his desk. With the maps and the diagrams spread out before him, he meticulously went over the plan. As always, in the end he had to decide on everything alone. He needed time to sit quietly and think through the problems that might crop up during the operation, take into account the new intelligence information he had received, polish the plan, and prepare the detailed briefing he would give to the entire force. He knew that the next day, amid the frenzy of briefings, preparations, drills, and presentations to the higher-ups, he would have no chance to do this. The plan Yoni had ready by the next morning, Muki says, "included lots of specifics we hadn't considered. He'd really worked it out to the end. He presented it complete, down to the last detail."[22]

It may be that then, as he sat alone in his office, he saw for the first time the full significance of the operation and the risks it entailed. The people of

Israel had yet to recover from the devastating blow of the Yom Kippur War in 1973. In many ways, the morale of the country had only deteriorated in the three years since. If the operation failed — if the hostages, or most of them, were killed, and if the elite forces of Israel's army were captured or wiped out, far from the country's borders — the effect on the country's spirit would be crushing. His first responsibility was to ensure that the hostages and his men returned safely to Israel. Yet beyond that, he felt his responsibility to the country weighing fully upon him.

"He was very, very thorough, down to the smallest details," remembers Yiftah Reicher, his second-in-command. "He spent the entire night thinking about what had to be done during the mission. It was a case of his obsession with detail, which clashed, really, with his more abstract way of thinking, with his wide view of things — and which also made him more worried than the others."

Yoni considered the issues soberly that night, but he also had absolute confidence in the Unit's ability to carry out the mission, and in his own ability to prepare his forces and lead them — not just successfully, but with the very minimum of casualties. He was well aware of his own talents as a combat officer; everyone who had seen him in battle was aware of them. "Yoni was top of the line," says former Chief of Staff Rafael Eitan, who first got to know him during the battle for the Golan Heights in the Yom Kippur War, which Eitan has called "the ultimate test. "If you compare him to other officers his age, men who were battalion commanders in the paratroops then and are generals today, he was head and shoulders above them. They're great officers, but I'd have to say Yoni was on an entirely different level."

From time to time Yoni left his office to check on matters, such as how the work on the jeeps was being done. In the middle of the night he made a brief visit to the nearby base where the paratroops and Golani men had begun to assemble and where the dry run would be held the next day. Lt. Col. Rami Dotan,* the Infantry and Paratroops Command's quartermaster, met him there. Dotan was preparing the base for the arriving soldiers; urgently needing a work detail to put up tents and move equipment, he had no choice but to ask the commander of the Parachute Training School to lend him air force cadets who

---

* Not to be confused with the air force officer of the same name who was later jailed for corruption in connection with deals with U.S. defense firms.

were at the facility learning to jump. Using cadet aviators was against the army's standing orders, but after arguing with Dotan, the commander gave in and sent them over. It was also Dotan's job to provide combat equipment for the paratroops and Golani forces and to begin preparing the props for simulating the raid, such as the pair of buses that would stand for the new terminal.

Yoni and Dotan knew each other well from the time when Yoni had served as a battalion commander in the Armored Corps and Dotan had been quartermaster for his division. Dotan says Yoni's reason for coming in the middle of the night was apparently to check how the other units' preparations were progressing, even though they were outside his responsibility. "It was typical of him . . . that he was concerned about what was happening outside his immediate area of responsibility," says Dotan. "It was the first time I saw Yoni before the operation. I saw him for three or four minutes. We slapped each other on the back, chatted, said 'How are things?' And you felt that this was a solid guy. But you felt something else, too: that he had the whole world on his shoulders."

Avi, meanwhile went to an intelligence base to receive new information. Among other things, he met with several people who had served in Uganda and who were being debriefed. By now the Intelligence Branch had thrown itself full force into gathering every possible crumb of information on the airport at Entebbe.

During the night, after countless phone calls, it was arranged that the Infantry and Paratroops Command would provide the Unit with Israeli-made Buffalo armored personnel carriers, the only armored vehicles that could fit aboard a C-130. These phone conversations were necessarily curtailed, as Yoni had given a general order that, in any calls made from the Unit, the other party was not to understand that preparations were underway for a rescue operation at Entebbe. To prevent accidental leaks, he had also ordered the operators not to give the soldiers lines to call home. Around dawn, Amitzur Kafri, the weaponry officer, and Yisrael, the tactical vehicles man, left with several drivers to bring the APCs from the base where they were stored. Yoni kept the option open of using the Land Rovers for the peripheral defenses, though. The Buffalos had just been put into service, and the Unit had never tried them. Before making the final decision to take them to Entebbe, Yoni wanted to check them out and make sure they were usable. Meanwhile, Tamir was working on the communications, and at dawn he drove to the General Staff to help prepare the communications net for the operation.

Before daybreak, Ehud also returned to Yoni's office. When he had left Yoni a few hours before, he had gone to the Kiryah with the just-formulated preliminary plan in hand. There he had met with men from the air force and other branches of service and begun developing the blueprint for coordination between the ground forces and the air force. At 1:00 a.m., he and Dan Shomron, along with Maj. Iddo Embar of the air force, had gone to the prime minister's office in the Kiryah. The three were supposed to present the plan for the operation to Rabin. Chief of Staff Motta Gur met them outside the office and asked to be shown what they had. "We spread the map out on the table in front of him and start showing him the different stages. Little by little, for the first time, Motta begins to grasp that he's looking at an operation that's doable under the circumstances we face. . . . And Motta says: 'Okay, leave this to me. I'll present the plan to the prime minister. You guys get back to work.' "[23]

When they came out of the prime minister's office, Iddo recalls, the scene that met them in the Kiryah was "total darkness. The only car parked outside is the one we've come in. Compare that to what you see for every operation in Lebanon, even the smallest one . . . when the lights are all burning and everyone's at work. Here there's only a tiny group of people working, which is already buckling under the load. . . . It just drives home that the General Staff isn't taking this seriously yet."

Ehud returned to the Unit after his visit to the Kiryah. The afternoon before, when Yoni had barely begun to get involved in the effort, Dan Shomron had appointed Ehud commander of the assault on the old terminal, perhaps following a request by Ehud that he do so. In essence, that meant he would be in command of the Unit's forces, with Yoni under him. Shomron explains that he hardly knew Yoni, while he knew Ehud well and felt he could depend on him. Yoni, of course, was miffed by the move. True, he had authority for anything related to the Unit's operational decisions: He had led the planning meeting and had made the decisions there; he gave the Unit's briefings, he would oversee the practice runs, and he would give the men their orders during the mission. Yet the possibility remained that during the rescue itself, Ehud would be giving the orders, or at least that it would look that way from the outside. Ehud, for his part, did not want to miss the chance to lead a mission of such enormous significance. As one of the Unit's staff officers commented later, "Who wouldn't want to be in command of an operation like that?"

Yoni had no intention of letting the matter stand. The actual fighting force at Entebbe would be made up entirely of the Unit's men, and as the Unit's CO, he felt it imperative to have sole command over them. Already the afternoon before, when Muki had told him of Ehud's appointment, Yoni had said, "I don't see any alternative to my being in command."[24] True, he was happy to have advice from a man he respected highly, but he was dead set on working to keep Ehud from being in charge, even if only in a supervisory role.

Tamir says that when he had come to Yoni's office earlier, during the evening planning session, he had sensed for an instant from Yoni's glance and manner that he was uncomfortable with Ehud's presence. The other officers did not share that impression, though.

Now Ehud and Yoni sat alone, and undoubtedly there was tension between them, even if it remained beneath the surface. Ehud went over the entire plan with Yoni, and made a number of suggestions. Though he was taken up nearly completely with the coordinating and preparatory work at the Kiryah, he was unwilling to stop there. For now, at least, he had responsibility for the key part of the operation, and by his nature Ehud wanted to keep as close tabs as possible on what the Unit was doing — not just supervise from above and give general instructions — even though he knew Yoni well and knew he could depend on him.

After the two men finished going over the plan, they climbed into Ehud's car and drove home. They lived in the same apartment building — Yoni one floor below Ehud.

When he got to his apartment, Yoni had an hour or two to sleep before he had to go back to the Unit. On the kitchen table he left Bruria the four small notebook pages he had written to her earlier in the week about his sense of turmoil.

It was a letter full of sadness, but at the end some hope for the future came through. "I trust you, and me, and both of us, to succeed in living out our youth — you, your youth and your life, and me, my life and the last flicker of my youth.

"It'll be all right."

These were to be the last thoughts he would commit to writing.

Endnotes

1. Maj. Gen. Benny Peled, interview; and Eliezer Cohen and Zvi Lavi, *The Sky Is Not the Limit* (Tel Aviv: Ma'ariv, 1990), p. 534.

2. Shimon Peres, "Diary Entries," *Yediot Aharonot*, June 9, 1990, and July 6, 1990; and Cohen and Lavi, *The Sky Is Not the Limit*, p. 534.

3. Y. Ben-Porat, E. Haber, and Z. Schiff, *Flight 139* (Jerusalem: Zmora, Bitan, Modan, 1976), p. 170.

4. Lt. Col. Haim Oren and Col. Shai Tamari, interviews.

5. Israel Defense Forces (IDF) Radio, "To Entebbe and Back," June 1979.

6. Peres, "Diary Entries."

7. IDF Radio, "To Entebbe and Back."

8. Yitzhak Rabin, *Service Card* (Jerusalem: Ma'ariv, 1979), p. 126.

9. IDF Radio, "To Entebbe and Back."

10. The account of the meeting is based on Peres, "Diary Entries," and on interviews with Maj. Iddo Embar and Maj. Gen. Benny Peled.

11. Peres, "Diary Entries"; and Shimon Peres, *Entebbe Diary* (Jerusalem: Eidanim, 1991), p. 79.

12. Peres, "Diary Entries."

13. Lt. Col. Amnon Biran, interview.

14. Ben-Porat, Haber, and Schiff, *Flight 139* , p. 215.

15. Ibid.

16. Moshe Barak (Bichovsky), interview.

17. Avi Livneh (Weiss), interview.

18. Ibid.

19. Ibid.

20. There is some difficulty in determining the exact size of the Unit's initial force due to the conflicting numbers which Muki mentions in his August 1976 interview (34 men at one point, but at another, when he mentions the number of men on each vehicle, they add up to only 31) and the number which Amir, for example, recalls, which was only 29 men. While the interviews with Amir were conducted ten years or so after the one with Muki, it is nevertheless probable that the number he gives is the correct one; for despite the proximity of Muki's interview to the raid, it is evident that the interviewee is not well acquainted with the details of the plan and the makeup of the force, and mis-states, among others, the number of teams comprising the assault party and the number of APCs used by the Unit.

21. Ibid.

22. IDF Radio, "Special Broadcast in Memory of Lt. Col. Jonathan Netanyahu," August 6, 1976.

23. Maj. Iddo Embar, interview.

24. Avi Livneh, interview.

The summit at Masada, overlooking the Dead Sea.

CHAPTER II

We're at the Bar-Meirs' apartment. I leave the living room, where my mother is chatting with Martha Bar-Meir and Tsvi, her husband, and look around for my brothers, who have disappeared on me. I go into Barry Bar-Meir's room at the end of the hall, the room where Yoni spent his leaves while he was in the army, and find the two of them, Yoni and Bibi, sitting on the bed. Barry isn't here; he's left for Italy to study medicine. Yoni is studying math and philosophy at the Hebrew University in Jerusalem after a year at Harvard.

There's an air of conspiracy in the way both of them suddenly turn their heads toward the door as I enter. When I ask them why, Yoni tells me that he's thinking of returning to the army, to Bibi's unit, and makes me swear I'll keep it to myself.

"Tell Uzi to take a look at my service record," says Yoni, going back to his conversation with Bibi. "If he does, I think there's a good chance he'll agree to take me."

"A good chance? He'll snap you up in an instant," says Bibi, and then adds: "That's the problem." There's no hint of happiness in his voice.

Yoni seems encouraged, as if he hasn't noticed the undertone in Bibi's words. "Tell him that if he needs an officer, and you're not willing to go to Officers' Training School, I'll take your place."

"I don't think you really see what you're getting yourself into," says Bibi. "You'll be older than any of the other officers with the same position. And besides, it's no job for a married man. You'll hardly ever get home."

"Bibi, I know what I want and what I'm getting into. Tell him everything I said, including the part about the service record."

Bibi won't let up: "Come back to the army if you want, but to a higher position. It doesn't fit your age or your experience to be a squad leader. And besides, the Unit. . . ." Then he stops, as though he can't quite explain his reservations, even to himself. Gradually, watching his brother's enthusiasm, he gets caught up in it, too, and starts describing all the opportunities that will open up for Yoni. Yet there's something forced about the way his words rush out. As for me, the youngest brother, I'm exhilarated by the scene — by what's being said in half-whispers, by the revelations I'm hearing for the first time.

When we're standing, about to rejoin the "grown-ups" at the far end of the apartment, Yoni warns us not to tell anyone about his intentions — even Tutti, his wife. "I'll tell her when I make a final decision," he says. "Until then, there's no reason to bother her with it." Even though I'm only 16, it strikes me as strange to hear a married man talk that way. True, I know his trait of having to decide alone about anything really important to him. But the words still grate in my ears.

* * *

Yoni has long since enlisted, I've been drafted, and we're walking together, in uniform, in the Judean Desert. The sun beats down on our heads and sweat pours over our bodies. With us are two other soldiers, fellow members of my squad. Nissim, excited to be with a high-ranking commander of the Unit, picks up the pace. A jerrycan of water is strapped to his back, yet he walks at great speed as if it were nothing. I'm already completely exhausted from spending the last two nights at solo orienteering in the Galilee (nearly half our time in training was spent learning to find our way in any terrain, even at night, by memorizing the map in advance). Why can't I sleep like the other guys do during the days between those nights, when we all stretch out in some olive or eucalyptus grove? Why don't the flies on their faces or the hard clods sticking into their backs wake them up, too? Yoni is relishing the orienteering — the exertion, the primeval scenery, and most of all, it seems to me, walking with young soldiers. Still, I can see he's also having a hard time in this heat. Once in a while, when we stop to drink from our canteens, the four of us talk about the sights around us, the orienteering, and the blistering heat. "Sometimes," says Yoni, "when you're walking in real hellish heat, much worse than this, worse than you can take, you look for any shred of shade you can find just to rest for a minute. You'll even stick your head under a lousy thistle, as long as it gives your eyes some shade."

Now it's my turn to carry the jerrycan, and I begin to fall behind a little bit.

"You're in the desert with another person, and you only have one canteen of water," Bibi once presented Yoni with a classic Talmudic dilemma. The three of us were boys, and we were talking in the hall of our house. "Either of you would need to drink all the water in the canteen to save himself. You can't split it. What would you do, take it for yourself or give it to the other person?"

Yoni thought a minute before answering. Then he said, "It would depend on who the other person was. If it were Iddo, let's say, I'd give him the water." I looked at my big brother, who was then 15 years old, and I knew: He'd do it.

Nissim turns around. "Give me the jerrycan. I'll carry it," he calls.

I shrug my shoulders in refusal, and run to catch up with the others. Later, when Yoni offers his help, I pass the load to him.

We're the first ones to reach the finish line, at the foot of Masada.* Yisrael, who had brought Yoni and has met him here with the car, has already made a big cooler of lemonade and a pile of french fries. I sit and drink from one of the tall glasses we've "borrowed" from a restaurant on Dizengoff Square in downtown Tel Aviv where we go on nights out. Time after time I draw cold liquid from the cooler and pour it into my mouth. My need is bottomless. We sit there around the cooler, the five of us, and eat fries. They taste so good that soon Yisrael has to remind me that I should leave some for the others who are on their way. The shadow of the cliffs has already spread over us and the slope leading down to the looking-glass waters of the Dead Sea. The others still haven't arrived; I'm thoroughly content. Yoni finishes eating, says goodbye, and drives with Yisrael to the Unit's base. We stay on for another day of orienteering.

* * *

We're at Ein Fit on the north side of the Golan Heights for urban combat exercises. This is our second time here, and this time the exercises are more elaborate than the last. The deserted town is beautiful, and the plants growing wild in its midst only add to its allure. The houses have stood empty now for nearly four years since the Syrian officers who lived in them abandoned them during the Six

---

* The mountain fortress on the shores of the Dead Sea, which was the last Jewish stronghold in the revolt against Rome. It was besieged by the Roman legions for three years between A.D. 70–73, until it finally fell. In the end, the Jewish families there chose suicide over enslavement.

Day War. The streets of the town slope down and converge at a small square; the spring at its center is enclosed by a wall built, like the houses and the low walls separating them, of black basalt. Between exercises we get some time to rest, and after we wash our sweat-drenched faces with clear spring water, we stretch out around the spring. The open spaces of the northern Golan are spread out before us. Above us lies Za'ura, another ghost town, while below and further off, on the crest of a hill, stands the Crusader castle of Kala'at Namrud. Against the wet skin of my face blows a bracing gust of wind. For this moment, looking out from these heights, I feel as if all the world were mine.

Yoni arrives for the week's concluding exercise. I'm leading the team responsible for covering fire in one of the drills. We're briefed by our commander, and then Yoni adds a few comments before we begin. Among other things, he discusses covering fire. "There's an important rule for the force providing holding fire," he says. "You've got to be ready to act, immediately, under any conditions, to defend the main force — even if it engages the enemy unexpectedly or too soon. You've got to lay down the covering fire without any delay, even if you're still moving and you haven't taken up your position." At the start of the drill, my commander reminds me of what Yoni said, and I can already see that they plan to engage the main force while I'm still moving towards my position. I run through an alley with my team. As I expect, the engagement comes early, and I open fire immediately. The drill itself, like most drills, follows a predictable pattern, but the lesson is etched into my memory.

That day we conduct another exercise, in which we take a group of houses. During one part I make a clumsy assault — my body upright and exposed, my movements slow and awkward. Yoni dresses me down, as he does others who have performed poorly, and then he demonstrates how to cut across the courtyard between the houses to burst into the building on the far side. For the first time in my life I get to see how someone moves when he's a soldier in every limb, every muscle, every step. His control of his body is absolute. Fast, agile, he leaps from a window into the courtyard, fires from behind the cover of a half-ruined wall, darts forward in a crouch under the wide window next to the door of the far house, and bursts through the door in a blaze of gunfire. The whole performance lasts but a few seconds. "That's how you do it," he says as he stands, still panting a bit, before us.

* * *

We're gathered — a very large group — on the lawn between the officers' quarters and the hut of the canteen. We're leaving soon for an extended tour in the Gaza Strip to take part in the final stages of Southern Command chief Maj. Gen. Ariel Sharon's 1971 campaign to wipe out Gaza's terror network. Yoni, who will be in command of our force in Gaza, has brought a veteran paratroops officer who has served there recently to give his impressions. In the middle of the briefing, the officer remembers a particular incident and starts laying into certain members of the Shin Bet security service working in Gaza. He turns to Yoni, who's standing to one side, and says, "You just can't believe a word some of them say, not one word. Let me tell you. . . ." We're all ears now, hoping at last to hear something really juicy — after all, this is officers' gossip.

But such talk is anathema to Yoni, especially when it's in front of us. "That's not important now," he says, cutting the man off in mid-sentence and trying to steer him back on course. He sounds uncomfortable, almost apologetic — the officer, after all, is only trying to help us.

A week or two later, in the Gaza Strip, Yoni is briefing us. It's afternoon, and we're sitting in an overheated room in a base in the city of Gaza. This won't be our first action in Gaza, but it will be bigger than anything we've done yet. Yoni is sitting next to a sketch of the objective, and explains the plan for the raid on a large building in the refugee camp, which is suspected of being a terrorist base. We crowd around him. It's the first time I'm taking part in an action that requires a real plan of operation, and I'm astonished by the quantity of detail Yoni deals with in planning a small assault in an area under Israeli control. The raid is set for that night, under Yoni's command. He explains how the various forces will be deployed, how we'll advance in order to seal off all of the clan's houses simultaneously from several directions, and how we'll enter the building. He goes over each part of the operation in depth — simply, detail after detail, as if he has been doing this for decades — to make sure there are no misunderstandings. In the brief pauses between subjects, as he glances at the points he's listed in his notepad, he squeezes his lips tightly together. The expression is so familiar; I've seen it every time I've watched him thinking something over seriously or concentrating on some task. His lips relax now as he goes on to the next stage of the assault, and a smile of pride passes over my own lips.

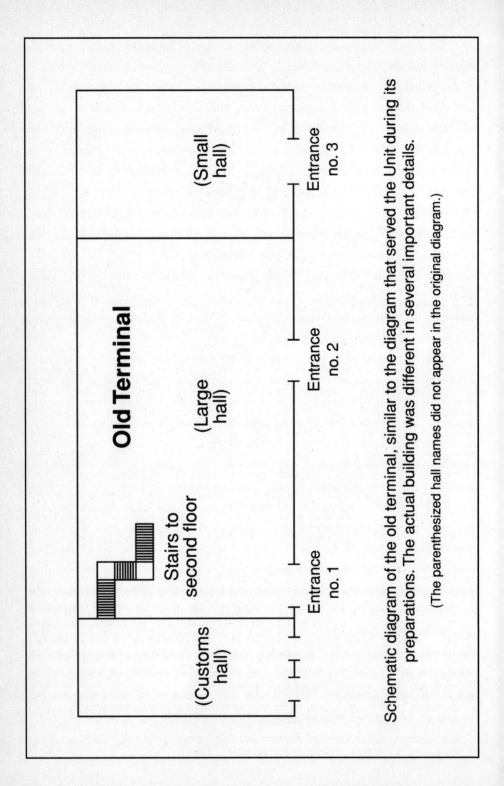

Schematic diagram of the old terminal, similar to the diagram that served the Unit during its preparations. The actual building was different in several important details.

(The parenthesized hall names did not appear in the original diagram.)

CHAPTER III

Amir Ofer hitchhiked to the Unit early Friday morning after a sleepless night. When Yoni's secretary had phoned him at midnight and told him to report to the base in the morning, he got suspicious. "Are we going far?" he asked.

"Very far," she said, and Amir understood. He was one of the group of soldiers who had recently been given their customary pre-discharge leave, and he figured that, as seasoned soldiers, he and his comrades would be assigned to the front edge of the assault. Memories flashed through his mind of earlier rescue operations during his time in the Unit — from Ma'alot* through the Savoy Hotel,** where a member of his squad, Itamar Ben-David, had been killed — and the thoughts of what awaited him kept him awake. In the morning, as he approached the base, he saw that it was buzzing with activity. When he spotted the mock-up of the old terminal, knocked together near the fence at daybreak out of

---

* On the night of May 15, 1974, three terrorists, members of the Democratic Front for the Liberation of Palestine, broke into an apartment in the Israeli town of Ma'alot near the Lebanese border, killed three members of one family, and then went on to take 88 hostages in a Ma'alot school — almost all children from another town on an overnight field trip. When, after 16 hours of negotiations, the Unit stormed the building, the terrorists began shooting hostages. Twenty-two children were killed and 56 wounded. A soldier also died in the assault. All three terrorists were killed.

** On March 5, 1975, eight terrorists from Yasir Arafat's Fatah faction of the PLO landed on the beach at Tel Aviv, seized the Savoy Hotel, and took those inside it hostage. The Unit attacked, killing seven of the terrorists and capturing the remaining one. Three soldiers and eight civilian hostages died in the incident.

burlap sheeting and strips of white tape, he knew that his guess about why he'd been called back to the base had been right.

Inside the base, he ran into Amnon Peled, his commander, who'd arrived the night before. Amnon hadn't yet been filled in on the details, but he already had an idea of what the mission involved. He, too, figured that he and his men would be at the front of the rescue force, even though he had not yet been told just who was on the list. Amir tried to draw some details out of him.

"There's going to be an operation to free the hostages at Entebbe," Amnon told him. "The Unit will spearhead it, and our team will be the tip of the spearhead."

He might have made the remark with mock melodrama, but Amir took it with dead seriousness. "When I heard that, it really scared me. . . . I felt like a huge weight had come down on me. Anyone who says he's not afraid in situations like that is either very brave or very stupid. Me, I was really scared." As it turned out, he had reason to be afraid. Amnon and his men would indeed be the tip of the spearhead, and Amir would be the first Israeli soldier to burst into the hall where the hostages were being held.

When he left Amnon, Amir went looking for the younger soldier to whom he'd passed on his ammo vest before going on furlough. Once he had his old, comfortable vest back, he went over to the supply room to get his equipment, including as many magazines as the vest would hold. Soldiers were already swarming around the counters, in the start of a commotion that would continue all day and night as men received everything on the detailed lists that had been prepared for them.

Out of habit, Amir asked for all the usual equipment. Then he stopped to look at it for a moment. Holding a helicopter landing light in his hand, it finally dawned on him where they were actually going. "We're flying to Uganda, at the end of the earth practically, and I'm asking the guy for a landing light," he said to himself. "What helicopter is going to show up to get us out of there?" He gave the signal back to the supply clerk, then took his pile of equipment to a room in a neighboring barracks to get his ammo vest ready before the briefings and drills began.

Meanwhile, Yoni was giving the "warning orders" for the operation — initial instructions to begin preparations — to the Unit's officers. A few of them had missed the briefing he'd given the night before. Now they heard for the first time, in broad outline, the plan for the mission, including details Yoni had added in his office, while working alone in the late hours of the night. One point in the plan was that Yoni and the other members of his command team would be the first ones to storm the old terminal, through the main entrance of the hall where the hostages were being held. The officers tried unsuccessfully to convince him that he and the command team should take positions further to the rear and leave it to others to storm the hall. Other soldiers told Yoni the same thing when they ran into him outside his office later. "When it comes to the skills, the weapons and all that," one soldier put it, "we've got it down much more than your command team, because we're training all the time."

"But Yoni insisted he would stay in the first team to go in," says Shlomo Reisman, one of the men who talked to Yoni, "especially since Ehud Barak was supposed to be outside and acting as some sort of super-commander." The crucial moment in the whole operation would be the entry into the rooms. For in a hostage rescue, a soldier goes in while ignoring the most basic rules of personal defense in urban combat. He can't throw a grenade into the room or spray it with fire first, and once he's inside, he has to try to distinguish between hostages and terrorists before he starts shooting. And when he does open fire, he can only use single rounds, aiming at particular targets, to avoid hitting the hostages. "For the soldier, it's practically suicide," explains one of the Unit's officers. "You go in knowing you've got one hand tied behind your back."[1] Yoni knew this one moment could decide the entire battle, even if everything else — the landing, crossing the airport, the ruse — went off without a hitch. A second's hesitation would mean disaster. And because of the unprecedented number of hostages, the death toll might easily dwarf even that of the Ma'alot massacre.

And so, says Shlomo, "Yoni wasn't willing to listen to our objections. I think he saw how important it was to set a personal example." What the decision meant for his own safety wasn't lost on his men. "Yoni had every possible reason not to be with the men storming the hall. Putting himself there, of his own free will, taking such a dangerous role — it took real courage, or at least a remarkable sense of responsibility," says Amir.

Once the initial orders were given, a time was set for briefing the entire force later in the morning. The officers dispersed to assign tasks to their men and to begin drills. Yoni and several staff officers left for a nearby base, where Infantry and Paratroops Commander Dan Shomron had set himself up with his staff and would issue his formal battle orders.

Shomron ended the briefing by telling the Unit commanders that they would present their operational plans to him during the morning, and Yoni and his officers returned to their base. Biran, Shomron's intelligence officer, came along. He had some 8mm home movies to leave with the Unit. The night before, during a joint staff meeting of the Infantry and Paratroops Command and the air force, an air force fueling officer had come over to Biran and given him the phone number of a company sergeant who had served in Uganda. "He has movies of the airport," he told Biran. That night Biran drove to the sergeant's house, and found he indeed had two movies that he had filmed at Entebbe: One of Idi Amin taking off for Israel, the other of the pope's arrival in Uganda. He took both, together with the movie projector. He even took the extension cord.

The movies, which he now screened for Yoni and the others, had been shot from atop the old control tower. "The picture they gave was really frightening. The five-story tower had complete command of the entire area — particularly of the entrances to the terminal," Biran recalls. Later in the morning, Biran showed Col. Matan Vilna'i, who would lead the paratroops, a TV news clip that gave a rapid shot of the new terminal. For the first time, Vilna'i got some concept of the building his men were supposed to take. He also stopped by the Unit to get information, as did other outsiders, since the Unit had amassed the most up-to-date, precise intelligence on the airport.

Officers came in and out of Yoni's office constantly, and the deluge of phone calls didn't let up. One of the men who came to see him was Master Sergeant Danny Dagan, at 42 the "old man" of the Unit. Despite the difference of 12 years between him and Yoni — perhaps partly because of it — they had become friends. They had first gotten to know each other during the Yom Kippur War, nearly three years before.

After two years and countless obstacles, Danny succeeded, with Yoni's intercession, in signing up as a career soldier attached to the Unit. His job was training men how to use vehicles.

The tie deepened after Danny showed up at Yoni's apartment one weekend to tell him about a serious problem that had come up in the Unit. "From that talk on, I had the feeling that this was someone really special," says Danny. The two men — along with Danny's wife and Yoni's girlfriend — became closer.

"I told him more about myself than he told me about himself. I never really knew how close he felt to me, or how much I mattered to him. I didn't know how things balanced out. We got together pretty often, at least as often as we could, what with the work in the Unit. We'd spend some time together, eat dinner. I really felt great around him. He was quite educated, way beyond me. Me, I'd learned from hard knocks. With Yoni, everything was a lot deeper. We were very different . . . but he had something so special that it felt good just to have a guy like that around."

Before going into Yoni's office, Danny had talked to Maj. Shaul Mofaz, whom Yoni had put in charge of the peripheral defense force at Entebbe. The two agreed that Danny would give the men a short demonstration of how to drive the armored vehicles, and at the same time check out the new APCs. "I want to be in the operation," he told Shaul at the end of the conversation. "I want to be on your team."

Shaul, who knew Danny well from working with him over the past year, stared at the older man. If they had to do things on foot, Shaul thought, there was no way Danny would be up to it. And yet it was difficult to say no, and he ended up agreeing. "But Yoni is going to have to okay it," he told Danny.

Danny found Yoni sitting by himself with documents and maps spread out before him on the desk. He was still completing the plans, dealing with new problems like the narrow road connecting the town of Entebbe to the open area north of the terminal. The road had been spotted that morning in an old aerial photograph the Unit had received, and now it, too, required attention. Yoni looked up from the desk as Danny came in.

"Now, the big question," Danny said to him. "I'm in on this. . . ."

"Yoni looked at me," Danny recounts, "and didn't know what to say. On one hand, I was close to him. On the other, I already had a lot of children, I wasn't so young, and I wasn't exactly your typical unit commando."

Danny looked for a way to convince Yoni.

"This fight belongs to the whole Jewish people, not just the Unit," he said, alluding to the fact that officially he was not a member of the Unit. "I think you've got to take me." Yoni didn't answer.

"Listen," Danny added, "when it comes to wheels, I'm the best in the world. It doesn't matter that I'm old. Something happens to those machines, I'll be able to take care of it better than anybody."

Yoni looked at him for a long moment. "You're in," he said.

Danny could barely hold in his excitement. Then, suddenly, he burst out: "What'll we do about my wife's party?" Her birthday party was set for Friday night — that evening.

"Leave it to me," said Yoni, and asked his secretary to put him through to Danny's wife.

"I want to tell you something," he said when she got on the line.

"You're not coming," she understood immediately, "neither of you."

"Irena, I promise that on Sunday, Danny and I are going to throw you a bash like there's never been. . . ."

Danny didn't stay in the room long enough to hear the end of the conversation. He hurried out before Yoni had time to change his mind. From that moment until the operation began, he took care to keep his distance from Yoni as much as possible, lest his heavy appearance and grey hair give his friend second thoughts.

Danny had seen combat more than once, as far back as the Sinai Campaign against Egypt 20 years before. But because of his age and present duties, he wasn't thought of as a combat soldier, and including him in the mission sparked resentment among the Unit's men, especially since putting him on the list necessarily meant taking someone else off. The fight over who would go was fierce and non-stop. It was clear that the most veteran soldiers and the combat officers would be counted in, and that younger men who had joined the Unit only recently were likely to stay home. But in between were men part way through their service. The battle was over them. Officers created an immense stir to get their own men included and constantly battered Yoni with requests. Paradoxically, not one of them believed there was the slightest chance that the operation would be implemented. That Friday they all expected that the top brass wouldn't dare approve it. Yet each of them still wanted to have every one of his men included. Despite contrary indications, maybe it would, after all, take place — and then how would it feel to have missed the mission of a lifetime?

"We hassled Yoni incessantly about including our men. It was awful," says Omer Bar-Lev, one of the officers. "At one point, he yelled at me: 'Get the hell out of here, I'm sick of listening to you!' So I had to go about it indirectly. I went to Shaul and said, 'Listen, Shaul, do you really want so-and-so from someone else's squad with you in the APC? I suggest you take a serious guy you know from my squad.' He said, 'You're right, fine,' and another one of my men was in."

So it's easy to understand the frustration that some felt when word got out that Danny was joining the force, and that the staff officers were, too. Among the latter was Yohai Brenner, Yoni's head of staff. He, too, was relatively old, 36, a seasoned combat veteran. Before joining the Unit, he had been the production manager at his kibbutz and had been planning to return to the army and take a transfer course from infantry to the Armored Corps. His desire to return to active service was a response to the deaths of three close friends from his kibbutz, all company commanders, in the Yom Kippur War. Early in the summer of 1975, a few months before he was due to begin the transfer course, he received a phone call from Yoni, who had apparently heard of him from a member of his kibbutz who served in the Unit. "We met at the Kiryah and talked, and I answered his questions. I told him where I had been in the army, what I had done, and what I was doing now. We just chatted, too. Yoni told me he had a few candidates for the job, four or five, and that within two weeks he would interview them all and decide who he'd accept. He told me that he was about to take over the command from Giora, that he was building himself a new staff — at the time I didn't yet have any idea what kind of work he was talking about — and that he was short of people. Two weeks later I got a call from him, telling me I had the job."

Yohai would be a machine gunner in Shaul's armored personnel carrier, next to Danny Dagan, who would be the driver. While feverishly attending to countless organizational details, Yohai made sure not to miss any of the drills and simulations.

In the meantime, Amitzur and Yisrael had returned with the APCs from their storage base, and work had begun on checking them and outfitting them with communications devices, ammunition, and heavy arms. Among the weapons were Dragon anti-tank missiles, included in case the Unit encountered

Ugandan armor. There were also grenade launchers, which were unfamiliar to the Unit's men. But Yoni wanted to take them to increase the force's firepower, and during the day the soldiers were given a short demonstration in handling them.

Later in the morning, men from the Unit took the APCs and Land Rovers to another site, where several Hercules planes had been brought. There they began to practice loading the vehicles, checking how to fit three on board the first plane and finding the best way to secure them. An attempt was also made to load vehicles onto a tanker, but with most of the plane's hold already taken up by the huge fuel tank, the idea quickly proved impractical. Working with the Unit's men were the load masters — the men in charge of cargo — from the Hercules crews, who would also be going to Entebbe. Everything was rehearsed over and over to cut yet another two or three seconds off the time it took to unfasten the vehicles and secure them. Loading the vehicles, like unloading them, had to be done as fast as possible, to prevent any delays in leaving Entebbe.

In charge of the planes was Major Nati Dvir, the squadron's deputy commander, who would be the pilot of Hercules Two. He was surprised to run into Amos Ben-Avraham, a young officer in the Unit who had grown up on the same kibbutz as he had. Nati hadn't known that Ben-Avraham was serving with the Unit, both because of the age difference between them and because Nati had left the kibbutz a long time ago. "Suddenly, I see him — a little guy with freckles who gets on my plane, and takes the jeeps on and off." Naturally, they struck up a conversation — but only about their kibbutz. Not one word was spoken about the operation, because neither could be sure that the other knew the purpose of these drills.

Yoni showed up to see how things were going, probably on his way to or from the Kiryah. In the last year, he had attended many meetings there in connection with the Unit's missions. Unlike some other officers, he didn't stick around the Kiryah after finishing his business to make his presence known and rub shoulders with the top brass. "He hangs around the Kiryah too much," Yoni once said when Bibi asked him how a certain officer was doing. "You know, Bibi, someone who acts like that isn't an officer anymore. He's a politician." In the year since he had taken command of the Unit, Yoni had run into army politics more and more, and it only depressed him. He couldn't bear the way men conducted intrigues and ran personal PR campaigns to advance themselves. Perhaps for the first time, he was seeing corruption in the army with his own naive eyes, and for someone who wanted to believe the best, it was hard to take.

* * *

In mid-morning, Chief of Staff Gur, Operations Branch chief Adam, and the chief of the Mossad met with Defense Minister Peres. "We can implement this," Gur said of the plan that had now been developed. "But before we make the final decision, we still have to examine what the level of risk is."

Peres later wrote: "He was talking about the level of risk to which we would expose the hostages, and not the risk to our forces. Motta was worried that we would not know exactly where the people guarding the hostages were posted. In most operations connected to terror attacks against Israel or freeing hostages, we had had intelligence material."

Or, as Gur himself said at the meeting, "We may face a situation in which we've got no intelligence on the primary objective. The risk this time is greater than we've ever taken on ourselves before."[2]

At 10:30 a.m., Gur met with Prime Minister Rabin. "For the first time, the chief of staff presented an operational plan that, overall, looked reasonable and implementable," Rabin would write. "I felt uneasy about two central aspects of it: how the force could reach the area while preserving the element of surprise, and how to rapidly take control of the area held by the terrorists and the Ugandans before they had the chance to kill the hostages."[3] Rabin would also note that he refused to rely on the possibility of refueling the planes at Entebbe; he preferred that they stop in Kenya to take on fuel, even without advance permission from the Kenyans.

* * *

The lengthy summary of the intelligence on the old terminal arrived now. Based on information provided by the released passengers in Paris and gathered by Levine, it reached the base after Yoni returned from the Kiryah and, as far as the men involved can remember, before the general briefing he was about to give. The cable included details about the layout of the halls where the hostages were being held, provided information on the terrorists and the Ugandans, and more. Avi read the cable to Yoni, who copied down some new facts that seemed important to him in his note pad. He made a few changes in the plan of operation in line with the new information. Then the two of them headed for the briefing room.

It was just before noon. The room was packed; even the younger men who weren't slated to take part in the operation were present. A diagram of the airport and a schematic drawing of the rooms and entrances of the old terminal had been set up on the dais. The list of the personnel for the operation, tentatively divided into teams, had already been prepared.

The briefing began, as always, with the intelligence officer surveying the available information. One hundred and six hostages were being held in the old terminal at Entebbe Airport, Avi said. Which hall they were in remained a question. Until two days before, the Israeli hostages had been held in the small hall on the ground floor, and the others in the adjacent large hall. After the release of all the non-Israelis except the Air France flight crew and some Jews of other nationalities, the remaining hostages might have been moved into the large hall, kept in the small hall, or divided between the two. Most likely was that they were all concentrated in the large hall, which was easier to control because of an interior staircase leading to a landing in the left rear of the hall. A small opening between the two halls made it possible to cross from one to the other, but only while crouching. Seven to ten terrorists, armed with pistols and submachine guns, took turns standing guard over the hostages, patrolling from time to time inside the halls. It appeared possible that the terrorists had placed explosives in the building, but according to the reports that had arrived from eyewitnesses in Paris, they were almost certainly dummies. Common sense also said that the Ugandan army would not have allowed the terrorists to plant real bombs on the ground floor while soldiers were staying on the floor above.

According to the most recent intelligence report, 60 to 100 armed Ugandans were guarding the building; other reports suggested that the number was much higher. The soldiers were working hand in hand with the terrorists. The Ugandans might be deployed in a line about 50 yards from the front of the building, with the soldiers spaced about 10 yards apart from each other; at least once they had also been spotted on the roof. But at the time of night for which the raid was planned, it was possible that most of them would be inside the building, on the second floor.

To the west of the terminal building and almost contiguous with it, Avi continued, was the control tower, which dominated the surrounding area. About 200 yards to the east was the military base, where one or two battalions of ground troops were stationed, along with Ugandan air force Migs. A road connected the north of the terminal with the town of Entebbe. Most of the town stood on a hill overlooking the runways; Amin's presidential palace, guarded by a garrison of troops, was in the town. The buildings at the edge of the town, at the bottom of the hill's southern slope, stood close to the airport boundaries and the old terminal. Just north and west of the terminal were dozens of small airport service buildings. The hijacked airliner was parked at the end of the diagonal runway, southeast of the terminal.

Avi finished speaking. Yoni rose from his seat in the first row and climbed to the dais. In his hand he held a pad in which he had made notes for the briefing early that morning. He glanced at it as he spoke. His voice was calm and vigorous. And yet, some men noticed that there were signs of exhaustion in his face.

He laid out the plan for the operation. The first plane would bring three "soft" vehicles — two jeeps and an additional car, probably a Mercedes. The next two planes would carry the Unit's four APCs. The fourth plane was designated for evacuating the hostages, and would also carry the medical staff and facilities. The Unit's mission was to take control of the old terminal, wipe out the terrorists, free the hostages, eliminate any threat posed by Ugandan soldiers inside and around the building, block the arrival of any Ugandan reinforcements, get the freed hostages to the fourth plane, and guard the other planes and the rest of the Israeli force from the rear until they had finished pulling out of Entebbe.

The primary mission, eliminating the immediate threat from the terrorists, would be carried out by the force arriving in the first plane, which would disembark near the new terminal and proceed in the Mercedes and jeeps. Yoni explained the idea of tricking the Ugandan soldiers by using these vehicles and by having all the men in them wear camouflage fatigues and green berets (which would be changed to white caps once the assault began, to avoid errors in identification). It had to be assumed that Ugandan sentries would surround the building, which made it crucial to try to delay or prevent them from opening fire — which they were likely to do if they realized that a hostile force was approaching.

Any effective fire by the Ugandans could slow the assault force's advance toward the terminal. If the sentries fell for the ruse and let the cars pass, the force could drive almost to the corner of the building. The men would then get out and move toward the doors at a fast walk, since running might arouse suspicion. If the sentries got wind of something or tried to check who the men approaching the terminal were, an attempt would be made to eliminate them with silenced weapons or, if there was no choice, with regular weapons. The moment the Ugandans discovered what was happening or loud gunfire began, the top priority would be to get to the terminal and wipe out the terrorists as fast as possible. The Mercedes would carry two teams, one assigned to each of the halls where the hostages were likely to be. If the jeeps were delayed by fighting of any kind, the teams in the Mercedes would keep going alone, and each would storm its hall as planned.

Yoni moved on to detail the objectives of the teams. In contrast to other rescue missions, the plans for this one had to take into account the chance that the hostages would not be in one place but in two separate halls, or even scattered in more rooms. The enemy would also be dispersed in various rooms, as well as outside the building. The hostages were in immediate danger not only from the terrorists in the room with them, but also from forces surrounding the building and covering the halls from a number of vantage points outside. At each of those points, the enemy had to be silenced totally. All parts of the building and of the area in front of it would have to be taken quickly and simultaneously.

A total of four teams would storm the two halls where the hostages were expected to be: one team was assigned for the first entrance to the large hall, two for the second entrance, and another for the sole door into the small hall. Capt. Giora Zusman was given command of the team assigned the entrance to the small hall, which was located beyond the large hall. Muki would lead the team assigned the western, and closest, entrance of the large hall. Yoni himself would command the first of two teams that would storm the large hall's second entrance. This was considered the most important door for several reasons: it was the central one; it provided greater command of the large hall than did the western entrance; and it was close to the opening to the small hall, which Yoni's team could use if it turned out that some of the hostages were being held in the second room.

A fifth team, under Amnon's command, would remain outside, apparently with Ehud, in reserve. However, while relating for now to Ehud as a senior commander who would be overseeing the force in the field, Yoni did not offer a precise definition of what his role would be. It seems likely that Yoni deliberately left this point unclear. "In any case, Yoni saw himself as the commander of his own force, of the Unit. If Ehud was going to be there in a supervisory role, fine," says Avi. "But from Yoni's point of view, it was absolutely clear that he would command the force carrying out this operation himself." It could be that by now Yoni had concluded, based on what he had been told by higher officers, that Ehud would not be taking part.

Amos Ben-Avraham had rushed back to the base for the briefing, along with the others who had been working with the planes. Now he heard that he would be one of the four men in Yoni's assault team. A few weeks before, he had conducted a combat exercise that Yoni had observed; he knew he had made a good impression and wondered if that was why Yoni had decided to put him on his own team. Amir Ofer, meanwhile, heard that his team, under Amnon's command, would not be storming the building, but would serve as a reserve force, and immediately felt that a great weight had been taken off him. His sense of relief would prove ephemeral, for an hour or two later everything was turned around, and Amnon's team was assigned to storm the central entrance.

Yoni moved on to the tasks of the other forces. Two teams under Yiftah, the Unit's second-in-command, would enter the west wing of the building, once the customs hall for arriving passengers. That was the part of the building that the Unit's men would reach first. Yiftah's main mission would be to move with one of his teams from there to the second floor and clean out the large number of Ugandan soldiers expected to be there. From this floor a door opened onto the landing above the large hall. The landing and the staircase leading from it to the floor of the hall provided complete control of the hall below, making it crucial to prevent any threat to the hostages and the rescue force from that direction.* If the need arose, Yiftah's team would also be able to fire from the doorway at terrorists in the large hall. The second team under Yiftah's command would remain downstairs. Its job would be to finish mopping up in the customs

---

* In addition, the Unit had received an inaccurate report that there was a glassed-in gallery on the second floor overlooking the large hall.

hall, secure the stairs to the second floor, and guard the rest of the building's southwest corner.

Another team, under Lt. Danny Arditi's command, would take the building's east end, where the terrorists' living quarters and some washrooms were located. It would also leave one man outside the building to secure the area from the east. One more small team would stay in the jeeps and provide covering fire if the need arose, paying particular attention to the roof and control tower.

If there were a delay in the arrival of the planes carrying the Unit's secondary force, the small advance force would also have to organize to defend itself and the hostages against attack. Barring unforeseen circumstances, though, broader peripheral defenses would arrive with the Unit's armored force of four APCs under Shaul Mofaz, which was scheduled to land six to seven minutes after the advance force.

Shaul's mission would be to prevent the approach of additional Ugandan forces and to eliminate opposition by any forces in the close vicinity of the terminal or in the wider area around it, particularly from the military base to the east and the town of Entebbe to the north. A pair of the APCs, under Udi's command, would be responsible for the area north of the terminal, and Yoni stressed how important it was for them to block off completely the old road leading from the town of Entebbe to the terminal area. Intelligence received during the preparations indicated that a company of Ugandan reinforcements was at the ready in the town and was capable of reaching the terminal within 20 to 30 minutes.

Shaul's four APCs would leave the airport last, after the evacuation of the hostages and the advance force. Udi's two APCs would leave first, followed by Shaul's pair on the last plane.

Some of the assault teams would be equipped with bullhorns, so they could give clear instructions to the hostages — particularly to tell them in the first moments of the attack to lie down and stay still. The hostages would not necessarily respond as they might in a similar situation within Israel, where they would expect the army to rescue them. At Entebbe, they'd be taken completely by surprise, and how they'd behave during the fighting was far less predictable. The bullhorns would also help afterwards to control the large number of hostages, some of whom might panic and try to flee the building.

During and after Yoni's presentation, the men raised questions. One was concerning precisely when the Unit's armored force would arrive. Yoni's plan called for the first pair of APCs to wait at the landing site for the other pair, which would arrive less than a minute later on the following plane. All four would then move under Shaul's command toward the old terminal. But the soldiers who would be storming the building wanted whatever reinforcements their small force would get to arrive as soon as possible, and argued that it would be better if the first two APCs headed for the terminal the minute they touched ground. By the time the actual operation began, Yoni had agreed that each pair of APCs should start for the old terminal on its own.

A question or two was also raised concerning the possibility that the force would not be able to take off from Entebbe after the raid for one reason or another. "We'll have a huge amount of firepower," Yoni answered, "and if worse comes to worst, we'll take our vehicles and commandeer any others we'll manage to find, and cut our way through to Kenya overland." For this purpose, maps would be provided showing the possible routes to the Kenyan border. The men laughed — only the Unit would come equipped with enough vehicles to carry all its forces, and the paratroops and Golani, they joked, would have to stay behind at the airport.

The men were also troubled that the force landing in the first plane would be outnumbered by the terrorists and Ugandan soldiers. Those assigned to storming the large hall were particularly concerned. There could be, they pointed out, as many as ten terrorists in the hall — more than the number of soldiers initially coming through the hall's two entrances. That, they argued, would violate the simple logic of combat, especially in a fight with terrorists holding hostages, when the attacking soldiers would be exposed and immensely vulnerable. Yoni's answer was that there was no choice. No more than three vehicles would fit on the first plane. Every man would have to read the battle quickly, as it unfolded, and help the others as circumstances dictated. The Unit's force would have the element of surprise working in its favor, he said, and Shaul would be arriving with reinforcements very soon after the assault. If everyone did what he was supposed to, there shouldn't be any problem overwhelming the terrorists and Ugandans and freeing the hostages, even with a relatively small number of fighters.

In that briefing, as on every occasion when he addressed his officers and men, Yoni was careful to project complete confidence that the operation would succeed fully. "Yoni went all out at this one, and he never stopped working to boost our motivation," says Omer Bar-Lev. It wasn't an act: Yoni was sure of himself and of his men. The problem was how to pass this confidence on to each and every man.

"Yoni wasn't uptight," says another soldier. "You saw him speaking — not disinterested, but completely calm and in control, and that gave us extra confidence through all the orders and briefings for the operation. Almost everyone else, when you first hear them speaking, it all sounds great, but when the shooting starts, everything changes. And you hear it even in their tone over the radio, you feel the tension. We'd heard from men who'd been with him in the Yom Kippur War that under fire, or when tension was high, he always kept his cool, never lost control, and we'd had the chance to see that ourselves a year before. When Yoni returned to the Unit, just before he took command, we were assigned to blow up a house in Lebanon where there were supposed to be terrorists. We showed up with bombs, explosives, lots of equipment, and arrived, I think, at an empty building. When we had finished firing and had blown up the house, we lost our discipline a little and started letting go, and instead of getting organized to withdraw, we all started blathering and talking about the stories we'd tell about it. All of a sudden flares went up, and some Lebanese armored car started shelling us. People got a little nervous. And I remember how Yoni suddenly took command, even though he wasn't officially the commander of the force. He said to get organized by teams, count off, make sure everyone was there, and begin moving out. From then on, we'd talk about how, when everyone was feeling the pressure and sort of losing their wits, Yoni was the one who wouldn't. And that's how it was through all the briefings for Entebbe. Everything was done with a definite purpose, without excitement or tension — very businesslike, and very orderly."[4]

Immediately after the briefing, all weapons to be used in the operation would be test-fired. In fact, the men had a great deal of work before them: getting their equipment, preparing and testing the vehicles, going through the drills, and learning the intelligence material, including diagrams and photos.

The meeting ended with a few concluding words from Yoni, and everyone rose to leave the hall. Only a few officers from outside the Unit were present, among them Brig. Gen. Avraham Arnan, who had founded the Unit almost 20 years earlier. Avraham was full of admiration for how thoroughly Yoni had prepared the briefing, and for his treatment of the various operational points. But other than Avraham, as far as anyone remembers, not one officer above Yoni's rank had shown up. This was extremely unusual for a pre-mission briefing, which normally drew top commanders, and perhaps it sharpened the feeling shared by the men that none of the top brass had any intention of going through with this operation, that no one was seriously thinking of sending them so far from Israel, thousands of miles into the heart of Africa.

* * *

After the briefing ended at noon, Yoni drove with Avi and Tamir to Dan Shomron's improvised headquarters nearby to get his approval of the Unit's plan for the operation. The three waited outside Shomron's office for several minutes while he finished up another meeting. Tamir stood to one side with Yoni and asked him what he thought the chances were of the operation going through. Yoni's assessment was that the key problem was getting the go-ahead from the prime minister and the cabinet. For them, he said, it would be a uniquely difficult decision.

Just then, Yoni was called to the phone to talk to the Operations Branch. He came back smiling, and said, "Ehud's gone. He cleared out." That morning Ehud Barak had gotten orders from Yekutiel Adam to leave for Kenya to arrange for the possibility that the planes might land there and refuel after the operation. From then on, Tamir sensed, Yoni acted differently; with Ehud's participation no longer hanging over him, he appeared more at ease. And so it seemed to Tamir that he entered Shomron's room a moment later with a certain excitement.

It took Yoni several minutes to outline his plan. No questions were asked, and no comments made. Shomron accepted it as it was, without amendment.[5]

Afterwards they returned to the Unit to continue the preparations. Apparently, because he now knew for certain that Ehud wasn't taking part, Yoni changed his own team's role in the assault to that of command group alone. It was to move with the first assault team, but it would not participate in storming the building and would remain several meters outside the terminal's central entrance. From there, Yoni would be able to keep control over the movement of forces into the terminal and the action inside, as well as over what was happening outside. If he needed to, he would also be able to enter immediately the hall where the hostages were held. For that purpose he decided to add another man, an experienced combat soldier he knew he could depend on, to the team, which already consisted of Tamir on communications, David Hasin, the doctor, and a combat medic. "I think Yoni chose to put himself in the spot where he'd best be able to switch quickly from heading a command team to taking part in the fighting," says Amir. "He set things up so that if there were a problem, even the slightest one, he would be able to take action. He knew that when it came down to it, at least he could always depend on himself."

The change in his role, made only a short time after the briefing, was only one of the revisions in the plan made during the 24 hours before the raid. Yoni didn't insist on sticking mindlessly to every detail he had laid out the night before. Most of the changes were made in response to new pieces of intelligence; the rest were products either of Yoni's own new ideas or of suggestions made by officers and men during the practice runs.

"It was never really planned from start to finish; because of the lack of time, it was put together in stages. Some of it wasn't even decided in the meeting room or the office, but during the simulation exercises," says Avi. "It was a very daring operation, with a lot of dangers, and I remember Yoni and I talking about how we could get it even better than we originally planned. He was really worried — you always had to keep in mind that there might be dozens of Ugandans on the roof, and new intelligence reports were pouring in constantly, and you began to say to yourself, 'I don't really know what's out there.' Yoni had sat alone in his office part of the time on Thursday night listing points to stress during the briefing to keep casualties to the minimum, given the risks . . . because altogether the picture that emerged was that this wasn't going to be a cakewalk. . . . Our starting point was that it would be hard to get back with everyone safe and sound, no matter how good or bad the Ugandan soldiers were. There were going to be dozens of them, and it would only take one or two of them opening fire for there to be fatalities. You were going to a place, and you didn't know exactly what it would be like — there would be rooms, crannies, a roof, darkness, and you wouldn't know where the fire was coming from. . . . And so during the training Yoni devoted a lot of attention to making sure, for instance, that we had effective enough weaponry. He wanted something good to use against that tower, something better than machine guns, like RPGs, that would really be able to silence it, and the same type of stuff for the armored reinforcements we had coming to the old terminal."

So while most of the basic plan remained in effect, new decisions were being made constantly about the weapons that would be used, the deployment of certain teams, the armored force's firing orders, whether or not to use blackface for the assault force, and other matters. During the practice runs, for instance, the officers decided that the men would be counted at the operation's end, and they agreed on the way to do it. "The plan was really open, and it changed many times," says Omer. "We only had a few hours to do everything. It was all so quick. It was a model of fast work and flexibility, of moving from one set of circumstances to another. It was the ultimate. Nothing could top it."

By the time Yoni returned from seeing Shomron, Amitzur had brought the Mercedes from a garage in the city. When it arrived, the men swarmed around it, hoping to be among those who'd get to ride in it during the operation. Yoni also examined it as soon as possible. "When he first came to see the Mercedes," Yisrael remembers, "his main concern was how many men it could seat without being too packed — how many you could fit up front next to the driver, for instance, and who they should be. He climbed inside the car, he walked around it, he looked it over from the point of view of ammo vests and rifles, considering among other things the possibility that a gun would accidently go off because the car was too crowded. And then, I think, he weighed putting one guy less in the back than he'd planned on."

The Mercedes the Unit had been supplied was a disaster — apparently because no one yet took the operation seriously. The car was white, and the movies and photos that had been gathered showed that Amin used black cars. That meant the car would have to be repainted. But that was the least of the problems. The chassis was old, the tires were worn, the battery was weak, and most important, the engine was shot. It would take long hard work to get it into good enough shape for the operation. Avi R., one of Unit's veteran mechanics, spent hours on just one of the parts that had to be repaired. "We lifted the hood, and I saw that the alternator was at an angle to the belt," he says. "Everything still turned, but not straight. Who knew how long the belt was going to last like that?

It could snap, and we weren't the kind that liked screw-ups. We didn't have a lathe to fix it, so everything was improvised. I took out the base of the alternator, and it turned out that the screws holding it went through holes that had gotten too big, which is why the alternator was crooked. I looked for something we could use instead of that base, but when I couldn't find anything I decided to fix it. I enlarged the holes even more, put in new threading, and screwed in special steel nuts that I also had to thread on the outside. The holes in the nuts were exactly the same diameter as the original screws that had been holding the alternator, but the screws were worn too, so we replaced them with new ones that fit."

But no sooner was one problem overcome than another was discovered. Next was a leak in the gas tank, which had to be emptied so that the hole could be plugged.

Even before this, Yoni had thought of getting a similar car as a back-up for the training exercises, in case the Mercedes didn't arrive or couldn't be used immediately. He knew Yisrael had a big, green Audi, so he called him into his office. The Audi, he knew, had only two seats, instead of the three in a stretch Mercedes, but it was the largest easily available civilian car. After asking the others in the room to leave for a moment, Yoni told Yisrael that he needed his car, and asked his permission to use it. "We'll need to get in and out of it quickly, a lot of times, and with weapons and equipment, and there's no doubt it will be damaged," he said. "But it's very important. We don't have another car."

"No problem," Yisrael answered, and gave Yoni the keys. Before Yisrael left the room, Yoni told him he'd make sure that any damage would be paid for.

As it turned out, the Audi was not used. The Mercedes arrived before the start of the training. The repairs were made before and between the exercises and on into Friday night and Saturday morning. Even then, the men had neither the time nor the tools they would have needed to fix everything wrong with the car. The paint job was completed only minutes before the force left for the operation; by then the car was drivable but was still in far from satisfactory condition. During the day, Danny Dagan went to Yoni's office and asked to pass a note to him. Danny had written that he was afraid they might not be able to use the Mercedes because it was in such poor shape. Yoni asked that they keep trying to fix it anyway; if that turned out to be impossible, they would have to take a third Land

Rover instead. Still, on the slip of paper Danny got back, Yoni had scribbled, "But it's very important that the Mercedes go."

At the same time, Avi's staff worked on paraphernalia for the exterior of the Mercedes. Little flags like those that could be seen in the pictures of Idi Amin's Mercedes were made to fly on the front of the car, and new license plates were cut from cardboard, painted the right color, and inscribed with Ugandan numbers.

In the early afternoon, Yoni and several of his officers held a meeting at the Unit with three officers from the Hercules squadron — the commander, Lt. Col. Shiki Shani, his second deputy, Maj. Avi Einstein, and Shlomo Ovadiah, chief navigator. The three would fly the first airplane, which would bring the Unit's assault force to Entebbe. The purpose of the meeting was to coordinate between the two key units carrying out the operation. "The planning had been done independently by the air force and the ground forces. Each one had laid out its own part separately," says Shani. "After the plans on both sides had been formulated, we met with Yoni and his men . . . and began weaving the threads together so that it would all work."[6]

They sat in Yoni's office for over an hour, with the various sketches spread out on the table. Yoni conducted the meeting. It was decided that the plane would put the Unit's men down on the strip linking the new runway, where it would land, to the old, diagonal runway. The direction in which they would get off the plane was set, as was the side on which they would pass by the plane. They worked through the other details involved in coordinating the operation between them, from small ones like the difference in height between the propellers and the cars that would pass under the wing, to big ones such as where the plane would wait for the released hostages.

"We sat and went over the most minute details, down to the technical aspects of the landing, taxiing, and positioning of the aircraft," says Shani. "We wanted to meet in a small forum to raise and answer questions about how we would respond to all sorts of little problems that might come up, which you never get to in large planning sessions. . . . Yoni handled the meeting very professionally — very organized and relaxed, the way it should be. He'd finish one item and move right on to the next. To a large extent we let the Unit call the shots for this operation, since we were basically providing them with a service. They had particular needs, and we had to try to meet them.

"Each unit presented its problems down to the last detail, because you never know where the needs of the two sides are going to meet. You're likely to think that something is irrelevant to the other guy when it isn't. I specifically remember that we talked about the problem of the runway lights. Yoni wanted to know what would happen if we arrived and the lights were out. He couldn't do anything to help, of course, but he definitely wanted to know. We explained to him the landing technique we had developed, which included using radar. . . . There at the Unit, we put on the final touches and made the final decisions — the kind that could be made only by the men who would actually carry out the raid. In the end we, the commanders of the forces, agreed on things, and that agreement is what counts in practice, regardless of what has been decided elsewhere."

This meeting was the first time Einstein heard which vehicles would be loaded onto each plane, and that his plane would land seven minutes before the others. It was also where he first heard about using the Mercedes, an idea that delighted him. In all, the more he learned about the ground operation and saw how the Unit worked, the more impressed he was. "It was the first contact I'd had with the Unit. I admired very much how efficient and to the point they were, and the way they focused on the right things. . . . As an outsider to this kind of thing, everything they were doing was beyond my comprehension. I didn't attend any of the briefings at the Unit, but just the matters we touched on in that discussion left me with an impression that they were getting down to the smallest details, and really covering everything. . . . The Unit really looked amazing, another world."

Shani recalls that the meeting was frequently interrupted by phone calls for Yoni, and that much of the time Yoni's hands were busy with a silenced revolver that had been brought to the office. Without thinking about it, he disassembled and reassembled the silencer; from time to time, he spun the gun's cylinder, making a long clicking sound. "Yoni was in his chair, with us sitting around him. Every once in a while the barrel would point in our direction. Having this pistol aimed at me every so often was something I really didn't enjoy too much."

Towards the end of the meeting, they also went over the technical side of the full-scale practice run planned for that evening. Afterwards, while still settling the last points, they went out to the porch in front of the office. There they were met by Nati Dvir, Shani's deputy, who had just arrived to serve as the squadron's liaison with the Unit for the evening's exercise. Shani was too busy to handle that job himself; from then until the start of the exercise he'd be concentrating on something else: Chief of Staff Gur had insisted that he and Einstein demonstrate to him that they could make a night landing on an unlit runway.

"I'm not worried about the Unit," Gur had said when he'd come to the squadron to talk to the pilots. "It doesn't make any difference to them whether it's Sdeh Dov Airport in Tel Aviv or Entebbe Airport in Uganda. The question is with you people, whether you can really land the troops there without any problems."* The squadron had in fact been working recently on a technique for landing the Hercules planes on a dark runway. But it hadn't been fully tested yet.

Gur and Air Force Chief Peled picked Sharm al-Sheikh at the southern tip of the Sinai Peninsula for the demonstration. There it would be possible to black out the airfield entirely, and the flight would require Shani to navigate a relatively long distance in the dark, simulating the conditions of the actual operation. Ironically, while Shani had full confidence in his ability to land in the dark at Entebbe, a completely unfamiliar airport, he was not at all certain about Sharm al-Sheikh, although it was well known to him. The landing strip at Entebbe was almost ideally suited for a landing without lights — the runway began at the shore and ran perpendicular to it, allowing the radar to clearly distinguish between the runway and the lake. At Sharm al-Sheikh, the runway was farther inland and ran parallel to the coast, making it much more difficult for the radar to identify it. Shani had therefore decided on his own initiative to fly to Sharm during the day for some practice runs before he had to perform the demonstration for Gur and Peled. He knew Gur would object if he found out, but he also knew that if he failed the demonstration, it would mean the end of the mission. And Shani certainly did not want the operation scratched because of a mistaken

---

* Gur undoubtedly intended to stress to the pilots the immense responsibility they would have. In reality, though, there was a huge difference — psychologically, and of course practically — between a rescue operation in territory under one's own control and a mission in distant territory completely controlled by hostile forces — especially when success depended on the element of surprise.

assessment of his squadron's capabilities by a "ground forces man," even if that man was the IDF's top commander.

Without wasting a moment, Shani and Einstein left the Unit and flew to the Sinai, a journey of just under an hour, to perform the approach and landing at Sharm al-Sheikh several times. They had to finish early enough to get back north by nightfall — so that they could take Gur and Peled back with them to the south.

At the Unit, feverish preparations continued non-stop. Adjustments were made in the cloth model of the terminal as more information on the building came in. The various teams had already begun practicing on the model, their commanders exactingly reviewing the drills while firming up the coordination between the different forces. As one team trained, another prepared equipment. Among other things, a trial was made to check whether the Mercedes could make it up the ramp into the Hercules while loaded down with nine soldiers. Yoni didn't participate in all of these exercises, but he didn't let his other responsibilities, including meetings at the Kiryah, keep him from coming to inspect the drills. "I remember him next to us, at our sides, shouting and urging us on," one soldier says.[7]

Throughout the planning and training, Yoni continually stressed several key points. "What I remember," says Avi, "from conversations we had while driving from place to place, was that he was contending with four central issues: First, how to reach the terminal without losing the element of surprise. Second, how to keep additional hostile forces from entering the terminal. Third was how to identify the terrorists inside the terminal, so we could hit them and not civilians. And finally, dealing with the problem of the control tower."

The time left before the large simulation and the operation itself was quickly ticking away. Every so often Yoni checked that the preparation of the equipment was proceeding apace. One of the Unit's officers remembers him dressing down the men working on equipping the jeeps when he saw that they were not ready by the deadline that had been set. Yoni held another meeting of the officers, at which he settled several more points. For instance, the plan now included scattering explosive charges on the runways near the old terminal as the Unit pulled out and returned to the planes. In the moments before takeoff, Yoni figured, the danger would be very high, since the troops would be inside the planes and defenseless. That's when the explosives would be set off, creating the impression that there was still an armed force in the field. This, it was hoped, would prevent or delay the Ugandans from advancing toward the new terminal during the crucial evacuation and takeoff stage.

At that meeting, too, Yoni decided that the Mercedes would indeed be used. It was now clear what repairs were needed, and another Mercedes could not be obtained, despite the requests the Unit had put in to the Defense Ministry. If the car broke down on the way from the plane to the terminal, Yoni said, the men in it would abandon it and continue onward in the jeeps.

A little after 2:00 p.m. Friday, a bus arrived packed with reserve officers from the Unit. They had returned from exercises in the south in preparation for the following week's armored maneuvers with the Unit's entire reserve force. At the beginning of the week, Yoni had appointed Alik Ron, a reserve officer, to be in charge of the exercise instead of Muki, who was busy working on the Entebbe mission. By the week's end, Yoni had new plans for Alik. Thursday night, during the planning for the operation, Yoni had decided to include Alik in the raid. He wanted Alik, both as an officer and as a fighter, to be alongside him in his own team and told Yohai to call him back that night. Yohai suggested it would be better to wait for Alik to get back to the Unit with the rest of the officers the next day. "If we call him now," he told Yoni, "it'll make the rest of the reserve officers suspicious. They'll descend on the Unit, and we'll be flooded by people demanding to be included in the operation." Yoni agreed, but also stated that Alik would not take part if he arrived after 2:00 p.m., when the combined exercises of the Unit's forces were scheduled to begin.

Yoni and Alik had known each other for years. When Yoni had left his university studies and returned to the army as a squad leader in the Unit, Alik had held the same position. Both were commanding soldiers at the start of their service. The two shared a room and often drilled their men together in the field. A warm friendship developed; in contrast to the usual tension between commanders of parallel squads, they didn't see themselves as competing with each other. Occasionally, Yoni would recommend to Alik a book he was reading, and once he tried to persuade Alik to smoke a pipe, as he did. "It's a very successful combination, a book and a pipe," he said, smiling. "Don't worry, I'll pick out a pipe that'll suit you just right." And as soon as he could, he brought a selection of pipes from home. He laid them out before Alik, examined them like a connoisseur, and finally picked one up and said, "This is a truly superb pipe, and it'll go splendidly with this book." Alik, who had never smoked before, experimented with it a little, but quickly dropped the idea.

They talked about training exercises, day-to-day things, this and that. "Yoni wasn't the type who rushed to become friends with everybody, and he wasn't really very open," Alik says. "You had to dig a little to get to know him. But once you did, the impression he made was tremendous." The two went through a lot together, including a stretch in the Gaza Strip hunting for terrorists, and most of the Yom Kippur War. At the time the war started, Alik had already been discharged, and he was called up as a reservist. Yoni was commanding a group composed mainly of young recruits, but Alik decided to join it. "It had to do with the relationship I had with him — the respect I had for him, and simply that I felt comfortable with him," Alik says.

Their respect for each other grew in combat. Alik was impressed by Yoni's ability to assess and direct a battle, and by his readiness to take any mission he was offered; in fact, he usually proposed missions for his force, brushing aside complaints from many of the men. Yoni, for his part, was impressed by how Alik worked under fire and by his abilities as an officer throughout the war. So it was just as natural for him to want Alik by his side at Entebbe as it had been for Alik to join his force during the war. It meant having a level-headed officer who wouldn't lose his cool if problems arose.

The reservists' ride back to the Unit didn't go quickly. The officers certainly knew about the Air France hijacking, and they even knew the subject was being discussed in the army and at the Unit in particular. But they had experience with such discussions and wrote them off as meaningless, without a chance of leading anywhere. On the way back they stopped for ice cream. When they arrived at the base, they hurried to clean their weapons and turn in their equipment, so they could leave for the weekend as soon as possible. Alik noticed the frenzied atmosphere on the base, but failed to make the connection with a possible action at Entebbe. When a staff officer came up and said, "Get over to Yoni, quick. You're late," he suddenly realized what was up.

When Yoni saw Alik walk into his office, he looked at his watch and said, "Look, you're half an hour late. Never mind, get moving and get yourself organized.

We're behind. We've got to hurry up and start practicing." He gave Alik a list of what he would need, and said that detailed explanations would come later; there was no time now. Before Alik walked out, Yoni warned him, "Do everything fast, but make sure the reservists don't catch on."

Alik went quickly to the supply room. The reserve officers were standing there turning in their equipment as he signed his out — and yet no one noticed. "They were so interested in getting home that they were oblivious. They just kept looking at the storeroom counter and at the bus that was waiting for them." The minutes ticked slowly by; Alik stood there tensely, afraid the men crowded around him would notice his strange behavior. He kept trying to cover the items he was receiving, like the camouflage fatigues and the green beret, which stood out as particularly odd. Finally, when he'd received everything he wanted, he moved to the next window — the armory. There he went to the trouble of returning the Galil assault rifle he had been shooting all week, in exchange for an AK-47 he had never test-fired. The Israeli-made Galil, which was just being brought into service, had fired well during the exercise, but by force of habit it never even occurred to Alik to take anything but an AK-47 on the operation.

He took the whole pile to one of the rooms in the officers' quarters and dumped it on a bed. As he quickly arranged everything, one of the other reserve officers walked in. "Well, we're going," he said.

"I'm not going with you," Alik said. "I'll get home later with Muki."

"You out of your mind? Muki'll be here till midnight. Come on, the bus is waiting. Let's go."

"Lay off, I'm tired," Alik insisted. "I'll lie down here with a paper and rest. Whenever Muki's ready, I'll go with him. I'm in no hurry."

The other man gave him a strange look. "Come on, you can sleep on the bus. What do you think the rest of us are going to do?"

The heap of equipment sat on the bed, under the reservist's eyes. Alik played up how tired he was. "Enough already," he said, yawning. "I'm practically asleep. In another second, I'm going to get into this bed and I'll be out."

The other man finally gave up. "Fine. You want to be crazy, it's your problem," he mumbled, and left to join the other officers waiting on the bus that would take them home.

After the reservist left, Alik peered through the crack of the door and waited impatiently for the bus to leave the base. Meanwhile he noticed the exercises underway with the vehicles just past the fence of the base. As soon as the bus disappeared, he burst out the door and ran to join the rest of the force.

Yoni briefly explained to Alik where he belonged, with him in the command team. He introduced him to the other members of the team, David and Tamir, who were already sitting alongside the other soldiers in the jeep. Alik hadn't met them before. "Whose squad are you from?" he asked David Hasin, the doctor, who looked so young that Alik thought he was one of the regular soldiers. After he heard that David was a doctor, he turned to Tamir. "And you?" he asked. "Signal officer," said Tamir. Since Alik had no time to find out what combat experience they had, he said only, "We can't talk now. Let me just say one thing. Every time I turn my head I want to see you guys next to me. That's all."

As it turned out, Alik was the only reservist from the Unit to take part in the operation. There were others who tried to join but didn't succeed. The Unit received more than a few phone calls that day from reservists who had heard rumors that a mission was planned and wanted to know where things stood. One or two even showed up in person, hoping to take part. All were turned away.

The exercises continued throughout the afternoon. The assault on the terminal was rehearsed again and again. The officers carefully timed how long it took to deplane, to drive to the old terminal, to jump from the cars and storm the building. "From the instant the vehicles stop, there can't be any delay. We have to get to the entrances as fast as possible," Yoni stressed over and over, repeating what he'd said at the briefing. "At the crucial moment, you each have to act as if you're the only one there, and it's all up to you." In the Mercedes, the soldiers practiced different positions for holding their weapons at the ready and firing them — AK-47 or pistol, left side or right, as the situation demanded — as Yoni, who was also the commander of the Mercedes, gave the orders. They practiced jumping out of the Mercedes and scrambling back into it. Yoni sat in front next to Amitzur, the driver. Behind Yoni, in the middle seat, sat Giora, next to Muki and another soldier. Packed into the back seat were four more men.

Around 4:00 p.m., Yoni drove to the Kiryah once more for a decisive one-on-one meeting with Shimon Peres. The defense minister believed the operation was essential, but he also feared a catastrophe. The price in lives that might be paid, even if the force made it back to Israel, weighed heavily on him. He had summoned Yoni to hear his estimation of the odds of success — and perhaps to get another chance to take stock of Yoni.

Yoni undoubtedly realized that he was going into a critical meeting. If Peres felt he lacked confidence or that he was overconfident and hadn't thought things through, it would be the end of the operation.

Yisrael was Yoni's driver again, and on the way to the Kiryah he started talking to him. After years of driving with Yoni, Yisrael was used to speaking to him with almost complete freedom, and he asked Yoni what he thought the chances were of the operation being approved. Yoni answered that, despite serious obstacles, he thought he'd "manage to get it through."

Suddenly, Yisrael understood that the operation could actually take place, that it was taking on a life of its own, and he was struck by doubt about the whole idea. On one hand, he saw how Yoni was pushing for it to happen; on the other, he wondered whether others shared Yoni's view. He hadn't been able to help but notice that virtually no one from the "outside" had come to the Unit to take stock of the preparations underway there.

"Yoni," he said, deadly serious, "are you really sure about this operation?"

"Yisrael," he said, "I've never been more certain of anything."

Yisrael pressed him. "Then what's in the way of getting it approved?"

"Look, I basically understand them. It means taking on a tremendous responsibility. I can see how it's hard for them to decide."

"Why haven't they shown up at the Unit? Why haven't we seen any of them yet?"

"I understand them," Yoni repeated without elaborating, and Yisrael felt from the way he answered as though he were somehow covering for them.

"What do you mean, you understand them? What's to understand? The guys at the Unit have been working almost 24 hours already. And other than you and Muki running around all the time, I haven't seen anybody."

Yoni said nothing he hadn't said already, and avoided responding directly to Yisrael's remark. Yisrael felt at that moment that Yoni, as commander, was alone on the battlefield.

When they reached the Kiryah gate, the sentry wouldn't let them in. "He wanted some kind of pass or another," Yisrael says. "Yoni was very tense. He got out of the car, pushed the guard aside, opened the gate himself, and told me, 'Drive!' and I drove in. Yoni left me there by myself to deal with all the sentries and the gate officer, and ran into the building. Only later, three hours after we returned to the Unit, he remembered what had happened and asked me if they'd detained me."

Yoni was forced to wait a few minutes before he was called into Peres' office. As he stood in the entrance hall, he was spotted by Rachel Rabinowitz, Chief of Staff Gur's secretary, whose office was nearby on the same floor. She was surprised to see Yoni there waiting by himself to meet with the defense minister — and even more surprised that the request for him to come had not gone through the chief of staff's office. "I asked somebody what the meeting was about," says Rachel, "and was told that Shimon Peres had asked him to come so that he could look him in the eyes and ask him straight, 'Yoni, can it be done?' That was the whole purpose of the meeting. Yoni stood there with maps in his hands, very preoccupied. . . . He was pressed for time and said that he was in a terrible hurry and they should let him in already."

The meeting lasted about three-quarters of an hour. Yoni explained the operation to Peres in precise detail. The various deception tactics, such as the Mercedes (about which Peres had already heard) appealed to the defense minister, as did the way Yoni presented the mission. "My impression was one of exactitude and imagination," Peres says, adding that Yoni's complete self-confidence had a strong influence on him. Deeply concerned about the dearth of intelligence data on hand, he questioned Yoni on the point. Yoni answered, "Do you know of any operation that wasn't carried out half-blind? Every operation is half-blind." Peres adds, "But Yoni was well aware of the problems and told me that the operation was absolutely doable. And as to the cost, he said we had every chance of coming out of it with almost no losses."

Yisrael remembers that Yoni left the meeting greatly encouraged, in contrast to the other meetings he'd had at the Kiryah that day. Yoni had seen how strongly Peres supported the operation, and he apparently felt that the defense minister would do everything in his power to see that it went ahead.

Meanwhile, Shani and Einstein were busy with their private exercises at Sharm al-Sheikh; and Shani's deputy, Nati Dvir, was giving the rest of the flight crews a detailed briefing for the simulation at the squadron headquarters. Also present were several reserve pilots, whom Shani had called up to take part, and Tzvika Har-Nevo, a veteran reserve navigator, whom Shani had slated for his own plane, Hercules One. Tzvika had been at his apartment Friday morning, preparing for his exams at the university, when he got a phone call telling him to be at the base by noon. It wasn't hard for him to guess why. He'd had enough time to go buy a newspaper, and on the way he'd met a woman he knew, the sister of one of the hostages.

"What's going to happen?" she had asked fearfully.

"It'll be all right," he told her, without being able to hint at what he thought would actually happen. "They're negotiating, and it'll be all right."

The woman had been close to hysteria as, indeed, were other relatives of the hostages. They had moved mountains to get their voices heard in the media and the government to make sure that their loved ones were not sacrificed for the sake of the principle of not giving in to terror — a principle that for some of them no longer seemed relevant. Among other Israelis, a feeling of helplessness and despair spread. People listened to the radio news broadcast every hour, and the picture seemed clear enough: The Arabs were about to win another victory, boosting their hubris and their strength. And Israel was helpless. Either it would give in to terror and release murderers from their cells, or would refuse to bend, and a hundred innocent people would be killed. There seemed to be no reasonable way out.

When Tzvika arrived at his base, he didn't recognize it. "Every path, every hallway was full of medical equipment. Huge stacks. "I'd never seen anything like it. Afterwards I realized they were going to set up a flying hospital."

Among the pilots at the afternoon briefing was Rami Levi, who arrived in his El Al uniform. He'd just flown a Boeing 707 back to Israel from London. When he landed the civil airliner at Lod, he found a young flight engineer from the Hercules squadron waiting to inform him that he had to go to the base at once.

Amnon Halivni, a former commander of the squadron, also returned to Israel that day as pilot of a civilian flight. Sitting in the cockpit after parking the plane, he saw an air force officer signaling to him from the ground to deplane immediately.

After Nati's briefing, the squadron's officers sat around the briefing-room table and discussed various points concerning the operation with Benny Peled and Yekutiel Adam. The rosters for the planes had already been drawn up. Halivni, who had served for several years in an Israeli military delegation to Uganda, interjected that he thought he, rather than Shani, should be the lead pilot. He pointed out that he knew Africa well — the air routes, the weather patterns, and Entebbe Airport in particular, at least as it had been in 1970. Another reserve pilot supported him in this. When Shani and Einstein returned to the base from their exercise at Sharm al-Sheikh, Shani was told there was a chance that one of the reserve pilots would take his place as leader. Shani was completely opposed to the idea, creating a dispute almost identical to the one over whether Ehud or Yoni would command the Unit's force. The difference was that this one was settled almost as soon as it arose. Peled simply asked Shani whether he was sure of his ability to carry out the mission. Shani answered with a flat "yes," and Peled as well as Adam — who had decided to send Ehud to Kenya that morning and thereby removed him from the operation — informed those present that the squadron had one commander, Shani, and that he would lead it for the raid.

The two reserve officers' suggestion doesn't appear to have resulted from any lack of confidence in Shani, but from professional considerations undoubtedly mixed with their own personal desires. "Shani was considered, from an operational standpoint . . . to be top-notch," says one of the squadron's officers who was there. Another officer from the squadron says he is convinced that Shani was "the best Hercules squadron commander we ever had. He was a first-rate lead pilot, the right man in the right place to do the job."

Shani and Einstein now took Gur and Peled to their Hercules and set off again for the Sinai. Einstein didn't believe for a minute that the operation would materialize, but he still wanted the chief of staff to be impressed with the landing, at least so that the flight team would not serve as an excuse for the rescue not taking place. At the airfield at Sharm, the order had been given to turn off every last light, and the field was totally dark when they made their approach that night. On the ground there wasn't a hint of anything visible to help the airmen find the runway. Einstein sat in the right-hand seat and peered out the windshield, trying to help Shani locate the runway in the final approach. Until that night, the two men had never performed a landing of this type.

Just as Shani had feared, the radar failed to identify the runway accurately, and instead homed in on the fence parallel to the taxiway. As a result, the plane came in for the landing over the taxiway rather than the main runway. When Shani turned on the airplane's lights and realized the mistake, he quickly banked to the left, straightened out over the main runway, and continued the descent. The wheels of the plane almost touched ground, but Shani avoided completing the actual landing, since the noise might attract unwanted attention from local Beduins, or even soldiers at the base, to the unusual activity at the airport on this otherwise quiet Sabbath eve. Actually touching down was in any case unnecessary to make the demonstration's point, and the plane rose away from the ground again. Gur, who was sitting behind Shani, realized there had been some sort of mistake.

Shani made another approach. This time the plane was in a better position relative to the main runway, though still not perfect. "I knew you could do it all along," Gur said happily to the airmen sitting in front of him, and slapped them on their backs. The pilots had no way of knowing whether the chief of staff, as someone who wasn't a pilot, had understood how imprecise even the second approach had been. But they kept their doubts to themselves.

The demonstration over, the Hercules turned north to take Gur and Peled to the site where the simulation of the raid would take place. At that hour of the night, the ground was still faintly lit by the moon. But the next night, in Africa, at the time for which the landing was planned, the moon would have already dropped below the horizon. The darkness that would envelop them might help keep the planes from being detected, but it would also make it extremely hard for the pilots to find the runway with the naked eye. Shani and Einstein were aware of this, but said nothing. They had no desire to add another point against the operation to their superiors' considerations. And until the operation itself, no one said a word about the difficulty created by the setting of the moon. Shani had decided anyway that, moon or no moon, if the runway lights weren't lit, he would turn on the plane's landing lights during the final stage of the descent after the radar had led him to the runway.

But even if the radar couldn't identify the darkened runway, Shani was absolutely determined to land at Entebbe. "If I see that the field is dark," he told Peled, "and the radar doesn't find the runway, I'll get on the radio and tell the control tower in English that I'm East African Airlines Flight 70 with a general electrical failure, in a state of emergency. Then I'll say, 'Please turn on the runway lights immediately!' There isn't a controller in the world who wouldn't flip the switch if he heard that. He won't be crazy enough to take the risk of causing a plane with 200 passengers on board to crash. He'll turn on the lights and we'll land. By the time he's figured out what's going on, the operation will be over. So what are you worried about?"

But Peled wasn't worried. He believed in his pilots, and he told Shani that it was a good idea, and to use it if he had to, but to keep it to himself.

The Unit's men now awaited the chief of staff so they could begin the simulation. Before the exercise, Yoni held another briefing for the Unit's commanders. "We talked about everything — about the plan, and about contingencies and how to respond," says Avi. "We went down to the smallest details, reviewed exactly what everyone was supposed to do. And then the subject of the Migs came up. Do we attack them? To the best of my recollection, the decision was that if there were a threat from that direction, we should open fire, but if everything was dark and quiet and nothing was happening, not to make a fireworks display out of it." Then Yoni gave one more briefing for the entire force.

Yoni had already held one full-scale simulation during the day. Muki, who was to command the teams storming the building, led the charge after the men left the vehicles. Initially, Yoni had put the teams in a different order, with Muki and his team third. Yoni had wanted Giora's team, which was to take the far hall, to be at the front, followed by the three teams storming the large hall. That way the men would come through the three main entrances simultaneously. Muki, however, says that he requested to be the one who would lead the advance. To convince Yoni, he pointed to past experience that showed that if the man in the lead was held up, the result was disaster. A short, stormy argument broke out, but Yoni remained unmoved. Finally, Muki said, "If you were in my place, where would you choose to be?" Muki recalls that Yoni smiled, and without a word pointed to the top of the list. In fact, Muki later found that the orders had been changed and he had been put at the front of the assault group. To the right of his team, out front, would be Yoni and his command team.

For the second simulation, Yoni had two soldiers play the role of Ugandans. "During the preparations for the raid," Muki explains, "Yoni foresaw a situation whereby we encountered two Ugandan guards . . . and our response in such a case was to take out the two guards with silencers."[8] Though it was known that there were sentries near the terminal, Yoni posted them further away, along the access strip leading to the building. "It makes sense for them to post guards here," he said.[9]

Besides the Unit's men, the men from the paratroops and Golani were also awaiting the beginning of the simulation. Among them was Sgt. Surin Hershko, who was about to go on leave before being discharged. His paratroop battalion had been on the Golan Heights when he and 14 other men had been called to come down to the coastal plain. In the middle of Thursday night they had arrived at the site where the simulation would be conducted Friday, and had slept there on the ground in sleeping bags. Sometime Friday they were told that an assault was being planned on a building three stories high in which there were terrorists. Not a word was said about Entebbe, and the assault was supposedly going to take place in Lebanon. But once they saw the transport planes arrive and were asked in the morning to board a tanker to see how many people could be packed on board, an explanation that they were preparing to go to Entebbe would have been superfluous. For most of the day, until the simulation, they had little to do. They sat talking among themselves and watched their officers meet and work on plans. Once in a while Surin saw a certain lieutenant colonel whom he had met in the past. It was Yoni.

"I had been sergeant of a mortar platoon," says Surin, telling how he met Yoni, who was then in the Armored Corps. "From time to time they'd send me with a team from my platoon to provide mortar support in exercises with tank battalions. Twice I was assigned to Yoni's battalion. I sat with him during the meetings to plan the exercises and the part I was to take in them. I saw a very forceful officer. . . . As for mortars, he was on top of the subject. Usually, when I went to an exercise like that, I knew I was going to do whatever I wanted, because in any case the battalion commander wouldn't understand what I was up to. I'd fire whenever and however I wanted so there'd be some smoke on the field, and that would be enough to make him happy. But with Yoni it didn't work like that. He knew what to ask for and when to ask for it. And in the battalion itself they had a special feeling for him. They really admired him. I remember one time when I went on an exercise with my team, they gave me a driver for the half-track carrying the mortar. It was Yoni's personal driver, the driver of his car. 'Watch this,' he kept telling me. 'Look how he directs what's going on in the exercise, how he's on top of everything, how he gives orders.' I was amazed. I'd never seen a driver so interested in following an exercise before."

Surin says he had no special qualms about a mission to Entebbe. He trusted his commanders and had faith that they could bring him back in one piece. Before the simulation, he and his friends were told they should get out of the plane and head for the "building" designated by marking tape. The next day, Saturday, they received a more detailed briefing, and were finally told that they were going to Entebbe that day, and that their role would be to take the new passenger terminal. Surin's team, with his company commander in charge, would go to the roof to ensure that there were no Ugandan troops there. Any Ugandan soldiers they encountered would be considered hostile, they were told. They were not to harm civilians, but were to move them to the first floor of the building. The hostages, they were told, had been held in the other terminal, the old one — but there was no way of knowing whether the captives had been moved to the new terminal over the last 24 hours. If that happened, they would have to be the ones to rescue them.

Gur returned from Sharm al-Sheikh around 10:00 p.m. on Friday. He went first to Yoni's office where, together with Adam, Shomron, and other senior officers, he heard Yoni briefly present the Unit's plan for the operation, the essentials of which they already knew. A short discussion followed. Gur stressed the problem of the control tower; Yoni explained that he planned to silence it in the first stage, using the covering force in the jeeps, and later with additional firepower from the APCs. After the short meeting, they all drove to the site where the simulation was about to begin.

In the exercise, the planes taxied down the runway as though they had just landed. First to jump down from the lead Hercules were members of the elite paratroops commando unit, who quickly placed signal lights along both sides of the runway. The signals would mark the runway for the remaining planes if the regular runway lights had been out to begin with or had been turned off after the first plane arrived.* When the first plane came to a halt, the hold was opened to allow the Mercedes and the two jeeps to roll down the ramp. Amitzur Kafri, the driver of the Mercedes, turned the key in the ignition. Nothing happened. The engine refused to start, and the exercise almost failed before it had begun. Amitzur shouted to the jeep behind him to give the car a jolt to shake up the starter. The blow did the trick, the car started, and the vehicles drove off the plane and headed for the mock-up of the old terminal.

After they turned left onto the access road to the terminal, they encountered the two sentries Yoni had posted. "The two soldiers who acted as 'guards' on the runway," explains Muki, were "suspicious" of the arriving vehicles and "ordered us to stop. We did, and Yoni 'shot' at them with a silencer. We then continued toward the terminal." In all this "we practiced according to the plan," sums up Muki.[10] The men then leapt out of the vehicles and Muki led the charge across the front of the building, with Yoni running beside him. The men rushed through the entrances between the jute sheets and fired a few blanks. Yoni directed everything, including the arrival of his armored forces right after the assault, and the evacuation of the hostages and the Unit's men afterwards. Gur was beside the men throughout the exercise — in his car during the drive from the plane to the terminal, and then on foot during the assault.

To Peled, the air force commander, the sight of soldiers running every which way in the dark looked like near-chaos. But Chief of Staff Gur, who'd come up through the infantry, understood what he'd seen and was pleased. Hagai Regev, Gur's adjutant, also accompanied the Unit's force during its "assault." Yoni and Regev knew each other from the Yom Kippur War, when Yoni and the forces under him had joined the Seventh Armored Brigade, where Regev was serving, for the push through the Syrian lines. From then on, they had remained in touch and had gotten together on occasion. "During the exercise, I had the feeling he was trying to tell me something," says Regev. "He was tired — maybe even a little sick, but certainly exhausted. And what he basically said, though not in so many words, was, 'Tell the boss it's all right,

---

* Using the signal lights at Entebbe was the idea of Col. Matan Vilna'i, the commander of the paratroops. Not long before, he and his men had been practicing nighttime landings under field conditions with the Hercules squadron, and the use of such portable lights to mark landing strips was a product of the exercises.

that we're ready.' . . . It seemed to me he felt that maybe the exercise hadn't been good enough, that maybe it had caused some lack of confidence among the brass who had to make the decision. . . . What he wanted was for me to pass on a message, that perhaps he couldn't say to them himself, because it might create suspicion that something wasn't quite right. And the message was: 'It's all right. Tell them not to worry. They don't know how these things are done, but we know what we're doing.' But again, I remember him being so tired. It was physical exhaustion, from the work-load he had, not mental. At least that's how it seemed to me."

Gur made only a few comments to Yoni after the simulation. He wasn't pleased with how heavily the jeeps were packed, fearing that the crowding would get in the men's way when they needed to act. "It looked like a pile of men moving along, not like a jeep," remembers Brig. Gen. Ben-Gal. Gur demanded that there be fewer men in each Land Rover. Yoni said he thought it would be fine as is, and that they had worked this way before without problems. But Gur insisted, and in the end they agreed to take one man off each jeep.

When the men heard this, says Alik, "It was tense. The glances started. It's that same old moment when everyone starts looking around, trying to find the 'someone' who'll be dropped. I felt like an outsider. I was a reservist. It would have been natural for me to start staring at the ground, shuffling my feet. But not this time. From the minute Yoni called me in, it was clear to me: That's it. Now no one could drop me. This time when they started looking around I said to myself, *No one's going to be able to drop me now.*"

Most of the discussion between Gur and Yoni following the simulation took place in a field tent that had been put up the previous night and which had served as mess hall that day for the paratroops and Golani men. There Gur called together the senior officers who had been present for the drill and asked what they thought of the mission's chances. For about an hour, they sat on wooden benches around folding tables on which Rami Dotan had taken care to have slices of watermelon waiting. What Gur heard, both from officers who were to take part in the operation and from the others present, was favorable, beginning with Shomron's comments. The raid, they said, would probably come off. If the first plane succeeded in landing, Shomron said, the operation would succeed. It all depended on that first plane, he stressed.

Gur now had to decide whether to recommend to the cabinet to go ahead. He had been positively impressed by the performance of the principal and secondary forces; now all that remained was for him to make a final decision. Without his unequivocal endorsement, sending the men into action was inconceivable.

At that moment, Gur must surely have felt the full burden of his responsibility as the country's supreme military commander. His first responsibility was to the men under him, who on his orders would set out for a target thousands of miles away, about which so little was known. Yet failure could have consequences beyond those of any military initiative the country had ever taken. The question was not merely how few or how many hostages or troops would be killed, the answer serving as a yardstick of the operation's success. Everyone's minds were on two harsh scenarios. The first was that all of the hostages would be slaughtered without the troops ever being able to reach them. The second, which no one even dared voice, was that the cream of Israel's fighters and officers would run into problems and be unable to withdraw by air. In the best case, they would then have to take on the Ugandan army and fight their way 120 miles to the Kenyan border. In the worst case, everyone would be taken prisoner or simply wiped out. That would be not only a military disaster, but an unprecedented foreign policy catastrophe. And the ultimate military responsibility would fall on the shoulders of the chief of staff who had recommended that the government take such a mad course.

Gur looked into the faces of the officers around him and listened to them speak. He tried to assess their spirit and, undoubtedly, his own as well.

"The officers in the tent, sitting around the tables underneath the kerosene lamp, each said in his turn what he thought were the chances of this operation succeeding," recalls Shaul Mofaz. "But in the end everyone waited to hear from Yoni, the commander of the operation. The 'go' or 'no go' for the operation depended on what he would say."[11]

As in his meeting with Peres earlier that day, Yoni understood the great importance of the tone of his comments and the weight he put on each word. "I had the impression," says Muki, "that Yoni tried hard to give even, balanced answers, so he wouldn't sound arrogant, even though I'm sure he thought that there were no problems, that it would go well. He said that, seeing how the exercises had gone, he couldn't envision any special difficulties . . . and that from the intelligence data it seemed to him that the operation was not only feasible, but that the risks were acceptable."

"Yoni said that if the plane landed at Entebbe and the Unit's force got going, the job would be carried out quickly and successfully," says Shaul.

Yoni's comments had their effect on Gur. "Yoni said," Muki recalls, "that he had every reason to believe that, if the hostages were in fact still there, the Unit, with the methods and men at its disposal, could pull it off. It was fairly natural for Yoni to think that, but he also had good reason for his thinking. His bottom line was: 'It can be done.' I saw Motta's reaction, and I'm convinced that those words of Yoni's gave Gur and other top officers the confidence they needed to push on with it and to get the go-ahead from the cabinet."[12]

Others who were present agree. Dotan, who sat to one side, watching the discussion without taking part, says, "Whether or not you want to, you can see what's happening. You see the people, their expressions, and you can tell whom Motta is looking at. He's looking at Yoni. When it comes to what the officers said, Motta got the confidence to go through with it . . . from Yoni, I'm 100 percent convinced."

"I think that Yoni's [positive] response stemmed, first of all, from his conviction that we must carry out this mission," explains Mofaz. "Secondly, it stemmed from his faith in the soldiers . . . and to no small degree, from his belief in his own ability to command and lead the men."

When the meeting ended, Gur announced that he would recommend to the defense minister that the operation be approved. It was one of the most courageous decisions ever made by a chief of staff. Now, Gur said, it was up to the cabinet. In the meantime, the planes and the vehicles for the operation would be moved during the night to Lod Airport, to be ready to leave for Uganda the next day.

The men stood. Some stepped outside the tent, others stayed inside another minute or two to exchange a few words. There were only a few voices, hardly above whispers. The feeling, one officer recalls, was of "silence in the face of the enemy."

As Yoni moved towards the opening of the tent, he took Dotan's shoulder and said, "It'll be all right." His tone, rather than cocky, was dead serious, as though he were promising himself, too, that it would all end well. "He was the man," says Dotan, "who would determine the outcome in the first moments of battle, the critical moments which, if something went amiss, could cause the whole mission to end up in chaos. His responsibility was a hundred times greater than that of the other officers there, and you could feel it. When he said, 'It'll be all right,' he projected a commitment that we'd really come out of this okay . . . I felt it, and it gave me strength."

Ben-Gal was also impressed with how serious Yoni seemed. "If you know a person well, it's enough to look at him or be around him for a few minutes to get a real sense of what's going on with him. . . . I saw something in Yoni's bearing way beyond anything I'd seen in him before, more grave, intense, something profound, much more than during the war."

Perhaps because Ben-Gal was particularly close to Yoni, he also noticed something else. "I had the feeling he was going into this exhausted. He told me he was terribly tired, and that he still had a lot of things to do. But beyond that, he looked troubled. Something was weighing down on him."

The officers left the site of the exercise with their troops. The Unit's men returned to their base. It was after midnight, and a great deal of work remained to be done. For one thing, the vehicles still weren't ready. The repair work and paint job on the Mercedes had yet to be completed, and small, important details like placing the Ugandan flags on the front had to be taken care of. The men had to finish outfitting themselves and preparing everything for inspection in the morning. And everyone, officers and men, had to study the intelligence material in their mission files, especially the layout of the terminal and the runways and the open areas around it. Until now, they hadn't had time.

Yoni met with his officers, giving them an intelligence update and reviewing the exercise with them. Afterward he sat with Alik, and, using the sketches scattered over his desk, quickly explained the deployment of forces and the plan for the operation. Alik's principal role, Yoni said, would be to manage the command team if Yoni had to leave it to intervene personally in any part of the action.

The Unit's men dispersed to the jobs before them — except for a few officers who gathered in a room near the flagpole. They'd been struck by a deep sense of apprehension. Until the simulation, no one had believed the operation would take place. Yes, they'd checked that their men were equipped at each of the inspections, they'd made comments during the drills, they'd fought bitterly to have their men put on the mission roster — but that only showed what half their minds was telling them. The other half said it was wasted effort. Now the chief of staff had endorsed the operation, the vehicles were about to be moved to Lod in the dead of night to be loaded on the planes, and it finally hit them that, despite everything, it could really happen. It really could. Gur would make his recommendation to the defense minister and the prime minister. The two of them, with nearly blind faith in the Unit's ability to do anything, would rule in favor and get the cabinet to approve.

Early that morning, they'd heard the mission plan from Yoni for the first time. Now, after a mere 18 hours of frenzied work and drills, the preparations were declared complete, and they were about to fly off to Entebbe. For a "special" operation of this kind, the officers were accustomed to work out a thousand and one details, to practice for months on end, to be prepared, so that every man knew what he should be doing every second of the way. Nothing should be left to chance. For an operation like this, you had to practice on a real building that would give a genuine sense of what would actually happen in the field, and not on a few pieces of burlap and masking tape. The plan should be polished and finalized weeks in advance, so that everyone was comfortable with it. The intelligence should be reliable enough to provide maximum confidence that the operation would be a success. And this time, one of the officers recalls, "we felt like everyone was leading everyone on. The troops weren't ready, the dry run wasn't a dry run, the vehicles weren't real vehicles, the preparations weren't real preparations, the intelligence wasn't real intelligence, it was all a load of baloney. We felt like the Unit was fooling itself and the army, the Infantry and Paratroops chief was fooling his superiors, and on up."

The conversation reached the point of someone suggesting that they go over Yoni's head, even over the heads of the top brass, straight to one of the ministers, so that the cabinet would know what the situation really was.

At that moment, late on the night before the operation, they felt burdened by doubts and had little faith in the chance of success. For the most part, that mood was a product of the objective conditions they faced. But it was also an expression of the dissatisfaction that two or three of them felt with Yoni's leadership — a discontent that had waxed and waned during his year as their commander, but had never been resolved. Yoni was aware of their ongoing opposition to him; because he was sensitive, perhaps too sensitive for a commander, it was an open sore for him. True, some of the young officers who had once been dead set against him had become enthusiastic supporters, and one or two others had completed their military service and left. But there were still a few determined opponents. Undoubtedly, some of their criticism stemmed from real mistakes Yoni had made during the year, but the underlying reasons were almost certainly personal. And the opposition, as is so common, had taken root, become obstinate, a matter of principle. Everything was automatically subject to criticism, and that included Yoni's plan for the mission and what he did to carry it out. Even after the operation had ended in success, they would continue to insist that "Yoni didn't think of everything, didn't prepare for every possibility."

Of course, he hadn't. Under these circumstances, with the minutes ticking away toward the terrorists' deadline, to think of everything was humanly impossible. And if someone else had prepared the operation, he might well have thought of details that Yoni failed to consider, or have even planned a different kind of operation. Yoni himself knew that the plan and the preparations were imperfect, but he was sure that they were enough for success. Even more, he believed in his men and his officers, including his opponents, and believed that when it mattered, most of them would do whatever the situation demanded. And he believed in himself.

"We young officers," explains one, "put our faith more in the technical side of the plan and training, and less in our own underlying ability and that of our men, in our resourcefulness, initiative, flexibility."

To be fair, it must be said that the officers' concerns weren't due to fear of combat. Their performance in the mission would demonstrate their courage. And it wasn't just Yoni's opponents who felt uneasy after the simulation, the last drill before the operation. Several other officers who didn't take part in that late-night discussion — officers who had fought at Yoni's side in the Yom Kippur War and trusted him in battle as they trusted no one else — felt the same. The hasty preparations, the complexity of the mission, and the negative experience from past rescue operations had their effect, as did the doubts and hesitations that strike every man who sets out on a fateful mission.

In the end, the group broke up without deciding to speak to anyone at all. But less than 24 hours before they were to land on Ugandan soil, officers who had serious reservations about the mission held key positions in it. Such a mood in an operation whose success or failure hinged on the performance of a few men in the course of a few seconds, held the potential for disaster.

The next day, with his words and his example, Yoni would completely reverse that mood.

Outfitting and inspections, cleaning guns, preparing the vehicles, and coordinating countless matters within and without the Unit continued deep into the night. In Amir and Shlomo's room, as in others', the men switched the lights off periodically to adjust the sighting lights mounted on their rifles, in case the hall where the hostages were held turned out to be dark. Without the lights, it would be impossible to tell whom they were shooting at. "The whole time I kept remembering the trauma of the Savoy Hotel," says Shlomo, who was wounded in that action. "The minute we reached the building, the terrorists set off their explosives. The whole building went dark, and with all the dust from the blast you couldn't see a thing. I was thinking that something like that could happen here, too. The only way you'd be able to see anything would be with your sighting light. You find the enemy with the narrow beam and take aim, but if the light isn't accurately aligned, you won't hit him. So in the room we'd prop up the rifles on something stable and look through the sights, then turn off the lights and press on the button, and make sure that the point of light was falling precisely on the spot we'd aimed at with the sights. It was a matter of life and death."

There were not enough lights fitting the AK-47 to go around, so some of the soldiers had to take less reliable Israeli-made Uzis, for which sighting lights were available. Ilan Blumer, one of the men in the assault force, took the Uzi he was issued to the nearby shooting range and test-fired it, using every clip in his ammo vest to make sure that they all worked.

Anyone who hadn't yet filled his clips with bullets and his vest pouches with grenades now did so. Everyone took as many grenades and bullets as his vest could hold. The men were told to make sure they had a second clip fastened to the one they'd load into their guns, so that they could load the second one the instant they'd emptied the first. Amir arranged a kit for breaking open doors in his pack and tried out different ways to carry both the pack and a bullhorn. One man in each team had to carry this equipment; since no one wanted the job, they drew lots. Amir had been the one to lose the draw in Amnon's team and got stuck with the extra gear.

Some of the men managed to grab a few hours of sleep. Others, whose assignments forced them to keep working, were up all night. Yet others stayed up because they were simply unable to fall asleep.

Bukhris was getting worried. At 2:00 a.m., he was told that another soldier from his squad had been dropped from the operation, leaving him as the last man from the squad still on the roster for Entebbe — and as the youngest man on it. It had only been a few weeks since he'd finished the Unit's long training course. The rest of the men in his squad had received the Unit's emblem at the traditional, well-attended nighttime ceremony. But a stress fracture in his foot had kept Bukhris from taking part in the long, grueling exercise that was the "final exam." After his foot healed, he and another soldier had done the exercise themselves. At the end, Yoni put them through a live-fire drill at an ancient battle site. Then their ceremony took place.

"This time we don't have the whole Unit here. It's just us," Yoni told the two sweaty soldiers. "But that doesn't take anything away from the event. Just the opposite. Of all of these ceremonies I've conducted, this is the most moving one for me, because this private ceremony creates a special bond between me, as the commander of the Unit, and each of you." He drew from his pocket the little wings of the Unit, handed the men the emblems, and shook their hands. They couldn't see the wings in the dark, but could only feel them with their fingers.

Yoni was taken by the intimacy of the event. Nothing was more important to him than his tie with the men of the rank-and-file. But as the years went by and he moved up the ranks, this connection had become harder to maintain, particularly once he took command of the Unit. For Yoni, creating an appearance of personal connection — giving the usual commander's external, superficial impression of "friendship," intended purely as PR — was simply out of the question. He hated pretense; anything fake in relations with people, even a "hearty" but meaningless smile, ran against his whole nature. When a broad smile lit up his face, it came from inside, unconsciously, without any intention to please.

Giving Bukhris and the other soldier their wings had provided Yoni a brief opportunity to be close to his men. He had offered them a ride back to the base in his car, rather than on the truck that had come to pick them up. On the way, before the two exhausted soldiers fell asleep, he had asked about their personal backgrounds. And so he heard that Bukhris's parents had come to Israel from Tunisia, that Bukhris was one of seven brothers, and that he had studied at a boarding school before he was drafted.

It's doubtful that Bukhris had more than a chance or two to look at his wings before the eve of the operation. The Unit's emblem was a secret, along with the names of those who served in the Unit, and Bukhris's wings adorned not his chest, but the inside of a drawer.

Now, late Friday night, with just a few hours left before the force was to leave the base, Bukhris feared that Yoni would drop him from the list as well. On the basis of seniority, he knew, he was next in line. He found one of the officers. "What are my chances of really going?" he asked anxiously.

"You they'll never cut," the other man answered, as if stating an obvious fact.

Bukhris didn't ask what made him so sure. He contented himself with the answer he'd received, and went back to his room to prepare his gear for the morning inspection. For him, the long day was almost over. He was sure the Unit would carry out its mission successfully, and that he'd do his job as a machine-gunner in Yiftah's second team well. "But one other thing was obvious to me," says Bukhris. "If they damaged our planes, there'd be no coming back. Maybe they didn't spell it out, but it stood to reason that that's how it would be."

He lay down two hours before the wake-up, and slept with a feeling of great relief that he, too, would be flying to an unknown spot on the equator, from which he could not be sure he would return.

Amir Ofer was among those who didn't bother going to sleep. He knew that both fear and excitement would keep him awake anyway. The fear wasn't a matter of lacking confidence in his commanders; it was something physical, the gut fear felt by almost every soldier going into battle. Only the night before, the secretary had phoned him to say that they were going "very far." And now he was really about to embark on that journey. "Either it'll be the IDF's most successful operation of all time, or its biggest failure," he told another soldier in his room.

In the hours left before the morning inspection, he sat and studied his mission file, reviewing the diagrams and photos over and over again so that he wouldn't get mixed up, miss the hall where the hostages were supposed to be, and enter another one. True, according to the plan he was supposed to go through the central entrance second, after Amnon, his commander, who would certainly know which entryway to storm, but one couldn't rely on that alone. He had to be ready for anything. He also examined the large map of Africa, and looked at the overland escape route: the roadway leading from Entebbe, along the north shore of Lake Victoria, to the border of Kenya.

Danny Dagan had also glanced at the map and the road. The distance to Kenya was 120 miles, and in the APC — whose tank he had filled to the top, and on which he had stowed a few spare jerrycans of gas — he had enough fuel to make it to the border. But right now he had more immediate concerns. The tires on the Mercedes were worn out; in some spots you could see the belts. "Of course, the Mercedes had to drive only two or three miles, but nine or ten men would be riding in it, and the tires had to be good," says Danny. Amitzur called a friend, who put him and Danny in touch with the owner of a Mercedes garage. That night Danny drove to a warehouse in Jaffa and took five new tires. On the back of a napkin from a local restaurant, Danny signed a note promising to pay the garage owner for the tires within a week.

But even after changing the tires, Danny was worried about the condition of the Mercedes, and wanted to replace it with another car. He reported to Yoni that he didn't believe the car was fit for use. "Are you sure?" Yoni asked. Danny told him that he had a friend with a large, black Fury that could seat nine. Yoni seized on the idea. "Great, try to get it," he told him. Danny drove to his friend's house in the middle of the night, and without telling him what he needed the car for, asked permission to use it for a day or two.

After Danny phoned the Kiryah and got official assurance that the army would cover any damage to the car, he called Yoni and told him they would be able to use it. "How long is it?" Yoni remembered to ask. When Danny reported back that the Fury was two feet longer that the Mercedes, Yoni had to rule out using it. There wouldn't be enough room for it on the plane. The Unit would have to make do with the Mercedes, and Yoni simply hoped that the starter, and everything else, would work during the crucial minutes.

Tamir, whose parents had returned to Israel that day from a stay abroad, received permission from Yoni to go home and come back in the morning. The rest of the officers of Tamir's age, like the other men, were ordered not to leave the base. But young officers often treat such orders as meant to be broken, especially when they don't believe that the operation involved will ever take place. "At the time, A. and I were going home for the evening every time we'd finish an exercise," says one officer. "We thought about whether we should leave this time too, and decided we would. We took a D-200 pick-up and left. We got as far as the intersection outside the base when the hood popped up in front of our faces. We looked at each other and thought: *Maybe we shouldn't go after all.* We put the hood down, turned around, and went back to the Unit."

Yoni was at his office. "We worked into the small hours of that morning," says Avi. "Yoni went over many things that still needed to be stressed or checked, tying up all the loose ends." In addition, Yoni sat with Avi and discussed a different matter, crucial to Israeli security and still classified to this day, to which the Unit was devoting most of its time in those days. The two of them had a key meeting with certain persons scheduled for the next day, and it couldn't be postponed. There was no choice but for Avi, at least, to make the meeting, and so they had decided together that he would not go to Entebbe. "Yoni sat with me," says Avi, "and discussed things connected with the other matter we had to take care of, but his head was really in Entebbe. He said he was sorry that commitments to outside people would keep me from taking part in the operation. . . . In any case, the assumption was that the chances of getting the go-ahead were still slim... Even then I don't think anyone was convinced we were going to do it. . . . Yoni told me, 'Avi, why waste your time on it?' "

When Yoni finished his work, he had only a few hours left to sleep. He knew he had to get some rest now, before the operation. He went home and got into the shower. Bruria remembers that when she came into the bathroom, it seemed to her that he'd fallen asleep there — standing with water pouring over his head, his back against the wall, his eyes shut. They set the alarm for early in the morning to give themselves a few minutes to talk about the note he'd left her the night before. Now, in the middle of the night, there was no time for thoughts and reflections. All Yoni wanted to do was to close his eyes. He climbed under the covers and fell asleep.

Endnotes

1. Giora Zusman, interview.
2. The comments by Gur and Peres are from Shimon Peres, *Entebbe Diary* (Jerusalem: Eidanim, 1991), p. 96.
3. Yitzhak Rabin, *Service Card* (Jerusalem: Ma'ariv, 1979), p. 528–529.
4. Ilan Blumer, interview.
5. Avi Livneh and Tamir, interviews.
6. IDF Radio, "To Entebbe and Back," June 1979.
7. Alex Davidi, taped recollection.
8. *Ma'ariv*, July 4, 1986, from an interview conducted August 1976.
9. Bukhris, interview.
10. Interview, August 1976 (printed in *Maariv*, July 4, 1986). An assertion has been made that there was no plan to silently shoot the guards in case they wanted to examine the convoy and that such a contingency was not rehearsed. This assertion is erroneous. In addition to the quote from Muki on page 91, see also Muki's statement on page 93 and Avi's statement on page 38. Capt. Giora Zusman sums it up thus: "We discussed the necessity of being ready to take out the Ugandans. If we were approached [by them] — no games, just shoot. And that's exactly what happened. [We decided] that if we see a Ugandan soldier on the way who will threaten us with his weapon, or perform any other threatening action, we will shoot him with silencers. The whole idea behind us taking the silencers was for just such an eventuality."
11. From a lecture at Bar-Ilan University, May 16, 2000.
12. Israel Television, "Now Is the Time," May 12, 1986.

Listening to a briefing on the Golan Heights, Yom Kippur War, 1973

CHAPTER IV

O ther people's stories join my own memories. They settle together into my mind — not in a jumble but in a line, each memory leading to the next, forming the road to Yoni's death at Entebbe.

It's been 16 years since the Yom Kippur War, and my friend from my days in the Unit has a hard time finding the exact spot where the battle took place. We drive a bit north from Nafah, toward Wast Junction. The road rises and falls, and each time we drop into a depression, we lose sight of the surrounding plateau with its low stone walls. On an uphill stretch, before we get to the top, he says, "Here's the place." We stop and get out.

"The Syrian commandos were scattered here, to the left of the road," he explains. "The helicopters that had brought them had already flown back to the east." Yoni's force had been assigned to defend the main military headquarters on the Golan Heights, at Nafah, and one of his teams had spotted the helicopters landing. As soon as he received the report, he gave the order to get in the half-tracks — the Syrian force couldn't be given time to get organized. Within minutes, everyone who had managed to grab a place on the half-tracks, about 40 men, had left.

Heading in the general direction of where the commandos had landed, they passed a force from the Golani infantry brigade that had already exchanged fire with the Syrians and sustained casualties. Yoni was unable to get a clear picture from them of precisely where the Syrians were, and he advanced a little further. He stopped the half-tracks where we'd just stopped the car, and the men climbed out.

I remember a description I heard years before from Shai Avital, a young officer in the Unit at the time of the battle, of how it began: "Suddenly, they opened up with pretty heavy fire, while we were still standing out in the open next to the half-tracks. Luckily, we crouched and the shells and bullets flew over us. But one of the officers was hit, and he died later of his wounds."[1]

So this is where Gideon Avidov, my team-mate from the service who went on to be a squad-commander, got hit, I note to myself, here on the road, just as he began combing the area for the Syrians. Says my friend: "We pulled him back to that little ditch by the side of the road, to the right, and we started treating his wounds. You have to understand that some of the Syrians were already firing from behind that wall, the close one." I look to my left, and see a long stone wall a few yards off, parallel to the road. "The Syrians were positioned on the ground just beyond it."

Shai was among those who advanced on the wall after the first burst of fire. As he told how it happened: "The Syrians had us where they wanted us — they had cover, and we were still out in the open, unprotected. . . . It could have been really bad. I could see the officer who'd been hit, only a few yards from me. There wasn't much shooting after that first barrage, and there was this feeling of suspense, that someone should do something. I remember I started getting scared, real scared. And what I saw then I'll remember the rest of my life. Suddenly, I see Yoni get up, perfectly calm, as though nothing was going on there at all. I remember that he had on a green helmet, without any camouflage netting. With his hands, he motions to us all to get up along with him — we'd all grabbed what cover we could — and he starts advancing, like it was a training exercise. He was upright, giving out orders right and left, advancing and shooting and calling out with that same calm he'd had in other actions, too. I remember the thought I had, as someone under him, as a soldier: Hell, if he can do that, I'm not giving in, either. I got up and started to fight."

We make our way across the field, between the scattered stones and the half-ruined walls.

Shai's story: "I managed to catch up with him. I was all worked up from the battle. Yoni told me to calm down, and asked how my ammo was holding out. I told him I didn't have much left. We'd been shooting quite a bit. He told me,

'When you kill them, do it with single rounds, like I taught you. It's much more accurate. Don't use bursts. Go on like I say.'

"Yoni didn't just run forward, he advanced carefully, in a real thought-out way. And that's the way we moved forward, combed the area and defeated them." Baruch Zuckerman was killed behind one of the walls, as he advanced at Yoni's side. We start looking for a tank emplacement in which about a dozen Syrian fighters took cover. It's hard to find, and when we finally do, it's shallow and flattened out from years of erosion.

I look over the area for a moment. There, up above, must be the spot from which Muki provided the covering fire. As he told it: "When I reached the top of the hill, I noticed a kind of depression in the ground, and soldiers shooting from it. I shouted to Yoni that he should cover me, and I'd storm the place. . . . I'd hardly shouted that there were Syrians there, and Yoni had already taken his men and in a matter of seconds he was charging them. The only thing left for me to do was cover him. . . . The picture that's engraved in my mind is of Yoni running first with eight of his men against ten Syrian commandos, and wiping them all out. That's the picture that always comes back to me: Yoni rushing toward the emplacement and shooting and leading his men in battle."

By now we're several hundred yards from the road. We turn back, picking our way through knee-high thistles. By the time Yoni and his men finished combing the area a second time and found the Syrians who had stayed at the rear, the battle had gone on for an hour and a half. I get in the car, still finding it hard to grasp the course of the battle and its outcome. The Unit suffered two dead and one wounded. The Syrian force, which had also numbered about 40 men, was completely wiped out. "To come out of it like that after being taken totally by surprise at close range, to organize a scattered force — it's thanks to Yoni that it turned out the way it did," said Shai. And Muki: "Yoni waged a battle here the likes of which I've never even read about."

Yoni himself summed up the battle in a laconic report he wrote after the war, and commented at the end, "This proves once again that a force of ours, fighting according to all the simple rules, will win. . . . Heavy covering fire has to be provided before every movement on the field. . . . The decisive stage is clearly reached when the enemy's mood shifts to one of defeat. The breaking point comes when the enemy is seized by the fear of death. That fear paralyzes men completely. . . . Until that point is reached, the enemy will continue to calculate his actions and constitute a dangerous opponent."

Yoni never told me the details of this battle, and I didn't ask. Only once did I hear him remark offhandedly, "Poor Syrians. What rotten luck to run into the best fighting unit in the world." And I thought, without saying it to him, that they'd had even worse luck: They'd run into him.

Yoni didn't tell our parents about the battle, either. Once he did say to our father, "You can't tell a good commander just by victory in battle. If you're willing to sacrifice enough people, you'll almost always win. The real measure of a good commander is that he wins with few losses."

* * *

The same picture of Yoni in battle repeats over and over. It portrays him at Entebbe, and it portrays his first battle, in 1966, when he was 20 — a retaliatory raid against terrorists at Samua in the West Bank, then under Jordanian rule. "It seems there are people," he wrote after that action, "who lose touch with reality under fire and don't know exactly what they're doing at the moment. And then there are people who feel no different than usual — or at least that's how I felt myself: no less concentration, no less sense of judgment, no less touch with reality, and practically no more tension than I feel any other day."

And the same picture depicts him late one night in the hills of Gush Etzion in Judea, in the early 1970s. "We were supposed to attack a house where terrorists were holed up," recounts Boaz Baron, a soldier who served under Yoni in the Haruv commando unit. "We went there four or five nights in a row, but we didn't get the go-ahead to attack. One night we hiked 12 miles through the mountains to get there. . . . On the last night, the lookout they'd posted outside suddenly spotted us. We froze in our tracks. Yoni, who realized that we had to go into action immediately, jumped over the stone wall alone, stood in the doorway and started shooting. . . . Afterwards, he was unhappy about how we'd carried out the attack, even though it was only our first battle. Only two of the five terrorists had been killed. The rest got away. . . . Yoni was quiet that night, withdrawn. We could feel that he wasn't pleased, that things hadn't gone the way they were supposed to. We didn't talk about it much. It was clear what had happened."

And more generally, Boaz says, "He wasn't just a commander, but also an educator. A great educator, I think. . . . He was special even in the way he disciplined someone. It could just be a tough conversation with him; that was punishment enough."

My thoughts move according to laws of their own; maybe it's the word "educator" that suddenly makes me think of what Yoni once told one of his soldiers, when he was a young platoon commander in the paratroops. "We were sitting in a dugout during some defensive exercise," the soldier remembers.[2] "Five of us had to share each battle ration, and only two could eat at a time. I happened to be the one who got to eat with Yoni. The man was hungry. He sat with the can of meat and the can of peas in front him, and for a minute he just wanted to eat, like a normal, hungry person. But he was also the platoon commander sitting next to one of his men, and it wasn't so nice for him to pounce on the food or eat too much. I could see him wavering, and it looked like the eating side won out this time. He ate a little more than his share. I saw that he was embarrassed that he'd eaten that extra amount. Of course, I had been looking for a chance to catch Yoni on something like this and point it out, so I asked him, 'What about the rest of the men?' He lowered his head and said, 'If you're ever a commander, don't do that.' Three-four years later, both of us commanders now, I was sitting with him, and it's interesting, it's that incident he brought up. 'You remember?' he said. 'I hope you don't eat your men's food.' "

The men of that paratroop platoon, Yoni's first soldiers, parted after that year of training; but even afterwards, they met once a year. "Every New Year's Day we'd get together at Dizengoff Square in Tel Aviv, and the turnout was almost always perfect," one of Yoni's soldiers says. "We'd go to a restaurant or a club and hang out until deep into the night. At those get-togethers, Yoni was one of us. He'd speak from the heart, pour out everything that had built up inside him. . . . When we realized how he felt about us, we developed a very powerful attachment to him.

Every year we'd always tell the same stories, relive the same experiences . . . and you could see how happy Yoni was, maybe because he had more of a tie to us. It wasn't like it got to be later, after he was promoted and his connection with the men under him got weaker. I think he was pretty introverted. If he didn't know someone well, if he didn't have a really close relationship with him, I don't know if he would have been able to start a personal conversation with him. But with us, he was just the opposite. He talked about everything in the world, even himself.

"At the last get-together, one of the guys didn't make it. Yoni couldn't understand it. How could somebody skip a reunion like this? What right did he have not to show? He couldn't see it . . . he almost went to get the guy. We said to him, 'Forget it, someone in his family died.' He just couldn't believe it.

"Every time, when the reunion was over, you could see that he was so sorry to leave, that he had no desire to go back to wherever he'd come from. He felt so good to be together with the guys. . . . He would drink with us, horse around, and always, half an hour or an hour before leaving, he'd go off to the side to drowse a bit. Then he'd come to, get up, say 'Take care, guys,' and disappear.

"The last time, he really danced and went wild all night, completely carefree. Toward morning he had to leave, to go back. Then we noticed: He didn't even shake hands with anybody. He just waved from a distance, said 'Goodbye,' and went. He was sad to go."

* * *

We drive on, to the north side of the Golan Heights. "Over here," my friend points to the right, "is the area where we broke through into the Syrian enclave." The night of the breakthrough, Yoni's force was attached to the 7th Brigade of the Armored Corps. That's when Yoni first met Avigdor Ben-Gal — Yanosh — the brigade commander.

Says Ben-Gal, "It was in some tent during the night, six or seven hours before the breakthrough. I think we were introduced by Rafael Eitan. It was right before the divisional briefing, and Raful said to me, 'Look, this is Yoni. He's under your command. Take him.' That was it. I put him in the first battalion to go through. . . . During the fighting, contact between us was really hurried, quick and dry, to the point. You got an order, you got your mission, you reported. But even then, somehow, I took to him. I was always glad when he showed up and we could talk.

"A few days later, he was called to Northern Command headquarters. Right in the middle of the war, they take him. I think they flew him in by copter to give him some mission elsewhere. I told him, 'Refuse anything they give you. You're coming back to us.' He said, 'Listen, I'm turning down anything else and coming back. All the rest is nonsense.' And he did. Later, they took him out a second time for something having to do with retaking Mt. Hermon. I was sorry they were taking him, and I'd known him, what, ten days? Maybe less."

The friendship between the two continued after the war. When Yoni finished the transfer course into the armored corps, he was put in with Ben-Gal's division, which was on the Golan Heights.

"As time went by, Yoni had a real effect on me," Ben-Gal says. "There was a pretty big gap in our ages. I was 40 and Yoni was thirty when he died, a difference of ten years. I was always senior in rank to him, but what drew me to him — since we were in the army, with all its hierarchy, I always had to approach him, not the other way around — was that I felt I could learn a lot from him. I appreciated him, in the full sense of the word, as a person whose strength and inner resources you could draw on. Everyone — it doesn't matter how old or what rank or what he does — looks for someone he can rely on, to feel stronger. In the army, in that kind of work, you particularly need that. It's only natural that the people who surround you wait for you to give them that support, and they're stronger by being around you. That's how I felt about everyone I worked with in the army, and without meaning to brag, I felt a little above them. But when I met Yoni, I felt here's someone who's above me in many ways, in most ways. I wanted his company so I could, to phrase it badly, take advantage of what he had, so some of it would rub off on me — in short, so I could lean on him.

"When I was with him, when I talked with him, I felt intellectually stimulated. It was as though I'd just read a good book. A book like that — it's an asset, it's uplifting. There was something impressive about him, a presence. But I don't think it's worth listing particular traits. It's more important to explain how a man feels than to give labels to everything."

* * *

We pass through a landscape of dun expanses, out of which round-peaked hills jut upward. On the horizon ahead looms Mt. Hermon. "You know," my friend, sitting beside me, continues, "at the time of the breakthrough there was heavy Syrian shelling. We moved away from the crossroads a bit and waited at the side of the road. There was nothing we could do but wait for the shelling to end. We all hugged the bottom of the half-track. Only Yoni stood and watched what was happening. We said, 'Yoni, get down.' But he kept standing. Why did he do it? There was nothing he could do anyway."

I hadn't heard this story before, but it's as if I had. Yoni remained standing, I think to myself, because it wasn't his nature to act differently. True, it was an unnecessary risk. He certainly would never have allowed the men under him to act like that. When it came to their safety, he was frightfully strict and careful. Once he even upbraided his brigade commander in the armored corps for appearing in his company compound without his bullet-proof vest. But to understand why he stood, you have to know that the natural, physical fear of death that almost everyone has — certainly a young man of 27 — was something Yoni never felt. As commander, even if there were nothing he could do at the moment, he'd watch and study the fighting.

A little later in the war, Yoni heard on the radio that Lt. Col. Yossi Ben-Hanan, commander of a tank battalion in Ben-Gal's 7th Brigade, remained wounded in the field after his attack on the hill of Tel-Shams had been repulsed. All but the dead and wounded had pulled back; and Yossi's tank, which had taken an enemy missile, was still at the foot of the hill while Yossi, wounded and bleeding, lay on the ground where he had been thrown by the blast. The driver of the tank hadn't been hurt, but had chosen to stay with his wounded commander and care for him rather than run for his own life. Yossi had managed to report to the rear on his situation with a portable transceiver Yoni had given him the day before. He and his driver were completely alone in what had been Syrian-controlled territory, and it was only a matter of time before the Syrians returned.

"We [Yoni's men] were eating battle rations outside Yanosh's brigade headquarters and following the battle on the radio. Suddenly, we heard that Yossi's force had been hit with missiles and stopped, and that he personally had to be pulled out of there," recalls Shai.

"I didn't exactly know what to do and how to extricate Yossi from there, since it was deep inside enemy territory," says Ben-Gal. "It was already dusk, with night-fall coming on. And then Yoni came to me, at his own initiative, and said, 'Give me the mission and I'll get him out of there.' "[3] Without a second's delay, a dozen men, including Muki, Giora, and Shai, went with him in two armored personnel carriers. "Friends of mine, officers from the 7th Brigade, said,

'Listen, Shai, what you're doing is suicide. It's nuts.' 'Shut up,' I told one, 'Don't talk like that in front of the men.' "

The two APCs, swaying and bumping in the rocky expanse, followed the treadmarks left by Yossi's tanks; then the men spotted the flames from a Syrian antitank jeep that had been hit in the battle and drove toward it. The hour was dusk, and by the time they reached the bottom of the hill, it was dark. Leaving the APCs, they continued on foot, running, until they reached Yossi. Yoni ordered several men to check the disabled Israeli tanks to make sure that there was no one in them, and strapped Yossi onto a stretcher. Then they hurried to pull out. Only a short while later, the Syrians arrived and towed the Israeli tanks to Damascus — with the bodies of crewmen that the soldiers from the Unit had apparently missed in the darkness.

"Yoni's arrival with his men saved me," Yossi said years later. "I owe my life to him."[4]

Just after the war, after visiting Yossi in the hospital, Yoni wrote him a letter. It praised Yossi's abilities as a combat officer, made no mention of the rescue, and said, "I was happy to hear you say, from inside that cast you were wrapped in, that the important thing is that you're here, that you're alive. . . . You reminded me very much of how I felt when I was lying in Rambam Hospital after the Six Day War, as the doctors around me discussed what would happen to my left arm. It seemed to me they were worried about an absolutely minor matter. What matters is to live; everything else is trivial."

* * *

My memories move on, passing one crossroads after another on the way to his last rush forward at Entebbe. I think of something he said to me during a conversation we had in the last year of his life. I was trying to convince him to act a certain way; Yoni, in a moment of openness, said he couldn't accept my advice because he looked at life differently from how I did. He said he couldn't think seriously about "tomorrow" and do the "rational" thing because he couldn't count on being alive when tomorrow came.

"My life belongs to me, and so does my death," Yoni had shot back at Bibi once, years earlier. It was just before another hostage rescue, when a hijacked Sabena airliner had been landed by Arab terrorists at Lod Airport in 1972. Yoni reached the scene minutes before the operation began. Bibi already had his gun, as did his men, ready to storm the plane. There was a standing order in the army against two brothers taking part in the same action, and Yoni, who wanted desperately to join the operation, demanded that Bibi let him fight in his place.

"How can I let my men fight while I sit on the sidelines?" Bibi argued.

Yoni answered, "Okay, you're right. So we'll both go in."

"Think of our parents," Bibi tried to persuade him. "Think of what would happen to them if we were both killed."

Yoni answered as he did: that he would be the master of both his life and his death.

But Ehud, who was the commander of the operation, would not let Yoni take part. And Yoni's anger quickly gave way to other feelings when he saw Bibi wounded after the gun battle.

To this day, I have no idea how Yoni succeeded in including me once in an operation he led. The aim of the operation was to abduct Syrian officers and exchange them for Israeli pilots and navigators long held in Syrian prisons. Perhaps it was easier to look the other way because I was assigned to a secondary force responsible for blocking a road. I saw Yoni for only a moment during the operation, but that was enough for me to understand the effect he could have — the look in his eye, the tone of his voice — on men in battle. Our force, under Muki Betser, had a marginal role, and we weren't around for the lion's share of the main action — overpowering the Syrian officers and the Lebanese gendarmes escorting them. The main force, led by Yoni and his second-in-command for the operation, Uzi Dayan, crossed into Lebanese territory in civilian cars to the area where the abduction was to take place, even as the Syrian convoy was heading west toward the same spot. Yoni's men pulled over by the side of the road and pretended to be a group of Lebanese having trouble with a car. Suddenly, Yoni's observation team reported that something had gone wrong. The Syrian convoy had been stopped by villagers who apparently suspected something, and had begun turning around. Yoni instantly ordered his men into the cars. After a short chase they overtook the Syrians and the Lebanese, and in the ensuing fire-fight overwhelmed them.

When we, Muki's force, approached from the roadblock in the west, only a few last shots could still be heard. The Syrian officers had already been captured

and gathered together. This was the first time my comrades and I had participated in fighting of any kind, and when I reached the area of the shooting, I
was as tense as I could be. Yoni stood on the road, calmly giving orders in a
forceful voice, without excitement, telling us what to do — and the tension
dropped. We were assigned by him to comb the area to the north for a lone
Syrian officer who had managed to escape during the fight. When we returned
several minutes later without the Syrian, Yoni was gone already. He'd left Uzi in
charge of bringing the prisoners and their vehicles to Israel, and had driven to
the nearby Arab village to oversee the search for an Arab car, possibly from the
convoy, that had fled there. When we crossed the border into Israel, trium-
phantly escorting the captured vehicles and the band of high-ranking prisoners, he wasn't with us.

* * *

We're driving past the area of the Golan where Yoni's tank battalion was
based. Yoni built the base; shortly after his death, it was renamed Camp Jonathan
and our family was given a tour. Entering the base we saw, painted in big black
letters on the wall of one a building, a few key sentences of Yoni's parting speech
to the battalion. The words had been reconstructed by members of the battalion
from memory after his death, more than a year after he'd addressed them — and
were strikingly close to the text of the speech we'd found in Yoni's papers.

"Kirsch, Yoni's second-in-command, assembled the entire battalion in a big
open area," says Yehezkel Kellner, one of the battalion's staff officers, describing
the change-of-command. "It was after some exercise. The tanks were arranged on
three sides of a large rectangle, facing inward. Yoni stood in front of them on an
APC and made his speech.

"I believe there can be no compromises on results," Yoni said. "Let us never
compromise in this battalion with results that are less than the best possible —
and even those let us improve," he said, giving his credo. "I believe in Israel, and
in the sense of collective responsibility that must accompany every man fighting
for the survival of his country."

"When he was done," continues Kellner, "he saluted the battalion to show
his esteem. That's how he wound up his command."

At the center of the base was Yoni's office, which at times had also served
him as a place of refuge, where he could let go of the army world of grey barracks

and paths marked with whitewashed stones and enter a different realm. "One night, I finished working at two or three in the morning, and I saw a light on in his office," recalls Kellner. "I went to see what was up. Yoni had been in the field all day, at a company exercise. I look in, and see him reading a book of poetry — Bialik, I think it was."

"At the time, if he slept two or three hours a night, it was a lot," says Ben-Gal, who was then Yoni's division commander. "He literally *lived* the battalion 24 hours a day. It's rare that you meet a person with such drive to succeed at something. Little by little, he built the battalion and shaped it, and exercises started to take proper shape.

"His first battalion exercise was an utter failure. It was basically a technical exercise, and it just went wrong, partly because of Yoni's inexperience with tanks, partly just because of bad luck. Sometimes, if you start on the wrong foot, nothing helps. It happens.

"I was sorry that the exercise he'd led had gone so poorly. I reviewed it for about 15 minutes in front of everyone, and then I said, 'Yoni, come.' I took him and analyzed what had happened from A to Z, blow by blow. I didn't know how he'd respond to my coming down on him so hard. I wasn't angry or shouting, but I was still criticizing in the most serious way possible, and sometimes that's the hardest thing to bear. I saw how he was writing everything down, not just saying 'Okay,' but asking questions and analyzing things himself. And suddenly I felt that instead of my reviewing one more standard exercise, we were having a real discussion. I'd say something, he'd speak, he'd ask and I'd answer, I'd elaborate on something, and so would he, and it turned into a real conversation between two people. We sat for four or five hours and talked about the exercise. We'd go off on a tangent about military history, philosophy, geography, and then go back to the exercise — all of it somehow connected to the matter at hand. I saw he had a desire to learn, be educated, understand. He didn't sit there like someone getting a reprimand, waiting for the lecture to be over and the humiliation to end so he could get out of there. He didn't want to leave. . . . I asked him, 'How long do you need before you can do the exercise over?' He said a week or two, and at the end of that time we held it again. Then you got to see what it means when someone can take what he learns and really put it into practice. It was first-rate. He didn't repeat one mistake he'd made the first time."

On Independence Day, almost a year after he'd taken command of the battalion, Yoni was supposed to go to Northern Command headquarters to receive the rank of lieutenant colonel from Rafael Eitan.

"He didn't have an Armored Corps black beret for the ceremony, just a regular, green work cap," recalls a staff officer. "In fact, he didn't have any of the different emblems or insignia either, like a Six Day War service ribbon. All of those little external symbols that they wear around every day in Tel Aviv in the Kiryah for people to see, he was missing. He'd go around the base with these tattered major's epaulets, and I had already told him once, half joking, that maybe it was time to get new ones. But before the ceremony, Haim Kirsch, his second-in-command, who was also a major, had given him a pair of his own epaulets, and I think maybe a belt, and between the two of us we got him everything he needed. After that, he hurried off to Northern Command to get his promotion."

As a battalion commander, Ben-Gal says, Yoni was "professionally and personally, one of the finest officers in the division, both in his ability to analyze the overall military picture, and in his personal ability to handle a tank. He knew all the tricks of the trade; he'd made a point of studying them. His unit was the best in the division. He infused it with his personality and turned it into the top battalion — in dry professional terms and in terms of morale and how much the men identified with the Unit.

"I wanted him to stay in the Armored Corps. I told him, 'We'll make you a deputy brigade commander after you finish your stint with the battalion. In my opinion you'll be a brigade commander in a short time.' I believed in his abilities, his leadership."

What would have happened if Yoni had stayed in the Armored Corps, I think to myself. "I tried to convince him not to go back to the Unit," Ben-Gal told me, and I can't get his words out of my mind. But my speculation is pointless, because there was never the slightest chance he would make any decision but the one he did.

Yoni came back to the Unit. He returned to the crucible where he had been formed, as he devotedly called it, and with that move, he became even more deeply alone.

* * *

"He struck me as a different type from the other commanders I'd known," says one of the Unit's staff officers. "To a great degree he was an intellectual. . . . He was quite a bit more mature than we. There were lots of things we couldn't understand then that I see differently today. . . . Only in the last few years have I begun to understand what it was he was doing. Then, we were too young to get it. And because we were young, the criticisms that some of us used to make of him were pretty harsh. But over the year he commanded the Unit, I had the chance to see him in wider forums, outside the Unit, and I began to have a different idea of who he was. . . . I was at his house once, and we talked about all sorts of things. He was sick and had asked me to come over. I realized then that the breadth of his knowledge was much greater than I'd imagined. That was when I began to change my mind about him, and to understand much more. First of all, I began to see that he noticed everything, even if he didn't always find it necessary to comment. When he thought it was important, he'd express his opinion. He could be forgiving, but only up to a certain point — if it went past that, he'd give you a kick in the pants. He wanted people to learn from their mistakes, to try to correct themselves and improve by their own initiative, and not because he'd used his authority. . . .

"He had much more experience in life than we, and it affected his behavior. He had a really good heart. You saw it in the little things, inside the Unit and outside.

"On one hand, he tried to develop a closeness, and the men were a lot less intimidated by him than by other top commanders. On the other hand, he was a riddle in a lot of ways. We didn't understand him, and I think he knew it."

In many respects, Yoni was an enigma to the enlisted men as well. "He was different," says one. "You could see that, despite his efforts to get close to us, he remained withdrawn, pensive. . . . When we went somewhere, or when we were waiting for a briefing to begin, he used to sit by himself with his pipe and a book. But when we were going out on the town in the evening and needed a car, we'd send a note into his conference room asking if we could have his car — something it takes a lot of impudence to ask the commander of the Unit — and we'd get it."

* * *

Another trip of mine, this time to the south, to Masada. I enter the big cistern on the south side of the mountain. I know that, not long before his death, Yoni climbed down these endless stairs until he reached the bottom of the empty cistern that had served the Jewish fighters of the revolt against Rome for three years. In his hand was the pamphlet given to visitors. Here, deep beneath the earth, on the cistern floor lit by shafts of light from openings in the ceiling high above, the air was cool and still. He could look at leisure through the pamphlet. On the last pages was the final speech of Elazar Ben-Yair, the leader of the Jewish fighters who were to take their own lives and those of their families just before the final Roman assault. In the silence of the cathedral-like space, with only Bruria at his side, he was caught by the words and read them aloud. She begged him to stop, but the lines spoken by the commander of Masada 2,000 years before came from his mouth and echoed between the stone walls:

> For death were we born, and for death did we give birth to our children. From death escape not even the most contented of men. But a life of disgrace and slavery . . . these evils were not decreed to be the fate of men from birth. . . . Surely, we will die before we will become the slaves of those who despise us, and free men will we remain as we leave the land of the living.

"To live," wrote Yoni in his last letter, just days before his death, "and as long as you possibly can." He didn't want to part from life. The question that stayed with him was: Which life to lead? In just going from one day to the next, he could see no point.

Endnotes
  1. Shai's and Muki's descriptions of the battle are taken from IDF Radio, "Special Broadcast in Memory of Lt. Col. Jonathan Netanyahu," August 6, 1976.
  2. Interview conducted by Danny Veseli of IDF Radio, July 1976.
  3. *Yoni*, documentary film, Israel, 2001, Semion Vinokur, director.
  4. IDF Radio, "Special Broadcast in Memory of Lt. Col. Jonathan Netanyahu," August 6, 1976.

The last photo taken of Yoni; a few weeks before Entebbe.

CHAPTER V

After a few hours sleep, Yoni awoke Saturday morning and ate breakfast with Bruria. Stretched out next to them on the floor of their apartment was Mor, their German shepherd. Yoni took the lemon meringue pie Bruria had bought and, as he sometimes did, ate straight from the pie pan. "I'll eat just half of it," he joked, "and then next time I'll eat half of the half that's left, so I'll always have some more pie to eat."

Bruria knew that the Unit was planning a rescue mission. While they ate, Yoni told her he was sure the government wouldn't have the courage to approve the operation, and that nothing would come of it. "It's possible that's what he thought," says Bruria, "but he might just have been saying it so I wouldn't worry."

"I'll probably be back in the afternoon for a few hours," he told her. "I'll see you then."

In response to her questions, Yoni started saying something about the troubled mood he'd been in, and that he'd expressed in the letter he'd written her a few days before. But the conversation didn't go far, perhaps partly due to lack of time. "I've got to run," he said when he realized he'd stayed longer than he'd planned.

After he had gone down to the car, in which his driver was already waiting, Bruria rushed downstairs and called to him, "Yoni, you forgot to say goodbye to Mor!" But the car was already on its way out of the lot, and he did not hear her.

The activity at the Unit still hadn't let up. The men were still busy with the last preparations and with laying out all their equipment on the ground for the final inspection. The staff officers continued coordinating the final details. Besides the inspection, Yoni gave a short briefing for everyone who was going. Then he phoned Hagai Regev, Chief of Staff Gur's adjutant. They were careful to speak only in veiled comments. Yoni wanted to hear from Hagai, who was at Gur's side constantly, whether the previous night's decision to go ahead remained firm. He also wanted to make sure that no one from outside the Unit would interfere at the last minute with its independence, or his as commander, during the raid. Hagai let him understand that nothing had changed on either point, then wished him luck.

Yoni put down the receiver. What he'd just heard undoubtedly made him very excited. Even now, he realized, after a long night of agonizing deliberations had passed in Tel Aviv since Gur had declared his backing for the operation, even with only a few hours left to H-hour, the operation continued to gather momentum. His brief respite at home had interrupted his own preparations, which had continued for over 24 hours. But events hadn't stopped because of his short time-out. The chance that he and his men would fly to Africa to free the captives looked more likely than ever.

Next Yoni sat with the commanders of the Unit's sub-forces to talk through tactics for each stage of the mission. Before the meeting, some of the junior officers approached their immediate superior, Giora. "On Saturday morning we found out that the mission was still on," he recalls. "I remember the feeling we had when we suddenly realized that things were happening for real." The officers said that, with the operation about to get underway, they did not feel good enough about it. "You've got to go to Yoni and tell him that the details just aren't all worked out," they said. The move, Giora says, stemmed from the "hasty way in which the operation was prepared, and from the tendency in the Unit of bringing up endless scenarios, from a tradition which says that before every action, you ask what you do if such and such happens. A lot of questions had come up this time — what happens if this or that team gets stuck, or if the terrorists are here and not there — and there was no time to settle everything." Giora went to Yoni, explained the situation and told him what was worrying the junior officers. "Yoni understood immediately that there was a problem here, and accepted what I told him." He assembled his officers in the room of his deputy, Yiftah, and the discussion began.

At the meeting, the officers went over the full range of questions that had arisen. One problem that came up was how to hold down enemy forces on the roof or in the control tower. As Giora remembers it, Yoni had ruled during previous briefings that, in the first seconds of the attack, the covering team would not fire on the high points unless shooting began from those spots. When the tactics session began, the officers didn't understand why the team shouldn't open fire immediately. But this point in Yoni's plan stemmed from the fact the the operation was a rescue mission, not a conventional assault on an enemy building. As always in such operations, preventing harm to the hostages entailed additional risks for the rescue force.

"We told Yoni, 'They'll shoot at us from there,' " says Giora. "But Yoni explained that the entire action would last between 30 and 60 seconds. During that time, Yoni was supposed to be at the front, and would have to decide if a team was stuck, and maybe to call another team to come in, or even to go in himself if there was a problem. When troops from five different teams enter a building at the same time and start shooting, there's noise and confusion, and it's hard to keep control. At first glance it looks simple, but in practice it's not, and especially if you want it to be over in a minute. So if he had a team above or behind him pouring heavy fire in the direction of the tower or the top floors, it would wreak so much havoc and make so much noise that he, as the commander, might lose control at the critical moment. He wouldn't be able to communicate with the different teams and shout his orders to them. Yoni's emphasis was on achieving the mission's goal of securing the rooms where the hostages were, and that depended on his being able to read what was happening in the battle during that very short bit of time. He insisted on withholding the cover fire, even though he was aware of the danger. He insisted that he have control over the heart of the operation."

The session was scheduled to last 15 minutes. It went on for an hour. "It was a productive hour," says Giora. "There was a lot of discussion about how things would be done under this kind of pressure. Different issues came up, and Yoni had to give them answers on the spot. . . . It was a real tactics session, like it should be. What happens if this team is knocked out, who replaces it, and so on. We raised these questions, and Yoni just decided on them and said: We'll do it this way or that. After an hour, we came out feeling completely different, feeling that a lot of things . . . that hadn't been clear were settled now. It was an excellent meeting."

When the hour was over, Yoni had to leave. He and several of the staff officers had to go to Lod for the last officers' briefing before the operation, and he asked Muki to finish up with the issues that were left to discuss.

On his way out of the office he called Ya'el Tatarkah, one of his secretaries, to say goodbye. Yoni seemed to her to be in a good mood. In answer to her question, he told her he was sure everyone would come back — but added, "as long as it didn't end in disaster." As he left, Ya'el noticed that he took with him a paperback in English that he'd been reading, a thriller by Alister MacLean called *The Way to Dusty Death*.

On his way across the base he ran into Yisrael. They stood together talking for a moment. Yisrael noticed that Yoni seemed introspective, thoughtful. "He felt he'd finished his battle over the operation, and now he was alone with his thoughts."

Suddenly, Yoni told him, "Listen, Yisrael, I'm going to salute the flag. Once in his life, a guy's got to salute the flag." He said it with all his heart, recalls Yisrael, and I felt that he really did salute. Not with his hand, but with his soul."

Even though Avi didn't want to go to Lod, saying it would be a waste of time, Yoni urged him to come along. "Come on, come with me," he said. Avi sensed that the ride to Lod deepened Yoni's recognition that the mission was about to take place. Yoni told him that he wanted to speak once again to the soldiers of the Unit, to tell them some additional things, before they set out.

"Also," relates Avi, "there was another side to our conversation, beyond the tactical aspect of the operation: the Zionist and human side. The importance of the mission really moved him, and he started talking about it with a lot of feeling. You start picturing where you're going, and thinking that if you pull it off and bring back more than a hundred Israelis, what an incredible accomplishment it would be. . . . Yoni also apologized that he had stuck me with other work, but said there was no choice, that someone had to take care of our ongoing responsibilities. . . . He was in a good mood, but immersed in his own thoughts. There was a lot running through his mind. . . . He was also concerned with the other matter, the one that was keeping me here while he was about to go. He said, 'Avi, I'm leaving you here. Take care of this, because we shouldn't mess it up.' "

They reached the squadron headquarters at Lod with a little time to spare before the briefing. Yoni saw Dr. Eran Dolev, who had once been the Unit's combat doctor. Eran had been asked by Dr. Ephraim Sneh, the Infantry and Paratroops Command's medical officer, to be responsible for the medical facilities that would be set up on the fourth plane, the one that would evacuate the hostages. Eran assembled a team of experienced physicians and medics, and they had prepared abundant supplies and equipment to care for the dozens of wounded that were expected. Yoni and Eran talked a bit about treatment of the wounded, and Eran reminded Yoni of another action of the Unit a few years earlier, in which a soldier had been hit. The man had lain wounded in enemy territory, with only one other Israeli by his side. Yoni, who had been relatively far from the scene, was the first to arrive. "After he finished his own task, he ran toward them," recalls Menahem Digli, who was commander of the Unit at the time. "He simply took the initiative and went to solve the problem. It was an episode that epitomized Yoni's way of doing things — the way he saw a problem, responded fast, and solved it first. He kept us in the picture by radio the whole time, and he was very quiet, no panic at all. He told us he was on his way, and he calmed down the soldier who was with the wounded man, 'We're on our way to you, stay calm.' " Yoni evacuated the wounded soldier; the doctor who treated him was Eran.

Now, at Lod, Eran returned to the question of casualties in the present operation and said their number would depend on whether the terrorists were taken by surprise.

"Yoni was very level-headed," Eran remembers. "I think he was in the kind of state of mind you sometimes see before exams. He had finished preparing and felt completely ready. . . . For him, the matter was taken care of, all that remained was to carry it out. My impression was that he was under no stress at all . . . but he was like a wound-up spring, ready... It also struck me that he really needed a haircut; his hair was down the back of his neck. And then I saw that he was tired — his responses were a bit slow."

While Yoni was standing in the squadron's briefing room, he heard that Amnon Halivni, the pilot of the fourth plane, had been stationed at Entebbe for a few years as a member of the Israeli military mission and knew the place well. "When he heard that, he pounced on me like a dog on a bone," Halivni recounts. " 'Just a minute,' he said, 'Can you tell me about the building?' "

They bent over either side of the long briefing-room table. Yoni spread out a chart of the airport, and began to interrogate Halivni. As the pilot answered Yoni's questions, he sketched a diagram of the building on a piece of paper.

"Yoni wanted to know details about the building, from the shed for firefighting equipment on the right end to the control tower on the left. He wanted to know where the stairs were, what kind of windows there were, what the approach to the entrances was like, and more. He was especially interested in how to get from room to room inside. He asked how you got from the customs hall for arriving passengers to the large departures hall. I told him there was a corridor hallway sandwiched between the two, but I couldn't answer his question about whether there were doorways from the two rooms into the corridor so that you could get from the arrivals hall to the departures hall that way." This could have been the first Yoni had heard of the corridor or of the entrance to it from the outside.

Yoni was also very interested in where the stairs to the second floor were. Halivni told him that, as far as he could remember, the entrance to the stairwell was on the other side of the building, and that to get to it from the entrance plaza on the south side, one had to cross through the building and come out on the north. (In fact, the entrance to the stairwell was indeed in the northern part of the building, past the customs hall, but not outside the building.) Likewise, Yoni wanted to know the exact location of the door on the second floor that opened onto the other staircase leading back down to the floor of the large hall. He went over details of other parts of the building with Halivni, and questioned him about the entrance plaza in the front, across which the assault force would run — whether there were any fences across it or other obstacles, and what the surface was like. Halivni also told him a few things about the control tower — most importantly, where to find the stairs leading up to the top.

"He asked about one more thing," says Halivni. " 'How do you think the Ugandan sentries will react to the Mercedes and the jeeps?' I told him: A Ugandan sentry plays by the rules all the way. It's not like an Israeli on guard duty at a gate. The Ugandan sentries do what they're supposed to, and follow the orders they're given. They're on their feet the whole night, without napping, and if a car comes, there's no messing around. They'll yell 'Stop!' or something like that, and they'll point their bayoneted rifles at you. And if you don't stop, they'll shoot, not because they think you're an enemy, but for fear of the punishment they'll get if they don't. . . . A Ugandan soldier might not be bright, but he's aggressive, and you've got to be careful with him."*

They talked for about 20 minutes, with Yoni asking questions and Halivni answering to the best of his ability. "He was anxious for info, trying to get more facts," recalls Halivni. "He left one clear impression: He was completely focused on the mission ahead of him. . . . As long as he thought he could learn something from me, he listened to every word. The moment he saw he'd extracted the relevant information, he moved on."

At 11:30 Saturday morning, Yekutiel Adam opened the briefing, the forum in which the top commanders would formally receive their final orders. Inside and outside the briefing room, high-ranking officers huddled together. A large diagram of the airport at Entebbe had been set up on the dais. Among those who spoke were Adam, Benny Peled, Dan Shomron, Matan Vilna'i, Shiki Shani, and Yoni. But most of those who would take part in the mission — officers and men — were not present, and the briefing was aimed mainly at going through the standard procedure.

When the briefing ended, Yoni went over to Shani. "Come show me again exactly where it is you're putting us down," he said. The request was typical of Yoni. While asking for his own sake, he undoubtedly also wanted to make sure there would be no misunderstanding on Shani's part about where and how the vehicles would be unloaded. They sat at the briefing room table and went over the diagram of the airport. Shani took the opportunity to tell Yoni that he intended to put the plane down at Entebbe even if the runway lights were dark and the radar failed to identify the runway. "It's the squadron's own private alternative plan," Shani said. "If we can't find the runway, we'll pretend to be a

---

* In fact, Israelis who served in Uganda were warned upon their arrival in the country about how Ugandan sentries tended to shoot with hardly a second thought. Halivni himself says that he used to raise his hands, despite his senior status in Uganda, when he approached a sentry at night.

civilian aircraft in distress, and ask the control tower to turn on the runway lights for us."

"Yoni liked the idea. He told me, 'That's a great plan,' " says Shani. "Then he ran off to tell someone in his group about it, as though it were a problem they'd been wrestling with, and here someone had come and given them a reasonable solution. After that, all sorts of senior officers got hold of him over there and wouldn't let go of him. I pulled out of there and sat outside on the grass with my pilots and talked."

Yoni made a deep impression on Shani. "We were the same rank, but I felt a respect for him the way you do for someone who is much higher up. It was a feeling based partly on what I'd seen of him myself and partly on stories going around. You had a combination of an extraordinary fighter and an intellectual. . . . I definitely had the image of someone out of the ordinary. He seemed like a hero out of our ancient past."

After the briefing, says Tzvika Har-Nevo, Shani's reserve navigator, the two of them saw Yoni pass a short distance away. Shani turned to Tzvika and made a comment that remained indelibly in his memory. "That's the greatest fighter Israel has ever had," he said.

The veteran navigator hardly expected to hear such a remark from his squadron commander, whom he'd known for years. "From Shani you'd get a compliment maybe once in half a century. He's a serious sort," explains Tzvika. "After all, we'd all been raised from childhood on stories about our heroes from the country's early years, and suddenly to hear this from a guy like Shani was really astounding."

And then Shani said, "And he's got a 50-50 chance of coming out of this alive."

During the morning, Gur, Adam, and Peled had met with Prime Minister Rabin, Defense Minister Peres, and Foreign Minister Yigal Allon. Earlier, Gur had received a report from the head of the Intelligence Branch, saying that in his judgment the available intelligence material was sufficient to permit going ahead. The army's plan for freeing the hostages was presented to the three ministers, and the chief of staff announced unequivocally his recommendation that it be implemented. On the basis of this recommendation, Rabin assembled the senior ministers, and after a short discussion in which Peres spoke strongly in favor of a military solution to the crisis, the ministers approved the plan. A meeting of the full cabinet was set for 2 p.m. There the final decision would be made.

The Unit's men had a respite of an hour or two before boarding the army bus for Lod. During and after the officers' tactics session there was not much left for them to do, since most of the preparations had been completed. Bukhris, the youngest member of the force, remembers this break as the toughest part of the whole operation — waiting, with little to do but think about what was coming and to take stock of himself and his life. Yael, Yoni's secretary, had gone to high school with Bukhris, and came up to him during the morning to encourage him. He was mulling over whether to leave something in writing for his family before setting out.

Danny Dagan and Amitzur Kafri were still so busy working on the Mercedes that they didn't notice the bus had left the base with the rest of the men. They finished putting the Ugandan flag on the antenna on the car's left side and another small pennant on the metal rod that had been welded to the front of the Mercedes. The license plates had already been switched to "Ugandan" ones made of cardboard. But they still weren't satisfied with the car's appearance. The nighttime paint job had left splotches of uneven color, and so the two continued to go over the car with can after can of black spray paint. Suddenly, Danny realized they were alone. They went to the center of the base to look for the rest of the force and saw that everyone had left. Quickly they folded the flags, covered the plates, climbed in and drove to the airport.

When they arrived there was still some time until takeoff. Amitzur backed the Mercedes into the hold of the first Hercules, which was standing out on the runway. The two Land Rovers were already inside, and all three vehicles were tied to the floor of the plane. In the meantime, the Unit's men had already met up with the members of the other, larger forces taking part in the operation. Bukhris remembers several paratroopers kissing goodbye to their company secretaries, who'd come with them to the airport.

Meanwhile, Avi Livneh had gone to a nearby base and came back with a packet of aerial photographs of the Entebbe airport.* These had been taken by a Mossad agent the day before, flying a small civilian plane. The photos ruled out

---

* Sometime later, a soldier from the Intelligence Corps also brought a packet of photos to Lod Airport and handed them to the men as the planes were about to take off.

the presence of a massive Ugandan force around the building or on the roof — at least at the time the information had been gathered. That reduced concerns about a high casualty toll and supported the assessment that the operation would succeed. Without that information, which the chief of staff had received verbally earlier, he would not have given his go-ahead.

Yoni told his men that they'd soon fly to Sharm al-Sheikh, and after a stopover there would go on to Entebbe. The cabinet was now meeting, he said, to decide on the operation. He added a few words of instructions for the operation, but left most of his final briefing for Sharm al-Sheikh, the last spot where he would have all the men together.

Only when Shaul Mofaz, the commander of the peripheral defense force, boarded plane No. Two, did he finally have a chance to arrange with Nati, the pilot, how they'd work together. They agreed, for instance, on the signals Nati would give the troops by blinking the interior lights when it was time to unchain the vehicles or open the cargo doors. Coordinating such matters at the last minute was out of character for both the air force and the Unit, but this was practically the first time they'd been able to talk to each other.

Peres and Gur arrived at Lod to see the forces off. Peres writes that when he got to Lod, the commanders of the different units came to ask him whether the cabinet would approve the mission. Shomron told Peres, "Shimon, don't worry. Everything will go fine." Yoni, says Peres, "came to shake my hand and tell me that the plan was 'tip-top.' "[1] Peres and Gur stayed only a few minutes before hurrying back to Tel Aviv, where the meeting of the full cabinet was about to begin.

Yoni and Avi still had time to review the new aerial photographs from Entebbe. "Intelligence was still pouring in from all sorts of directions," says Avi, "and we talked it over. Towards the end, when they were about to start getting on the planes, Yoni said to me, 'Come with me as far as Sharm al-Sheikh.' I said to him, 'Yoni, I'm here without a gun or anything, and you're telling me to come to Sharm? Then what? You all take off and I stay behind. It doesn't feel right.' In the end I convinced him there was no point in my going on to the Sinai with him. I went with him to the car to get his ammo vest and equipment bag." At Yoni's request, his driver had filled his canteens for him; he hadn't had time to do it himself.

"We agreed that I'd take his car, and come back with it to Lod the next morning to pick him up after the operation and take him back to the Unit," Avi says. "We shook hands, and I wished him luck. I could feel from his handshake that this wasn't just another operation, but something special. I felt, and I think he felt, even though I can't tell you for sure what was going on in his mind, that this handshake meant more, somehow, than a simple goodbye. He was smiling, but it was a smile that had a lot of meaning to it. He still thought to tell me, 'Do everything we agreed on, so we won't lose time on the other thing.' "

Ben-Gal, too, parted from Yoni here. "Yoni was the last one to board his plane. I was standing at the door. We shook hands. I told him, 'Don't worry. If something happens, we'll look after the widows.' Of course, I said it more as a joke than anything else. It never crossed my mind that he would be killed and would never come back. I didn't doubt for a second that he'd come back. He told me, 'It'll be all right, and give her my regards,' or 'Take care of her" — he said something like that, referring to Bruria. And that was the last time I saw him."

At 1:20 p.m., the four Hercules transports began taking off from Lod, along with a fifth plane that was brought to Sharm al-Sheikh in reserve. The planes took off at intervals of five minutes and flew in different directions so that it would not appear that they were taking part in an action against a specific target. At a certain distance from Lod each of the planes turned south. On the flight to Sharm al-Sheikh, Rami Levi flew the first plane instead of Shani, to get experience with an aircraft he hadn't flown in a long time. Before takeoff, a few mechanical problems had been detected in the plane, even though Shani had made sure earlier that the four planes picked for the mission underwent a thorough overhaul and that the mechanics repaired or replaced anything that might malfunction. The problems were minor and were quickly repaired, but they left Levi feeling uneasy.

Complete radio silence was maintained during the flight, mainly because there were Soviet surveillance ships not far from Israel's coast. The pilots flew at a very low altitude to elude Jordanian radar. Flying so low, along with the summer heat, caused tremendous turbulence, and the troops suffered severe nausea and vomiting. "It was horrible. I've flown a lot on these Hercules planes, but this was the worst flight of them all by far," remembers one soldier. "We sat in the jeep, and there were times when our heads pounded against the ceiling because the plane was rocking so badly. I thought that when we got to Entebbe and opened the hold, we'd all fall flat on the runway and wouldn't be able to move."[2] Shani felt guilty about the miserable flight even though there was nothing he could do about it. "You know you've got to carry them 7½ hours and afterwards they have to get out and fight, and here it's just the beginning of the flight and you're already knocking them dead." After more than an hour of turbulence that left the floors covered with vomit, the planes finally put down at Sharm al-Sheikh. Just then, radio silence was broken by the pilot of a plane belonging to Arkia, Israel's domestic airline, who noticed the landing and told the control tower — so that anyone else on a civilian wavelength could have heard: "Looks like there's a party going on down there."

The troops deplaned as ground crews rushed to fill the fuel tanks to the top. Even now, only a few men believed the operation would really take place. Shaul remembers wondering at the time of the landing where they could spend the night in the airport.

The paratroopers and the Golani soldiers gathered in one underground hangar, and the Unit's men in another. Many of them were worn out from the flight. Alik did not even have the strength to get off the plane. He asked Amitzur to bring him a change of clothing, and Amitzur brought over a jerrycan of water as well to wash his face. Alik changed his soiled clothes, descended from the plane, and lay for a long while in the sand until he recovered. David gave out anti-nausea pills to the Unit's men, as Dr. Dolev did among the other infantrymen. One soldier from Muki's assault team, who had thrown up repeatedly during the flight and was left dazed and weak, felt that he wouldn't be able to go on. To replace him, Yoni ordered Omer, the commander of one of the APCs, to transfer one of his men to the assault force. Omer chose Amos Goren, whom he trusted to open fire without hesitation when the time came. Yoni told Amos that he'd explain his precise role to him during the flight. In the meantime, Amos went to the soldier who'd pulled out and took his camouflage fatigues, bullhorn, and backpack, which contained explosives for opening doors.

A light meal was distributed to the troops. The soldiers ate and drank, and after a little while began to recover from the flight. Yoni once more reviewed the intelligence data, then spoke to the various teams. "Yoni personally briefed every one of the men, asking each if it was clear where he should be, where the rest of the men would be, and so on," recalls a soldier.[3] Apparently based on his conversation with Halivni, Yoni explained to Yiftah's team, which was to go up to the second floor, that the stairs were located beyond the first room they would enter.

He also gave final instructions to the peripheral defense force, emphasizing that it had to provide an "active blockade" around the old terminal. That didn't mean massive fire, or shooting at fleeing Ugandans who posed no threat; it did mean taking the initiative and thoroughly combing the area to prevent any penetration of forces from outside — and not hesitating to fire on defined targets. The intent was to turn the four APCs into a real security belt. Yoni again stressed the need to block the road leading from the town of Entebbe to the north side of the terminal.

"As things went on, there was a change in Yoni," says one soldier. "I think he was more relaxed. He seemed more at ease, as if he were in his element now."[4]

In addition to Yoni's short briefings, the commanders of the main sub-forces gave their own: Muki to the ground-floor teams, Yiftah to the men who would take the second floor, and Shaul to the periphery forces.

Yoni now gathered his men around him. Just then, they were called two or three times to come to the other hangar for a briefing with Shomron, but Yoni told them that it was more important at the moment for them to hear what he had to tell them. These would be his last words to the entire force. He knew that the things he would try to express and the feelings he would try to instill were critically important to the mission. He spoke briefly, but in these few minutes he succeeded in having the effect he needed.

"It wasn't your usual briefing," says Ilan Blumer. "It was a different sort, and left an impression on everyone."

Yoni started by reporting on the new intelligence material, including the assessment that the Ugandan security belt was thinner than had been thought, and repeated the broad outlines of the plan for the mission.

He then put aside the countless details and instructions that had been heaped on the men in 24 hours of hasty preparations, and spoke to the them about the heart of the matter. The objective was to save the hostages' lives, he said. Even when they were under fire, even if the hostages weren't exactly where they were supposed to be, no matter how unexpectedly things developed, everyone had to remember that goal and work toward achieving it. It had to be their first thought and guide their decisions at every stage of the operation.

The Unit's men were better than the terrorists, so that if everyone acted as logic and necessity demanded, they would quickly overcome the enemy, he said, expressing total confidence in their ability to carry out the mission according to plan. To the assault teams he emphasized again that the overriding concern was to reach the hostages as quickly as possible and eliminate the gunmen threatening them. Men would be wounded during the assault, he said, and no one was to stop to take care of them. The priority was to get to the hostages. Only after the terrorists had been wiped out would the wounded be treated.

"What Yoni said was short and completely to the point," says Shlomo.

"His instructions that everyone had to respond to developments in line with the purpose of the mission were exactly what a soldier needed to hear . . . it put things in the right perspective. When you cram a million details into a man's head in a single day, things gets confused. Then someone comes along and straightens it all out in two sentences."

Finally, he made some brief remarks about the significance of the mission — words that "touched your heart," as Yohai terms them, that can be reconstructed only in the broadest strokes: It was crucial not to compromise with the terrorists, he said. Israel, and the IDF, had an obligation not to give in to blackmail in such situations, even if that now meant that they had to go far from the country's borders to fight back. This was a mission of the first importance, he summed up. Everything was up to them; the entire nation was depending on them.

"During the briefing, I remember being struck by his eloquence," says Amir. "What he said gave me a tremendous amount of confidence. . . . You couldn't give a better briefing before a mission."

"It was a speech I'll never forget," says Alex Davidi, a soldier in Muki's team. "He gave us the confidence that we could do it. His leadership and his ability to affect us were simply above and beyond."

At the end of the briefing, Danny Dagan came up to Yoni, as did others, to glance at the new photographs of the terminal he was holding. "I put my hand on his shoulder. He nodded his head that everything would be all right, without saying a word. It gave me a good feeling."

Yoni gave Tamir a photo of the airport and a map of Uganda for a possible overland escape. "Hang on to these in case we need them," he said.

Among the aerial photographs was a close-up of the old terminal, showing that there was no substantial Ugandan security force outside the building or on its roof. It also showed two awnings, one leading to the second entrance to the main hall and another to the entrance of the small hall. The first entrance to the main hall, which was assigned to Muki and his team, had no awning.

Some of the men then went to the other hangar to hear Shomron. Thirty-one years after the Holocaust, he was saying, there were people who were once again conducting a "selection" of Jews to kill them. The men on this mission had the privilege, he said, to serve as the long arm of the IDF and to prevent history from repeating itself.

Muki recounts that after Yoni's briefing, he and Yoni went off for a few minutes to discuss some points concerning the mission. Suddenly Muki noticed that Shomron was standing and speaking to the rest of the force. He didn't realize that the Unit had been called earlier to hear Shomron's briefing, and somewhat angrily, he said to Yoni, "Look what's happening. They've forgotten who's the main force. They're talking to everyone but us. No one spoke to us."

"No, it's all right," said Yoni. "He called us over, but since we were giving the kind of briefing we were, he let us be."

"Listen," Muki said. "We're the ones doing the dirty work, we're the ones going off to get killed, and the guys on the front page tomorrow are going to be Shomron, Gur, and Rabin."

Yoni laughed.

Endnotes
1. Shimon Peres, *Entebbe Diary* (Jerusalem: Eidanim, 1991).
2. Shlomo Reisman, interview.
3. Eyal Yardenai, interview.
4. Shlomo Reisman, interview.

Reading at camp, 1964

CHAPTER VI

You know what 'liberty' means?" Yoni asks me. I'm eight years old. "It means freedom. That's why this bird is called a 'liberty' in Hebrew. Because he can't live without it."

Yoni and his friend, both 14, are standing in front of me in our yard. I'm sitting on the ground, my arm around the cage I've made: a cardboard box closed with a screen, with a sparrow inside.

A kid from the neighborhood, the kind who's always roaming the streets doing nothing in particular, found the bird in the small patch of woods by the school, and for some reason decided to give it to me. How attached I suddenly became to that fledgling! I padded the cage with dry grass, scattered bread crumbs in it, and put in a tiny dish of water. It was a perfect world, the work of my own hands, that I'd built for the little bird. Early the next morning, as I rushed around the side of the house to see my bird again, I heard a fierce hissing and was struck by fear. I started running. A large, spotted cat was pulling his claws across the top of the cage, trying to tear off the screen, his mouth wide open, fangs showing. He turned his head, caught sight of me and the stone I'd flung at him, and within a split-second had shut his mouth and nimbly disappeared over the fence. The bird behind the screen, tiny and grey, stood frozen in one corner. Only its beak moved non-stop, issuing one terrified squeak after another. My heart went out to the little bird.

I'd been sitting there a long time, guarding the cage and wondering what to do, when Yoni and his friend appeared. Now I try to come up with reasons to convince Yoni that the bird should stay with me, but he patiently explains to me what freedom is — for a bird that's meant to fly above and for people below.

"Moishy and I will take it back to the woods," he says after I explain where it came from. "We'll find a nest for it."

In the end he convinces me. Carefully, I open the screen. Yoni puts his hand through the narrow opening I made and scoops up the bird. They walk away from me on the dirt road that leads from our home to the woods.

When Yoni comes back, alone, he tells me simply that everything is all right — they found it a good nest. I don't ask questions. And I don't know whether he was trying to spare me something when he didn't take me with him to the woods.

* * *

I'm sitting in one of the two rooms of Yoni and Tutti's apartment. Yoni, now a university student, is studying, and I'm doing my own homework for high school. I ask Yoni to go over Tchernichowsky's "Before a Statue of Apollo" with me. After spending more than four years in America, I've been back in Israel for over a year, but I'm still having trouble with Hebrew poetry. The winter before it was Bibi who helped me with my essays on Bialik's poetry, sitting with me at night after coming home tired and sick on a short leave from basic training.

Little by little, as Yoni goes through the poem with me, the verses begin to take hold of him. This guileless enthusiasm of his for the lofty, the beautiful, is so familiar to me — it's the driving force in his life. Toward the middle of the poem he begins to read it aloud in a quiet voice, letting himself feel the melody of the words on his tongue:

> For I am first of them who return to thee,
> Now, as I throw off death throes of generations,
> Now, as I break the chains of the soul,
> My living soul, that clings to this good earth,
> Before life I bow down, before courage, beauty. . . .

His voice sounds pensive, adult, not quite the same as the voice I had heard reciting Jabotinsky's Hebrew translations of poetry years before, when he first discovered them. The family was sitting in the dining room in Philadelphia, and Yoni was late coming to the table. Finally, he appeared in the door, an open book in his hand, and read to us, almost against our wills, the translation of Edgar Allen Poe's "The Raven," and then of "Annabel Lee," marveling over the sounds and the moods of the poems. I wanted him to finish already and sit down. Yet even though his almost childish enthusiasm was irritating at the time (to me — an 11-year-old!), it's surprising how deeply this scene etched itself in my memory — the power with which he read those beautiful lines, the excitement in his voice, the way his eyes shone as they looked at the page. And it's curious that when I was older I searched for those translations, after the English originals failed to satisfy me. This time, in Jerusalem, I listen to him patiently and follow the words of the poem on the page as he reads. When we finish analyzing the poem, Tutti urges me to stay the night. Outside it's pouring rain. I refuse for some reason and go outside to wait for a bus. It's already dark, and it's cold, and the rain lashes my face.

* * *

"I was driving today," he tells Bibi and me. It's already a year since, in 11th grade, he got his American driver's license. "Suddenly, I realized I was driving fast, as I always do, and for a second the car skidded on the curve, and I thought, *Now I'll turn the wheel too hard, I won't step on the brakes fast enough, and that'll be it, my life's over.* Life suddenly felt so tangible, so valuable, that I started driving very slowly, carefully. It was as though my life were dangling by a thin thread, and if, at any instant, I weren't concentrating completely on every move I made, the thread would snap."

A year later, on a snowy winter day, I go up to the attic to be alone. I find Yoni's notebooks from 12th grade, before he went back to Israel to go into the army, and on one page there's a poem by Shakespeare. I read it slowly. I understand only parts of it, mostly with the help of a short composition he had written on it in class. But that's enough, because I've gotten the gist of it:

> Like as the waves make towards the pebbled shore,
> So do our minutes hasten to their end;
> Each changing place with that which goes before,
> In sequent toil all forwards do contend.[1]

* * *

We are sitting around the dining room table in our home in Jerusalem, having Sabbath lunch. Our parents sit at either end, and we children, all school age, sit on the sides. The white tablecloth is spread, on it are dishes and crumbs from the meal, and our voices fill the room with easy conversation. The open window facing us brims with the red flowers of the tree my mother had planted in the garden.

Yoni, on my right, sips the water in his glass. "Water," he says, in a tone full of pleasure. "There's so much flavor in it." He takes another sip — this time leaving the water in his mouth, swishing it once or twice from side to side, tasting it, finally letting it slip down his throat. He smiles to himself, satisfied. Life is worth more than anything to him at this moment; it tastes amazingly good.

Endnote
1. "Sonnet LX."

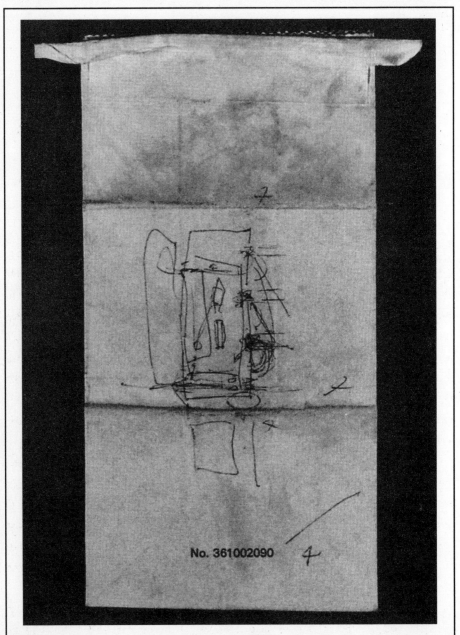

No. 361002090

The air-sickness bag, on which, during the flight to Entebbe, Yoni drew for Amos Goren a sketch of the terminal building and the assault pattern. The control tower is marked as a square at the bottom. The terminal building is marked as a rectangle, divided into halls, with the entrances marked. The oval circle at the corner of the building indicates the planned spot for parking the vehicles.

CHAPTER VII

W hen the cabinet meeting began at 2:00 p.m. on Saturday, Prime Minister Rabin and Defense Minister Peres expected it to be short, since both
of them supported the operation. But the debate went on far longer
than they'd anticipated. After Chief of Staff Gur presented an outline of the
operation, one of the ministers asked, "How many casualties do you expect?"
Gur said it was difficult to predict, but that, based on the simulation the night
before, he thought the mission would probably succeed. The losses were likely
to be low, but there was a chance that as many as 20 hostages would be killed.[1]
And, Gur admitted, one could never know what would happen in a military
action.

Success depended on absolute surprise. If the terrorists had even one minute's
warning, they could kill all the hostages with a few grenades and some bursts
from their AK-47s, and when the troops arrived, there would be no one left to
save. Furthermore, the force would go into action at a distance of a good many
hours' flight from Israel. With a hitch of any kind, there was definitely a risk that
not one man in the whole force would come home. And the men who were
going, Gur stressed, were Israel's finest.

Gur's remarks had an effect. A long, exhausting debate began, with many
questions asked and many reservations voiced. Without a doubt, it was one of
the toughest decisions an Israeli government had ever faced. Rabin made it clear
that if the raid failed, the government would have to resign. But when the final
vote was called, all hands were raised in favor. Only two days had passed since the
cabinet had voted, also unanimously, to give in to the demands of the PLO

splinter-group holding the plane. The new decision had been made by the cabinet as a whole — but the ultimate responsibility rested on Prime Minister Yitzhak Rabin.

At 3:30 p.m., more than an hour after the force put down at Sharm al-Sheikh, word came to go forward with the mission. In fact, the cabinet had not yet reached its decision, but in order to keep to the timetable, the order had been given to set out. The force could still be ordered home if the cabinet decided against the operation.

Yoni informed the Unit's men that they were taking off. "We're going to do it," he told them, as the roar of the just-started engines drowned out his voice.

"Yoni went around and told the men, who were surprised to hear they were actually going," says Shlomo. "Not that he was raring to fight, but he didn't look at all worried by the go-ahead either. You could see that he felt very comfortable, that he was finally starting to breathe easy." Others had the same impression — Yoni was relaxed and buoyant from the moment the order was given, and stayed that way throughout the flight.

Among the men, the general feeling was very positive, though not free of anxiety. They had felt confident even before, when they boarded the plane at Lod, but the feeling now grew much stronger. They believed in their ability to carry off the mission. "When we left Sharm al-Sheikh, I had a good feeling, that I was prepared for action. I don't remember any fear, even in the back of my mind, that I wasn't as ready as I should be," says one officer, who only 12 hours before, after the simulation and a harried day of preparations, had gone to sleep with a nagging fear that the Unit wasn't ready for the operation. And another officer, who had talked the night before with friends about how to keep the mission from being approved, says, "When we boarded the planes, we were extremely confident, and this confidence had been inspired, first and foremost, by Yoni." The men did not doubt any more that they would succeed in freeing the hostages. The only thing that still worried them was whether they would be able to get out of Entebbe. The possibility that they might be stranded in Africa, thousands of miles from Israel, didn't leave their minds.

The troops were told to hurry on board. To maintain secrecy, Yoni hadn't wanted the members of the assault force to put on their camouflage fatigues before they reached Sharm al-Sheikh, and on board the plane, he thought, it would simply be too crowded to change. Bukhris recalls that they stood on the runway, quickly pulling off their regular olive-drab uniforms and putting the mottled ones on.

At that moment Shomron passed by and started yelling, "What are you guys doing now? Who needs this nonsense?"

They finished dressing without responding to his shouts. "He was talking about our 'nonsense,' when the whole operation depended on the ruse, which we kept our mouths shut about," says Bukhris. "When you're about to go out on a mission like this, and suddenly an officer of that rank starts yelling at you, and about something that small that you need 20 seconds for . . . it really left a lousy taste in my mouth."

The four planes were loaded much more heavily than was permitted in training, and possibly more heavily than any Hercules transport had been loaded before. The fuel tanks were absolutely full, including the wing tanks. Besides the air force flight crew, Shani's Hercules One carried the Unit's assault force of 29 men and its three vehicles, as well as 52 paratroopers and part of Shomron's command team.

Hercules Two, Nati's plane, may have been even heavier. It carried two of the Unit's APCs and their 16 troops, Dan Shomron's command jeep and the other half of his team, and 17 more paratroopers.

Hercules Three, piloted by Major Aryeh, carried the Unit's other two APCs and their men, along with 30 Golani fighters and their jeep.

On board Hercules Four, Halivni's plane, were two Peugeot pickups, one for the Golani contingent, and the second to transport the fuel pump. The plane also carried the pump itself, the 10 members of the refueling crew, the 10-man medical team, and 20 more Golani soldiers.

The runway at Sharm al-Sheikh lies across a low hill, making it impossible to see the end while the plane is accelerating for takeoff. The Hercules was designed for improvised battle-field airstrips, and the pilots were used to making short takeoffs. They were unpleasantly surprised. The planes gained speed with great difficulty and, to the men at the controls, it seemed that the runway would end before the planes got off the ground. Making matters worse was the 100-degree desert heat, which cut the power of the engines by as much as a third. The trip down the runway, heading northward against the wind, seemed to last forever before the planes finally gathered enough speed to lift into the air.

After his plane had gained altitude, Shani wanted to turn around and begin heading south, but he found he couldn't. He was flying only two or three knots above the velocity at which the plane would stall, spin out of control, and crash. The Hercules refused to pick up speed, and every time Shani tried to make the turn, it began to shake, forcing him to straighten out again to keep from endangering the plane and its load. "No responsible pilot has ever handled an aircraft under such conditions," he says.

After a while the planes stabilized and made the turn southward toward Africa without mishap. They flew the length of the Red Sea only about 200 feet above the waves, to avoid Saudi radar on the east and Egyptian radar on the west. Still, the flight was considerably more comfortable than the previous one, because fewer air pockets form over water than over land. When the planes' radar detected a passing ship or the crewmen sighted one themselves, they swung as far away from it as possible, so no one below would notice the four military aircraft heading southward. That caused repeated deviations from the planned flight path, and each time it took careful navigation to return to the right course. In the daylight, the planes' pilots could still follow each other by sight, but when night fell they would have to manage with radar alone.

The flight path followed the narrow strip of sea a long way. The planes would stay at low altitude until reaching a certain set of coordinates, where they would begin climbing and turn south-southwest toward Ethiopia. Ethiopia had no radar that could effectively track combat aircraft at night; once there, they would be able to fly at 20,000 feet, which would require less fuel.

In the belly of Hercules One, the soldiers were packed together with barely any room to move. The paratroopers were crowded between the vehicles and the sides of the plane. The Unit's men had the middle, which meant sitting in or on the vehicles, lying on the floor under them, or sprawling out on the hoods of the cars or the roof of the Mercedes. It was quiet; the soldiers spoke only a few words to each other. For the most part, each was lost in his own thoughts, at times peering out the windows at the blue water and the shoreline where the Saudi Arabian desert met the sea.

The Flight Path

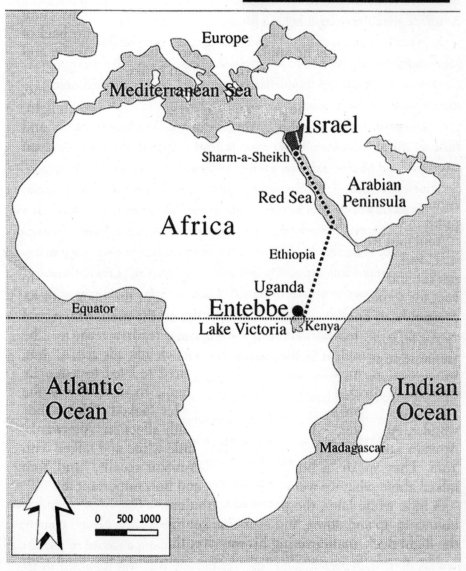

Wedged between the front of the Mercedes and the plane's rear cargo gate, Yoni and Muki explained to Amos Goren his role in the mission. All three sat leaning against the gate. Amos, who had been added to the assault force at the last minute to replace the soldier who had gotten sick on the first flight, was only vaguely familiar with the layout of the terminal and the tasks of the various teams. Yoni sketched the plan of the terminal and the assault routes on the back of an air sickness bag as he spoke. No matter what happens, he and Muki told Amos, he should stay right behind Muki.

"At exactly the moment when Yoni was explaining all this to me, we were informed that the government had given us the green light, that we were going to do this. . . . Yet he stayed completely calm . . . and went on explaining my job to me as though we were going to do an exercise."

The private briefing lasted about 20 minutes. When it ended, Amos took the bag, and after looking it over again, folded it up and put it in his pocket.

Yoni and Muki climbed into the Mercedes. They sat in the front seat, and Yoni took the book he had brought with him out of his pocket and started to read. He usually read when he was forced to wait for something, which was why he'd brought the book. But he probably also knew the effect it would have on the men, who would see that he, at least, wasn't tense. When he read one passage, he laughed to himself and said to Muki in mock admiration, "Listen, these are *real* men. What are we, compared to them?" Then he noticed Amitzur standing in front of them, fixing the way the Ugandan flag on the front of the Mercedes looked. "He's a boy wonder, Amitzur is," Yoni said to Muki with affection. Afterwards, Amitzur sat down in the Mercedes for a little while and talked with Yoni. They spoke "a little about life," Amitzur recalls, "and Yoni talked about what we were about to do, and how important it was."

A little while later, the plane hit turbulence. The Mercedes was bouncing up and down, and everyone got out. Yoni went forward to the flight deck, maneuvering his way over the vehicles.

The normally roomy flight deck was crowded to the limit with officers. Most were sitting on small wicker stools. Shani sat up front in the pilot's seat, with Einstein to his right in the copilot's place. Immediately behind them were the navigators. Rami Levi, the El Al pilot who had been attached to them, was looking over the Jeppesen guide. He was the one who was supposed to speak with the control tower at Entebbe if the need arose, and wanted to get his story straight. After examining the various airports in East Africa in the guide, he decided that it would be best to pose as a small Kenyan aircraft, taking off from Kisomo Airport in Kenya near the Ugandan border. Rami rehearsed the words he would use. Afterwards, he sat down on the floor of the plane with a map of Uganda spread out beside him, and passed the time preparing the flight pattern for the descent.

Einstein asked that someone pass him a piece of cake. The custom was for the load masters to provide food for the crew during the flight, since they had little to do once the cargo was loaded on board. And indeed they had put a cake on a tray at the back of the flight deck, and Yoni, who was sitting next to it, passed a piece up to Einstein. But the copilot sent it back, calling to Yoni, "No, I want a moist square from the middle, not one from the edge."

Yoni smiled and quipped, "Are these pilots ever spoiled! Poor things can't eat from the edge of the cake." He sent up another piece, and had some himself.

From time to time Yoni and Shomron would ask the navigator questions about their precise position and flight path. Shani conferred with Shomron and Yoni, and they agreed again that they would land no matter what, whether they found the runway lighted or dark. They both gave Shani full backing for his plan of pretending to be the pilot of a plane in distress if the lights were out. Yoni studied the new aerial photos yet again, and also went over a number of points with Shomron and Lt. Col. Haim Oren of the Infantry and Paratroops Command, including the exact time at which the two would arrive in their command jeep at the old terminal.[2]

Yoni also spoke a bit with Matan Vilna'i, who was on the flight deck, too. The two knew each other not only from the army, but from growing up in Jerusalem. In 1968, when he was studying at the Hebrew University and trying to decide whether to go back into the army, Yoni had gone to Vilna'i to ask his advice. "What would you do?" he asked. "Should I go back to my paratroops battalion and be a company commander, or should I go to Bibi's unit?" Vilna'i, who was then in the paratroops, answered without a moment's hesitation that if he were in Yoni's place, he'd choose the Unit. And within a few weeks, Yoni joined the Unit as a junior officer. Nearly eight years later, now the Unit's commander, he stood with Vilna'i on the flight deck of a plane heading south over Africa.

Yoni now talked with Lt. Col. Haim Oren, whom he knew from their joint service in the Haruv commando unit. At one point in the conversation, Yoni said, "If he's there, I'll kill him."

"Who are you talking about?" asked Haim.

"Idi Amin," said Yoni.

Haim was stunned. He urged Yoni to banish the thought from his mind, but his pleading fell on deaf ears. "You can't do something like that. It hasn't even been discussed. You'd have to ask for approval," Haim said.

"I don't intend to ask. If Idi Amin is there, I'm going to kill him," said Yoni, without offering explanations. From Yoni's point of view, the reasons were self-evident.

In a letter he had written to Tutti seven years before, he had said, "What an insane world we live in! In the 20th century we've landed on the moon, and there's still more to come. But the 20th century has also seen Hitler and his mass murders. And it saw the horrors of World War I. Yet we still haven't learned. Today we're seeing an entire people being wiped out by starvation [in Biafra], and still no one is concerned enough to get this ugly world to do anything about it. All of us — including Israel, including me — are caught up in our own wars, and there's not a single country willing to go in with its army and stop what's happening there. Of course not. No one wants to get involved. What strange animals people are."[3] Now he had firmly decided that if he saw this monster of a man named Idi Amin, who'd murdered hundreds of thousands of his countrymen, and who threw the victims of his torture chambers from the top floor of Kampala's fancy Nile Hotel, he wouldn't let him get away alive.

In the rear of the plane many of the men had dozed off, overcome by both the accumulated exhaustion of the week and the drowsiness induced by the anti-nausea pills. But many others couldn't fall asleep. Some busied themselves with simple tasks like checking their ammo vests or aligning their sighting lights yet again in the relative darkness of the plane after nightfall. Otherwise, there was little to do but sit and think about what was coming and what one had already done in life. Bukhris sat the entire time in his place in the jeep, wearing his ammo vest and rifle, his machine gun at his side, studying the faces of the soldiers around him.

Amir also did not shut his eyes for a moment, even though 2 days had passed since he'd last slept. "We were flying, and at a certain point we realized that we just weren't turning back, that we couldn't even if we wanted to, because there wasn't enough fuel. A lot of guys went to sleep . . . but I didn't manage to sleep the whole flight, not for a second. The whole time I was thinking and repeating over and over what I was supposed to do and how I was going to do it. I wasn't shaking with fear, but I was very tense."

Sometime during the flight, Muki called Amir and Amos over. The two had been assigned to handle the bullhorns, and Muki discussed with them what exactly the hostages should be told. They decided once again that, at the moment of battle, the captives should simply be instructed to lie flat on the ground.

Shlomo dozed on and off. At one point he woke up and walked around the plane to stretch his legs and see what was happening. When he spotted Yoni sitting in the Mercedes, calmly reading his book, he thought to himself that this was something really special. Surin, from the paratroops, who was sitting beside the car, was surprised that Yoni was reading an English book. Like most of the men around him, Surin was also unable to fall asleep — in large part because conditions were simply too cramped. Every time Surin wanted to straighten his legs a bit, he had to stick them under the Mercedes. It's not easy to fall asleep, he found, with a car bouncing up and down above you, coming within inches of your legs.

After a few hours, Yoni wanted to go to sleep. In the rear of the flight deck, there were two narrow cots stacked as a bunk bed. The bottom bed was broken, but the top one was intact and unoccupied. Shomron, who could see that Yoni was tired, told him, "You can have the bed. You sleep on the way there, and I'll sleep on the way back."[4] Yoni asked the navigator to wake him up half an hour or so before landing. He pulled a blue inflatable pillow from one of his pockets, blew it up, climbed onto the top bed, put the pillow under his head, and fell asleep almost immediately.

A little while later, Shani also wanted to go to sleep. Several hours were left before the landing. "I look back and see Yoni sleeping in that bed," says Shani. "Under normal conditions, if some battalion commander is resting there, I tell him politely but firmly to go rest in the rear of the plane. This time I couldn't bring myself to do it, because my theory was that the first group that storms that building, its chances of staying alive are 50-50. I said to myself: *He's taking a huge personal risk in this, that's for sure. He's grabbing some sleep here. So am I going to wake him up?* On the other hand, I also wanted to lie down. He was curled up on the edge. I lay down next to him, getting closer little by little till I was a few millimeters away from him."

Lying there, Shani closed his eyes, but they snapped open a minute later. He felt the weight of the responsibility he bore, and he could feel his heart pounding rapidly. Would he manage to land without trouble, he asked himself, or would he have to make several passes over the airport before he could put the plane down? In that case would the entire airport be awakened, the terrorists alerted, the hostages killed? Because of his failure to land the plane, would they be ordered home without carrying out the mission? Variations on these questions kept repeating themselves in his mind.

"I was afraid of a failure on the national level — not just that someone would be killed or wounded, but that we simply wouldn't succeed, that we'd cause a disaster," explains Shani. Gur's words from the day before — that responsibility for the operation's success rested with the pilots, since as Gur put it, it didn't make any difference to the Unit's men whether they were put down in Tel Aviv or Entebbe — echoed in his ears.

"I looked at Yoni from about an inch away, nose to nose, and he was sleeping like a baby, utterly at peace. I asked Tzvika, the navigator, when Yoni had gone to sleep, and he said, 'Listen, he went to sleep and said to wake him up a little while before the landing.' And I couldn't free myself from the thought: *Where does this calmness of his come from? Soon you're going into battle, and here you are, sleeping as if nothing's happening!* I got up and went back to my seat."[5]

After Shani got up, Rami Levi decided that he needed to stretch out. He moved Yoni a little in order to clear himself a place to sleep. "He turned over a bit, and went on sleeping. I lay down next to him to rest a while; I knew I wouldn't fall asleep. I didn't know who Yoni was. I just saw a lieutenant colonel in a camouflage uniform lying there, tired. I didn't know that he was the commander of the Unit, but I'd seen him on the flight deck. He was in charge of something, so it seemed to me. Now I said to myself, *These guys probably haven't slept in days.* I remember this thought going through my head: *And who knows if these aren't his last hours of sleep, maybe ever.*"

They woke Yoni when the plane was already nearing Lake Victoria. Most of the flight over Africa had been through Ethiopian airspace. From time to time, the pilots reported their locations, using code-words signifying designated points on the route.

The planes crossed the border out of Ethiopia over the huge Lake Rudolph, and continued south-southwest over the western reaches of Kenya. Despite their altitude, the high African clouds remained well above them, dropping rain on the planes now and then. On the radio, they heard the exchange between the Entebbe control tower and the pilot of a British Airways jet as it took off from the airport, exactly on schedule. At around 10:30 p.m. Israel time, they reached Lake Victoria, flying over the bay near the Kenyan town of Kisomo. They now ran into extremely stormy weather, and the static electricity in the highly charged air sent bursts of light dancing across the windshields of the planes. Here, three of the planes circled downward in the storm for about six minutes, hanging back to give the assault force time to carry out the primary action.

Hercules One flew on alone over Lake Victoria. Its flight path first took it westward, toward a large island south of Entebbe. From there it would be able to fly due north to the airport. Contact was now made for the first time with the Boeing 707 command plane that had caught up with Hercules One and was circling above. Here, out of radio range from Arab countries, they could speak Hebrew freely, without any codes. "Do you see the runway lights?" Peled asked Shani.

"Not yet," Shani answered.

As they flew through the storm over Lake Victoria, Yoni went back into the hold of the plane. Some of the men were still asleep. Yoni went around waking them up and telling them to put on their ammo vests and prepare for landing. Giora, who was dozing in the Mercedes, recalls that Yoni had a smile on his face when he woke him up. Yoni bent down to wake up Amitzur, who was asleep on the floor of the plane under the car. Shlomo pondered the perennial soldier's question of how many layers of clothing to wear — the storm outside told him nothing about whether it would be hot or cold in Uganda. Alik, who had slept for most of the flight on the hood of one of the jeeps, felt very hungry when he awoke. He had not eaten any of the food they'd been given at Sharm al-Sheikh, and now he went up to the flight deck to find something to take the edge off his hunger.

Rani Cohen, a young officer on Yiftah's team, had also been sleeping since the flight began. When they had taken off from Sharm al-Sheikh, word had not yet come that the raid had been approved, and Rani had gone to sleep, serenely certain that the order would soon come for the planes to return to Israel. When he awoke, he suddenly discovered he was about to land in Uganda. It was the first time that he had felt any tension whatsoever. He peered out a nearby window. The storm was already behind them, and the star-strewn sky lit the waters of Lake Victoria below. Rani went back to where he'd been sitting, went over in his mind the sequence of the actions the force would execute, and tried to envision the structure of the old terminal and its entrances.

The soldiers took their places in the vehicles. The landing approached, and the excitement among the soldiers reached a peak. Yoni now did something that none of them had ever seen before any other operation. He moved along the row of vehicles, walking on the jeeps, going from soldier to soldier, officer to officer, and with a word, a smile, an occasional handshake, encouraged his men.

"There was this reddish light, and I remember that we saw his face," tells Shlomo. "He wasn't wearing his beret, or his ammo vest or gun. . . . He spoke to all the men, smiled at us, said a few words of encouragement to each one. It was as though he were leaving us, as though he knew what was going to happen to him. He didn't issue any orders, but just tried to instill confidence. I remember that he shook hands with the youngest guy on the force. . . . He acted more like a friend. . . . I sensed he felt that from here on everything, or at least nearly everything, depended on these men. He'd seen a lot of combat, and quite a few of the soldiers there had seen none at all, or a lot less than he had. And I remember him going by, joking a little, exchanging a few words, easing the men's tension before battle."

"Remember," Yoni told them, "that we're the best soldiers who'll be there. There's nothing for us to be afraid of."

When he reached Arnon, he shook his hand and said, referring to the terrorists, "Don't hesitate to kill those bastards." He also shook hands with the men on his own team — David the doctor and Tamir the communications man. "It'll be all right," he told Tamir. "We'll do it without a hitch, don't worry." At the very back of his jeep, to the left, sat Bukhris. "What are you smiling about, Bukhris?"

Yoni said when he reached him, tousling the shock of dark hair on the young soldier's head.

"It created a sense of personal connection between him and all of us, the men who'd be doing the fighting," says Bukhris. "It's not like some commander way above you who hands down orders to the officers under him, and they pass the orders further down, until you, the grunt, can't even see the top of the pyramid. Yoni gave this feeling of a personal tie between the commander of the operation and the very last soldier in the force, which, in terms of age, was me. That encounter, right before we landed, left me with a very, very good feeling."

One of the officers of the Unit went over to Yoni and said, "Don't stay too near the assault force. Remember you're the commander of the Unit, and you can't be hit."

Yoni smiled at him, and said, "It'll be all right."[6] Then he shook hands with Muki.

Yoni went to the flight deck for a moment. The storm was behind them, and the sky was clear. Up ahead, it was already possible to see the runway lights at Entebbe. The strip was brightly lit for all to see, while the plane, flying without lights under cover of the darkness, was invisible from the ground. When the men on the flight deck saw the shining lights, there was a general feeling of relief — apparently no one was expecting them there.

Shani carefully continued bringing the plane down. It could not touch down too hard, lest its excessive weight cause the landing-gear tires to burst. Meanwhile, the crew also carried out the routine for a radar landing, so that if the Ugandans suddenly suspected something and shut off the lights at the last minute, Shani would still be able to try to land the plane.

"Everything all right?" came Benny Peled's voice from the airborne command center.

"A-okay," Shani answered, carefully keeping the excitement in his voice under control because he knew he was being recorded. "No problems."

From the flight deck, Yoni — along with Shomron and Vilna'i — examined the airport ahead. To the right of the runway was the new terminal, also lighted. Farther away to the east was the old terminal, less distinct, though the lights were on there, too. Yoni quickly returned to his men, and, after putting on his ammo vest, climbed into the front seat of the Mercedes. In front of him was the rear door of the plane. To his right, next to the window of the car, now stood Matan Vilnai, who had left the flight deck after him. Matan positioned himself near the side door, through which his paratroop commandos would leave to place the back-up lights on the runway.

The rear door now began to open, even before the plane touched down, and Yoni could see the black waters of Lake Victoria. He told Amitzur to start the Mercedes. The starter, which had been repaired at the Unit's base, did its job, and the engine came to life. Seconds later, they felt the jolt of the plane hitting the ground and could see the runway lights racing past them. Bukhris glanced at his watch. It was 11:01 p.m. Israel time — just after midnight on clocks in Uganda, the beginning of July 4, 1976.

The plane quickly cut speed. When it reached the middle of the runway, the ten soldiers of the paratroop commando team leapt to the tarmac, one after another, as the plane continued moving toward the Unit's deplaning point. At the same time the straps tying the vehicles to the floor of the plane were released.

Shani taxied to the access strip connecting the main runway to the diagonal, turned to the right, and brought the plane to a halt. He had delivered the Unit's assault force to its starting point.

The signal was given to lower the ramp all the way to the ground. Before it had even settled properly on the asphalt, the Mercedes had already pulled out and turned right, alongside the plane, with the two jeeps behind it.

"I saw them pass under the wing," says Shani. "The access strip was rather narrow, with a ditch running next to it, and I was afraid they were driving too close to us, and in a second the propeller was going to slice through the roof of the Mercedes. But they got by, and the three vehicles headed down the access strip and disappeared from sight."

After the Mercedes had moved a little away from the plane, Yoni turned around to make sure that the two jeeps were following. He ordered the soldiers sitting in the back seat to maintain visual contact with them, and told Amitzur to keep going. They kept to 40 miles per hour, the speed to be expected of someone driving innocently across the airport. Near them to the right, beyond a level field, was the new terminal building, awash with light. They were pulling away from it now and made a right onto the diagonal runway leading to the old terminal area.

The rumble of the plane's engines, which had accompanied them through the long hours of the flight, quickly faded behind them. Near-silence descended; all that could be heard was the hum of their own engines and the whir of the wheels on the asphalt. The air outside was heavy with a warm, tropical humidity. The feel of the air, along with the high grass by the sides of the runway, through which the men could see anthills as tall as men in the glow of the headlights, brought home to them that they were in a strange, unknown land. But those, like Amir, who had allowed their imaginations to portray Africa as something exotic, a land of lions and crocodiles, now found themselves in a surprisingly mundane scene, remarkably similar to every other airport in the world, including the one they'd left at Lod.

Yet they were not at Lod, but in hostile territory, exposed and visible to anyone who bothered to look, and protected to no small degree by the very unexpectedness of their presence there. In his seat in the jeep, Ilan felt as though he were trapped and exposed by the burning headlights of his own jeep, which announced his presence to the world and lit up the vehicle in front of him. Next to him sat Amir, who looked at the men around him as the distance between them and the objective grew smaller and wondered: Which of them will still be standing on his feet five minutes from now? Shlomo sat in the same jeep. He now picked out at a distance the dim lights emanating from the old terminal area, and strained his ears to hear any sounds. As one accustomed by experience to recognize the sounds of gunfire and explosions as harbingers of trouble, he expected to hear at any moment the telltale shots marking the beginning of the massacre of the hostages. But for now the silence remained unbroken.

It took about a minute to reach the approach road that led to the old terminal. Amitzur signaled left before turning the wheel and pulling onto the road. It was important to nurture any seed of hesitation among the Ugandans who might be hidden in the dark, beyond the headlights of the car, so that they would not open fire and delay them. The silhouette of the old terminal, and of the high control tower even closer to them, grew ever larger.

Suddenly, two Ugandan sentries appeared, standing on the approach road in the headlights of the Mercedes, one on the right side and the other on the left. Through Bukhris' mind flashed the image of the two "sentries" Yoni had posted in exactly the same place the night before during the simulation, and at that moment he knew: The mission would succeed.

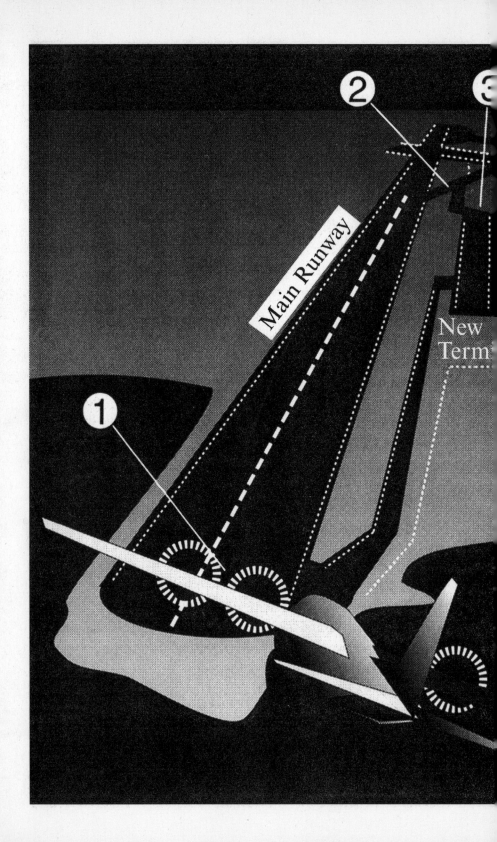

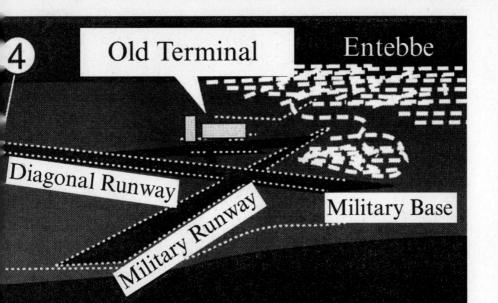

Old Terminal

Entebbe

Diagonal Runway

Military Runway

Military Base

Lake Victoria

The Landing

1. The first Hercules C-130 descends toward the main runway over Lake Victoria, bearing north.

2. After landing, the plane turns right toward the diagonal runway. The forces alight.

3. The paratroopers fan out and wait to take over the new terminal.

4. The Unit, under Yoni's command, heads on the diagonal runway toward the old terminal, where the hostages are held.

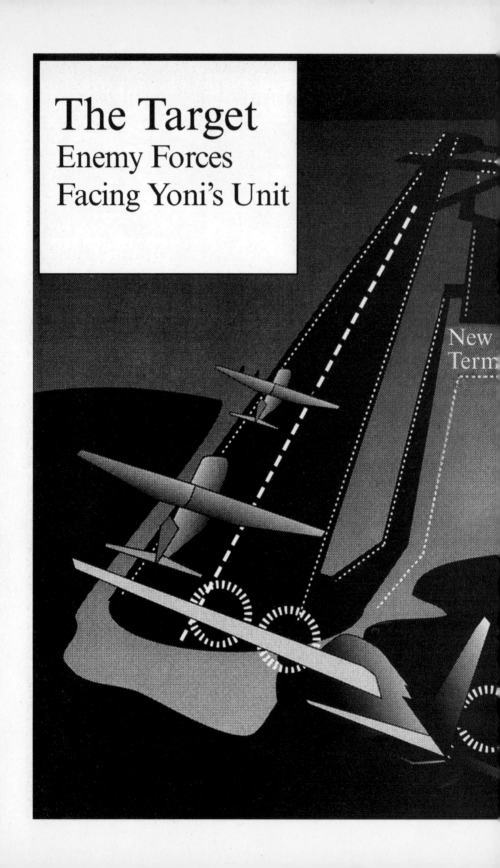

The Target
Enemy Forces
Facing Yoni's Unit

New
Term

ebbe
dan army
pany
and-by

Old Terminal

* Seven to ten terrorists
* Dozens of Ugandan soldiers in the building, control tower and outlying area holding **105 hostages**

Military Base

* Ugandan battalion
* Five Mig-21 jet fighters
* Three Mig-17 jet fighters

Lake Victoria

The sentry on the left vanished back into the darkness, while the one on the right advanced toward the Mercedes. He now acted precisely as Amnon Halivni had told Yoni he would that morning. After stamping his foot and calling out a warning, the sentry raised his rifle to his shoulder and aimed it at the Mercedes. The metallic noise of a rifle being cocked could be heard. It was obvious to almost everyone that the sentry had assumed a menacing pose and was demanding that the vehicles moving towards him stop and identify themselves — or he would shoot.[7] "I was sure the guard was about to fire," says Rani, "no 'ifs' about it." The Mercedes was about 20 yards from the Ugandan. Yoni instructed the men sitting next to the windows to ready pistols with silencers for action. It was for just such a turn of events that they had prepared at the Unit.

"It was obvious to me that the guard had to be taken out," explains Amir. According to the script, they were first to try to solve the problem, if possible, with silenced fire.

"Yoni was calm," recalls Amitzur, the driver. Yoni told him to approach the sentry on the left-hand side, and to slow down. The order was intended to reassure the sentry that they were indeed approaching him to identify themselves — and probably also intended to enable them to shoot more accurately. They closed in on the dark form of the soldier, who continued to aim his rifle at them. At the last instant, Muki shouted "Don't shoot!" not believing that the Ugandan would actually fire on them.*

But Yoni had no hesitation about what had to be done. As the Mercedes passed within a few yards of the sentry, Yoni gave the order to fire. The sentry looked surprised by what was happening. Both Yoni and Giora, who sat behind Yoni next to the right-hand window, opened fire with silenced pistols they thrust out the windows. The sentry staggered back and tottered. But even if the bullets had actually hit him, he was apparently not out of action.

---

* Judging by his testimony, Muki at that moment was under the misconception that the Mercedes was just by the control tower, while in fact it was some 200 yards away from it. He seems to have lost all conception of the subsequent ride from that point to the tower. Yoni must have been surprised at Muki's sudden cry not to shoot, which was in opposition to what had been planned and rehearsed and to what was called for both by the facts on the ground and by Halivni's description of the Ugandan guards' usual stubborness and determination.

The stillness was suddenly shattered by open, unsilenced fire. The source of the burst cannot be determined for certain; it may have come from one of the Israeli vehicles, or, according to some of the men, from the sentry who had been fired upon, or even from some other Ugandan soldier. In any case, even if it was not the sentry who had first opened unsilenced fire, it was clear he had not been taken out by the pistols, and it was imperative that he be eliminated at once. "One does not leave behind an armed soldier . . . who would use his weapon once he realized what you were going to do," explains Yiftah. Alex, who was sitting in the right-hand position in the rear seat of the Mercedes, thrust his unsilenced pistol out the window as well, and began shooting at the Ugandan, whom the Mercedes had passed by now. He fired six of the seven bullets in the clip of his Beretta and believes that the last bullets found their mark. Fire also came from the jeeps. The moment he heard unsilenced shooting, Amnon Peled opened fire with the machine gun mounted on the jeep, intending to finish off the sentry once and for all, as did others in the jeeps. The entire incident, from the first pistol shots to the elimination of the sentry, was over in an instant.

"We could not have approached the terminal building silently any closer than we did," sums up Amir. "We started shooting heavy fire, and had we not done that, I'm sure they [the sentries] would have fired on us."

With the first sentry eliminated, the second one reappeared. He was spotted running with all his might, but instead of fleeing into the darkness, he ran away from them on the asphalt, fully exposed, along the lights of the access road. He could not be left behind, since he could endanger the rear of the assault force. Bukhris, who was holding a machine gun in his hands, was given an order by Yiftah to open fire on him. Both the jeep from which he was firing and the Ugandan were in motion, and the first rounds missed the target. But then Bukhris laid a long burst in front of the Ugandan, and didn't release the trigger until he saw the soldier run right into the flying bullets and fall.

During this seconds-long firefight, the Mercedes had leapt forward. The moment the silence was broken, Yoni told Amitzur to drive on at top speed. They were very close to the old terminal, with the control tower rising in front of them no more than 200 yards away. They covered the distance in a few seconds. As they approached, Yoni probably saw several armed Ugandans in the lighted entrance area of the terminal. It was obvious that the latest aerial photos had been correct and that the massive Ugandan security belt reported originally did not exist. Yoni may have spotted one or more of the terrorists, armed with AK-47s, outside near the entrance to the large hall.* No one opened fire on the Israeli force yet. Yoni quickly read the situation and ordered Amitzur to turn left, before the control tower, and park the car next to it.[8] This was a different stopping point from the one that had been planned, which was 20 yards further ahead, between the tower and the terminal.[9] Yoni's assessment must have been that in this area, which was substantially darker than the plaza, the force would be less likely to be identified and less vulnerable to attack during the cumbersome process of getting out of the vehicles.

"Stop here," Yoni ordered Amitzur, and the Mercedes instantly came to a halt, tires screeching. "Leave the engine running," he said, and jumped out. The jeeps arrived right afterwards and pulled up behind the Mercedes. Men poured out of the vehicles in disorder as Yoni shouted at them to get out and storm the building. Not a single round had yet been fired as the first of them began to move toward the target, only a few dozen yards away. By now, any terrorist who had been outside must have moved into the hall. As the Unit's men ran, they formed a triangle, at the head of which were Muki, Yoni, and others, while the men who ran behind them gave the appearance of a fan. A number of men were still climbing out of the vehicles. Muki, who ran first, a little ahead of Yoni, fired a few bursts, one or two of which were perhaps aimed at a terrorist who came out of the hall for a second. It seems that one of the terrorists in the hall shouted at one point to his comrades, "The Ugandans have gone nuts — they're shooting at us!"[10] At least for this first moment, the

---

* The terrorists did not linger in the hall where the captives were held, but would come in to observe what was going on and leave after a minute or two. They guarded the hostages from outside, standing in the open area next to the terminal. Just seconds before the first shots were heard, one of the hostages, Ilan Har-Tuv, looked through the glass front of the hall and saw them having a lively conversation with a Libyan doctor and the manager of the civilian airport. Even though the hall was brightly lit, it was possible from inside to see clearly anyone in the outside area, since it was also lit. According to the hostages, there were also Ugandan soldiers outside, some of whom sat in armchairs. Another hostage, Sarah Davidson, remembers that the moment the first shots were heard, she saw the leader of the terrorists stand up from the low stone wall where he was sitting, grab his AK-47, and turn in the direction of the shooting.

terrorist was fooled by the ruse that had been intended primarily for the Ugandan guards.

Within seconds, the spearhead of the force reached the beginning of the terminal beyond the control tower. Here Muki Betser pulled to the left, toward the corner of the building. He flattened himself against the wall and began firing into the plaza, and the entire force suddenly stopped behind him. Yoni, who was standing to his right in the open, shouted several times: "Betser, forward! Forward, Betser!"[11] The delay that would lead to disaster, which Yoni had so feared, was taking shape before his eyes. To Shlomo Reisman, who was farther back, the force appeared at that instant, in the dim light, like something strange and awesome — the soldiers crouched, leaning forward, in their mottled fatigues, with the round sighting lights jutting up from the barrels of their guns. "Forward!" shouted Yoni again, impatiently. The loss of a fraction of a second, especially

Aerial photograph of the old terminal when it was still active. This photograph served the Unit in its preparation. During the raid, following their encounter with the Ugandan guards, Yoni and his men drove from the left on the access road (adjacent to the cluster of buildings).

when they were so close to the hostages, could have catastrophic consequences. "We knew," says Amos Goren, "that it was a matter of seconds before the terrorists would recover their wits" and would start to shoot the hostages.

The delay, though, continued but a few seconds, for Yoni decided to take action himself. Yoni now lunged forward, presumably at the instant Muki ceased his fire, and bypassed Muki. "Yoni kept shouting to run forward, and I remember him running forward and passing Muki," recalls Amos. "The one who was first out of the corner of the building was Yoni. Then he ran a little to the right, to let the men [who were meant to go inside the building] pass him."

"Once Yoni started to run, those who had hesitated ran too. . . . He pulled the line with him," says another soldier.[12] The fan began moving again. Thus, Yiftah, as soon as he saw Yoni begin to run past Muki, and understood what was going on, started running and also passed Muki.[13] With another soldier running behind him, he burst through the first entrance of the building, which would lead him to the second floor.

At the same time, Amir arrived from behind, running fast. When he'd climbed out of the jeep, he'd looked for his commander, Amnon Peled, whom he was supposed to follow, but whom he hadn't seen. Amir was convinced that Amnon was running on ahead of him, and he was afraid Amnon would charge into the building alone. In fact, Amnon had not yet finished extricating himself from the jeep, and was still at the rear. Amir began running as hard as he could, intending to catch up with his commander and reach his entrance as quickly as possible. To avoid being slowed down, he ran to the right and began to overtake the group of men behind Muki, while hearing Yoni's urgent shouts of "Forward!" Up ahead, he could see the door he was supposed to enter, and he kept overtaking the others. "I didn't care about anything else. I remembered what Yoni had told us, to run as hard as we could, and I ran as hard as I could."

Right behind Amir was Amnon, who was straining to catch up with the man who was supposed to follow him. He didn't even notice that the force had been held up, apparently reaching the edge of the building after Yoni had already passed Muki and the assault had resumed. It can't be said for certain who passed the edge of the building and entered the lit plaza first — Yoni, or Amir and Amnon. In any case, by the time they were running along the front of the building, Amir and Amnon had almost certainly passed Yoni. Because of his role, Yoni now ran more slowly so he could watch the entire force and check what it was doing, probably turning his head back and to the left to see how the assault was taking shape. "Go in!" Yoni managed to shout while still running forward. Now Muki began to run again, with Amos Goren and another soldier from his team on his heels.

Perhaps about 20 seconds had passed since the cars had stopped. Amir, with his commander, Amnon, behind him, was first in the line of assault, some distance from the front of the building. After them were Muki and Amos Goren, hugging more closely to the building and running almost parallel to Yoni, who was several yards from the front of the building, in a more exposed position in the plaza. It is possible that Giora, too, had overtaken Yoni and was now ahead of him. The rest of the force had fanned out behind them. With Yoni, about a yard behind him, ran Tamir and Alik, the members of his command team.

At this point or a little sooner, a Ugandan soldier jumped out from behind some crates on the right. He aimed his rifle towards the force and apparently also managed to shoot. He was immediately eliminated by bursts of fire from several soldiers — just as the wide windows of the hall were shattered by gunfire from one of the terrorists, who had figured out what was happening and started shooting through the glass.

Amos now saw, from the corner of his eye, that someone to his right had fallen. It was Yoni. He had been shot in the front of his chest and in his arm, by a burst from an AK-47.[14]

Yoni had almost managed to reach the point he had designated for his command team to deploy, and may have already slowed down and turned his head to the left to look to check how the force was advancing. At the time he was hit, he was roughly in front of the first door of the large hall,[15] and he probably had time to understand that Muki's team, which was supposed to go through this door, was running past it. Yoni crumpled forward and turned around; then his upper body straightened again. His face twisted, his arms went out to the sides, and his knees folded under him. He sank to the ground, sighing, and sprawled on his stomach.

"Yoni's wounded!" Tamir shouted. No one stopped to treat him, since his own orders had been that the wounded were not to be attended to until after the assault. The teams continued independently towards their respective objectives — parts of a machine that worked automatically, even without anyone in command, without a word from Yoni, who was lying immobile on the asphalt in front of the hall where the hostages were.

Amir was already opposite his entrance, the second door of the large hall, and had turned straight toward it. One of the terrorists was lying prone on the other side of the door and fired a short burst out of the hall from his AK-47. It may be that the gunman was not aiming at Amir, for if he was, says Amir, "I don't understand how he could possibly have missed me." Amir's memory is of hearing Tamir's shout that Yoni had been hit just before he charged into the room. In an instant, he spotted the terrorist's hand and shot him through the open door as he ran, at a range of about five yards. He saw that the terrorist had been hit and finished off, and he ran into the building without pausing.

Just as he had practiced, Amir turned right as soon as he crossed the threshold. Only then did he see that he was the only member of the Israeli force in the hall. But Amnon came in right behind him. Instead of turning right himself, as had been planned, he decided on the spot to go left. Perhaps he realized that there was no one covering the entire left side of the hall, since no one had come through the first door. Amnon saw two terrorists to the left, a man and a woman, both prone or crouched on the floor. They had just come into the hall from the outside and had already had time to train their guns on Amir, who had run a short way into the room and had passed by without noticing them. But before they had time to pull the triggers, Amnon shot them both. He ran toward them, kicking the AK-47s away from the bodies. "Amnon, don't advance!" Amir shouted, thinking he intended to move further into the hall.

After Amnon, Muki, Amos, and another soldier from Muki's team came in, all through the second door. Muki had run past the first entrance,[16] to which he had been assigned, and Amos, who had been added to Muki's team at the last minute and had been told on board the Hercules to stick to him no matter what, had simply followed his commander. After Muki entered the room, he shot at one of the terrorists that Amnon had already hit. The men now stood, weapons in hand, scouring the room for any movement. Suddenly, from the back of the room on the left, another gunman leapt up. Amos Goren opened fire and hit him in the chest, the bullets passing right through the shell of the AK-47 he was holding in his hands.[17]

All four of the terrorists who had been in the hall with the hostages, and had posed an immediate danger to them, had been eliminated. At that moment — seconds after Amir had killed the first terrorist, less than a minute after the force had encountered the Ugandan sentries, and about three minutes after it had rolled off the Hercules — the operation had essentially achieved success. It was a moment that Yoni, who had been hit only seconds before, never saw.

Meanwhile, men from the teams of Amnon and Muki, as well as from that of Amos Ben-Avraham, continued to pour in through the same door. Like those before them, they stayed close to the front of the hall at first.

Amir pressed the bullhorn to his lips and said in English and Hebrew: "Everyone down on the ground!" Had it not been for the bullhorn, his voice certainly would not have been heard, as he was so excited that he was barely able to get a sound out of his mouth. Most of the people remained prone on the floor, probably more because of shock at what was happening around them than because of Amir's instructions, but several of them did jump to their feet. Amnon and Amos Goren trained their rifles on a figure that rose in the far corner of the room, near the stairs. Even as they were squeezing their triggers, they realized that it was the figure of a little girl. They quickly jerked their guns upward. The bullets hit the wall above the girl's head. It's doubtful whether the small hostage understood that she had narrowly escaped death. A moment later an older man jumped up; the soldiers, realizing he was not a terrorist, shouted to one another not to fire at him.

But some were not so fortunate and were hit during the shooting. Three hostages lost their lives — two succumbing later to wounds sustained from Israeli fire; the third, Ida Borokovitch, killed on the spot, perhaps from the fire of one of the Arab gunmen.

IDF assessments before the operation had included the possibility of dozens of dead even in a "successful" operation. In fact, the swiftly executed assault caught the terrorists by surprise, and they had no chance to massacre the hostages. And conditions in the hall when the Unit's men arrived were nearly ideal: it was well lit, all of the hostages were in one room, and in the first instant of the

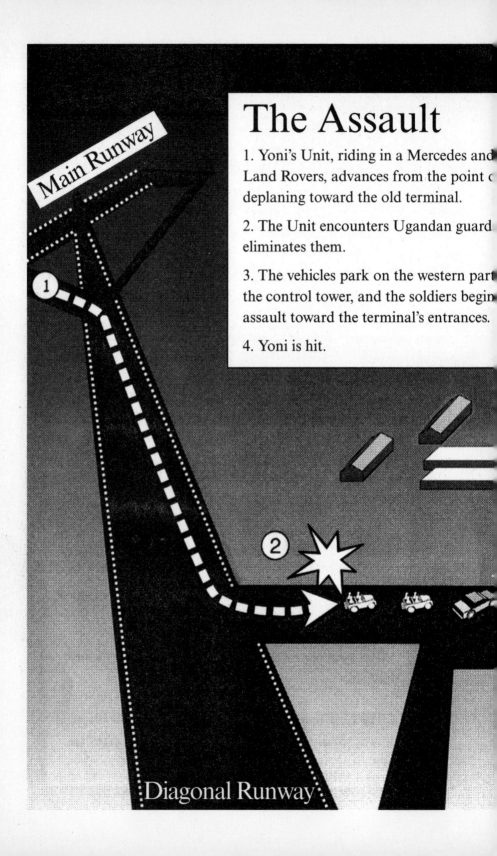

The Assault

1. Yoni's Unit, riding in a Mercedes and Land Rovers, advances from the point of deplaning toward the old terminal.

2. The Unit encounters Ugandan guards eliminates them.

3. The vehicles park on the western part the control tower, and the soldiers begin assault toward the terminal's entrances.

4. Yoni is hit.

Main Runway

Diagonal Runway

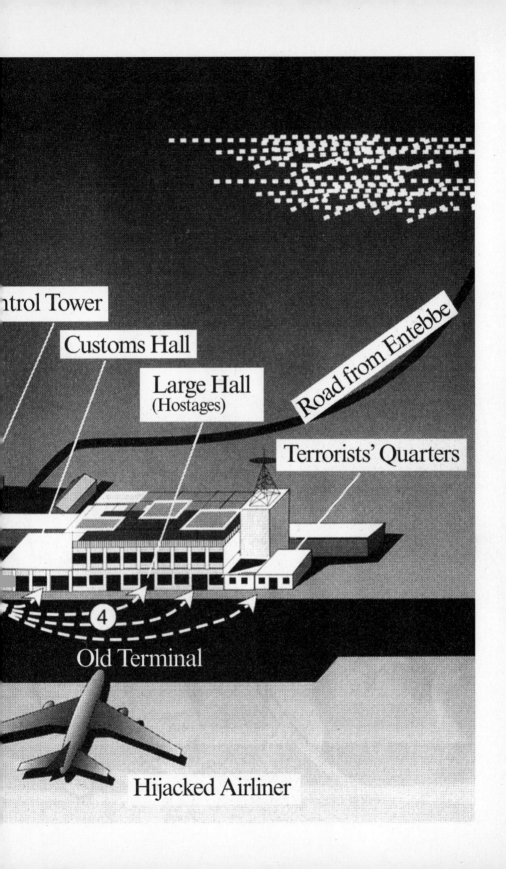

ntrol Tower

Customs Hall

Large Hall
(Hostages)

Road from Entebbe

Terrorists' Quarters

④

Old Terminal

Hijacked Airliner

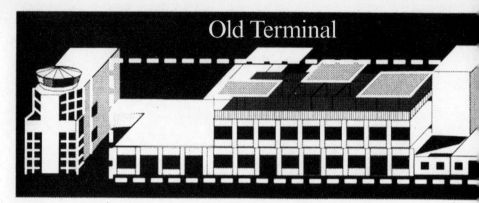

Old Terminal

The boxed-in area is detailed below

Customs
hall

Passage-
way

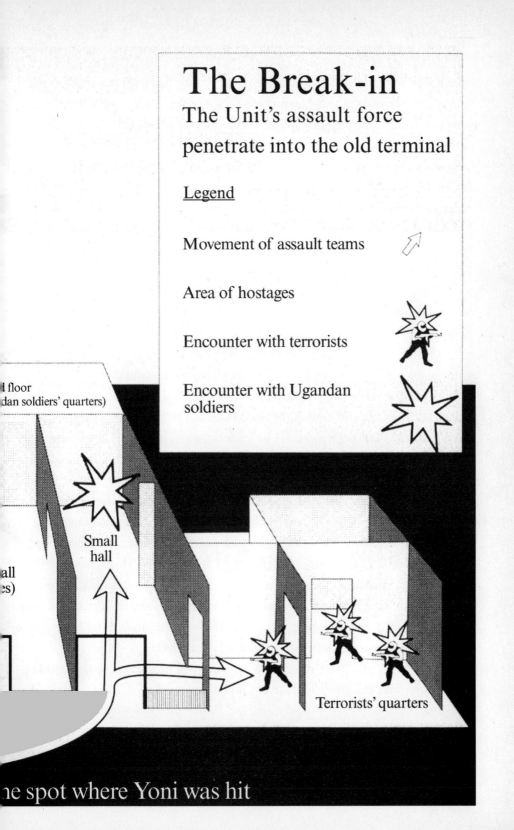

The Break-in
The Unit's assault force penetrate into the old terminal

Legend

Movement of assault teams

Area of hostages

Encounter with terrorists

Encounter with Ugandan soldiers

d floor
dan soldiers' quarters)

Small hall

all
es)

Terrorists' quarters

he spot where Yoni was hit

attack they were all still lying on the floor where they had been resting or sleeping — caught, like their captors, completely by surprise. So it was possible to hit the terrorists with lightning speed almost without endangering the hostages themselves, most of whom did not yet understand what was happening. Some had just woken up, and many were too stunned to even make a sound. Seconds earlier, when they had heard sounds of gunfire outside growing nearer, most had thought that their end had come and the massacre was about to begin. One hostage, Sarah Davidson, had thrown herself over her young son to shield him from the bullets, as the thought had flashed through her mind that it would not take long and death would come quickly.

Only one small boy reacted uninhibitedly to the Unit's actions in the hall. When he saw the shooting, he clapped his hands and shouted with glee, "Wow, great! Great!"

Orders in Hebrew filled the hall. One of the soldiers announced, "We've come to take you home," and the people began to understand that the inconceivable had indeed happened. After seemingly endless days of degradation, of repeated ultimatums and threats, of obedience to the orders of a shrill German woman whose brutality reminded one Holocaust survivor of her block warden at Birkenau; after the "selection" of the Jews, during which the German man had tried to calm them, just as his Nazi forebears once did, by saying that the separation from the others was intended to improve their conditions; after days of listening to the pronouncements of the clown-tyrant of Uganda, luxuriating in the international spotlight and amusing himself at the expense of the group of hostages who had fallen under his authority; after days in which they had been exposed to the burning hatred of the Arabs, some of whom were just waiting for the chance to pull the trigger and murder the accursed Jews; after many of them already saw death as inevitable and inescapable — salvation had suddenly come, in the form of young Israelis emerging from the night.

Simultaneously, the other teams took control of the rest of the building. Giora burst into the small hall farther down the building. This was where the Israeli hostages had been kept at first, and up until the moment he entered, it wasn't clear whether they were still being held there. In a glance he saw there were no captives here and sprayed the hall and the corridor leading off to its right with bullets. In the hall there were several beds with sheets, and it seemed to him that someone was lying in one of them (the bed later proved to be empty). In front of him, on the single table in the room, were piled the hostages' passports, and a number of suitcases stood on the floor. Giora sensed he was being fired upon from somewhere. When he had emptied his clip, he jumped back outside to replace it, since he was alone in the hall with no one to cover him. In the meantime, two soldiers from his team entered the hall and began advancing through it, firing. They reached a room that had been used as a kitchen on the far side of the hall, and when they had finished spraying it with bullets, they found two dead Ugandan soldiers inside.

Shlomo entered the small hall as well. He belonged to a different team, Amnon's, which was assigned to the large hall, and he'd entered this room by mistake. He had known he was supposed to come through the door after the one Muki entered, and that's what he did. But Muki had gone through the second door of the large hall rather than the first, and Shlomo ended up in the next hall. Ilan Blumer, another soldier in Amnon's team, did the same thing.

Even when he was in the hall, Shlomo didn't realize he was in the wrong place. "What are you doing in our hall?" he asked Giora. And when he saw that the room was empty of hostages, he added, "They've probably moved them to the new terminal."

While he had been outside replacing his clip, Giora had noticed that the team after his, Danny Arditi's, was unable to penetrate the terminal through the entrance it had been assigned. Danny's group was supposed to storm the VIP lounge at the far end of the building, which had served as living quarters for the terrorists. It was the team that ran last in the assault force, and as Danny had run along the front of the building, he'd seen Yoni sprawled out on the ground, with someone else stopped next to him. Danny paused for a fraction of a second, but when he heard someone nearby yell "Keep going!" he continued with his team toward their entrance. When they reached the door, they found it locked, and had difficulty breaking it open. One of Danny's men tried throwing a grenade through a window, but it apparently hit the frame or a bar across the opening and bounced back, exploding nearby and lightly wounding one of the men in the leg. Giora, who had noticed a corridor leading from his hall to the terrorists' quarters, shouted to Danny that he could enter his wing of the building and clean it out.

Giora and Shlomo entered the corridor, taking turns advancing while throwing grenades and firing continuously. Behind them was Tamir, Yoni's communications man, who had been left with nothing to do after Yoni had been hit and had joined Giora's team. While they were in one of the rooms, two people with frightened looks appeared out of the smoke. Their hands were lifted a little, as though they had not yet decided whether to raise them or not. The two moved toward Giora and passed by him. Shlomo began calling out in a mixture of English, Hebrew, and Arabic: "Stop! Who are you?" They didn't respond, but kept moving.

"They're terrorists!" Giora shouted to Shlomo, jumping out of his possible line of fire. "Shoot them!" Giora was unable to fire himself without endangering Shlomo, who was standing close to the two. So he yelled to Shlomo again: "Shoot them!"

Shlomo, still under the mistaken impression that he was in the vicinity of the large hall, answered, "No, they're hostages!"

But as the pair passed him, Shlomo suddenly noticed a grenade clipped to one of their belts and realized who they were. Again, he ordered them to stop. When they kept moving away from him toward the door, he finally sprayed them with a burst of fire. As one of them fell, Shlomo saw the blue flash of a detonator. "Grenade!" he shouted, throwing himself to the floor of an alcove to one side and dragging down Tamir, who had been standing next to him. The grenade, which may have been hidden in the terrorist's hand, exploded, but apart from Shlomo getting a tiny piece of shrapnel in his lip, none of the Israelis were wounded.

From there, they went on to clean out the area around the bathrooms, which was still full of smoke from a grenade that someone from Danny's team had thrown in through a window. When the smoke cleared, it became evident that no one was inside. Searching back through the area they had already secured, they discovered the body of another terrorist in the corridor (Giora remembers there being two bodies). It is not entirely clear when he was killed, and by whose fire. Meanwhile, Danny's men had succeeded in breaking in through a narrow window and mopping up part of the wing. Danny was assisted by Amos Ben-Avraham, who had been in the large hall but had seen earlier that nothing remained to be done there and had looked for another place where he could be of assistance.

While this was happening on the ground floor, Yiftah Reicher and his team were carrying out their mission on the second floor. In the initial assault, when

Yiftah entered the first door of the building, he made sure that the other two members of his team were behind him; then, without waiting for his second team, under Arnon Epstein's command, he immediately began executing his assignment. The three men quickly cleaned out the customs hall, killing several Ugandan soldiers, went out the other side of the room, and climbed the stairs to the second floor. When Yiftah reached the top of the stairs, two Ugandans were headed toward him, but he opened fire first and killed them. At the beginning of the hallway they found the door to the platform overlooking the large hall, but it was sealed with a steel grill. Yiftah posted one of his men in the corridor to watch this door and the entrance to the second floor, while he and Rani Cohen, his other soldier, continued mopping up. The end of the corridor opened into a large room that had once been a restaurant and now served as living quarters for the Ugandan soldiers. The room was full of blankets and sleeping bags. Only two minutes earlier, Ugandans had been sleeping there, but now no one was to be seen. They'd apparently made a lightning escape, leaping from the second floor window to the area behind the terminal.

Yiftah and Rani suddenly spotted the silhouette of a person and fired on it. When they heard glass shattering, they realized they'd fired on their own reflections in a mirror, just like in the movies. Afterwards they quickly returned to the hallway, and from there climbed several steps onto a large balcony that was actually the roof of the customs hall. They briefly searched it with their flashlights, but didn't see anyone. Looking up, they could see the exchange of fire with the control tower.

When they returned to the hallway, Yiftah made radio contact with Arnon's team. Arnon's men were already outside again in the plaza, after having gone inside the building but had failed to locate the stairs to the second floor, over which they were supposed to stand guard. It's easy to understand why they'd missed it, since the layout of this wing had been almost completely unknown to the Unit. Only at the last moment, at Sharm al-Sheikh, shortly after he had found out about it, had Yoni told Yiftah that to reach the staircase they had to cross through the customs hall to the other side of the building.

While searching for the stairwell, Arnon and his team shot several Ugandan soldiers that they ran into in a side room which Yiftah had not had time to clear. After combing the customs hall area and failing to find the staircase, they'd gone back outside. They could see that there was fire coming from the control tower, and Bukhris and another member of Arnon's team began returning fire. They moved away from the front of the terminal so that they could shoot more effectively.

The covering force in the jeeps was also shooting at the tower. At first the men fired from where Yoni had ordered the cars to stop for the assault. Then they realized that they were in a poor position — from where they were, they couldn't hit anyone shooting from the other side of the tower into the entrance plaza — so they drove out into the plaza. The stubborn Ugandan soldier who was posted on the top floor of the tower continued shooting bursts throughout the entire operation, including the later stage when the hostages were being evacuated, and even afterwards. Fortunately, his fire was ineffective, in part because the counterfire kept him from aiming properly, and no one was hit.

Now, a minute or two after the rooms had been stormed, Bukhris and Arnon spotted someone lying on his stomach further down the front of the building. They realized it was a member of the Unit who had been hit, and shouted, "Someone's wounded here!" as they ran toward him. Arnon turned over the wounded soldier, and then, in the light of the plaza, they saw that it was Yoni. "Doctor!" they shouted. David, who had positioned himself as planned next to the main entrance to the large hall, turned his head in the direction of the shout. He saw the wounded man sprawled on the ground a few yards away and came immediately. David's rule was never to leave a wounded man where he had fallen, and he dragged Yoni, who was unconscious, closer to the building, behind a low wall. The new location, too, like the rest of the entrance plaza, was still exposed to fire from the control tower.

David heard Muki trying to raise Yoni on the radio. Right after the terrorists had been eliminated, someone had reported to Muki that Yoni had been hit, but Muki relates that he thought he heard Yoni himself calling him over the radio a few seconds later. He kept trying to call him back until David informed him on the radio that Yoni had been hit, and that he was treating him.

Yoni was very pale, and David noted other signs indicating massive blood loss. It was clear that Yoni was seriously wounded. He saw no blood on his clothing, other than on his right arm, where he had been hit in the elbow, and deduced that the hemorrhage was primarily internal. The doctor cut off Yoni's ammunition belt and shirt with a knife, with Arnon helping him. At first he found only the exit wound left by the bullet on his back, near his thoracic spine. In spite of the good lighting in the plaza, he had a very hard time finding the entry wound; finally, he discovered a small slit under the collar bone, on the right side of Yoni's chest. The bleeding, then, was in fact internal, and nothing could be done to stop it. David realized that Yoni's condition was almost hopeless.

Muki informed the entire force over the radio that Yoni had been hit and added that he was assuming command. Earlier, while the soldiers were still combing the large hall for more terrorists, one of the hostages, who had recovered from his initial shock, had come over to Muki. The smell of gunpowder and the sharp odor of blood from the dead and wounded filled the room. "You've gotten all the ones that were here in the hall," he said. "There are just a few more in the next wing."

Those few more were the ones that Giora's team, accidentally joined by Shlomo and Ilan, had already wiped out. After they'd finished securing what had been the terrorists' living quarters, Shlomo had helped care for the wounded man from Danny's team and Ilan had gone over to the large hall, to which he had been originally assigned. When Amir saw his friend coming through the door, he was overcome with joy. Not having seen Shlomo and Ilan, the other two members of his team, in the large hall, he had grown increasingly worried that they'd been hit on the way to the building in the first moments of the assault. Amir had already pictured the worst: that they were gone, just like the man from their squad who'd died in the Savoy Hotel rescue operation. Still, when Ilan appeared, Amir didn't allow himself a display of joy. Instead, he picked up the gun of the terrorist he'd killed, and as gunshots from Yiftah's team echoed from the second floor, he said with a big smile, "Look at this great new AK-47 I got myself."

Coming downstairs after securing the second floor, Yiftah ran into more Ugandan soldiers, and shot them. Outside again, he joined Arnon, who headed the second team under his command. Along with several of his men, Yiftah now began cleaning out the long corridor that ran between the customs hall and the large hall and opened onto the northern entrance plaza. All that had been known in advance about this corridor, which actually led to the inner area of the terminal complex, was the little that Halivni had told Yoni at Lod.

Bukhris remained crouched next to the building, ready to fire again if need be at the control tower, which was quiet for the moment. Suddenly he felt a tap on his back and heard a few mumbled words he did not understand. He turned his head and saw the barrel of a rifle only inches from his face. At first, confused by the mottled uniform, he thought the man holding the gun was from his own force. But when he saw black skin, he shouted, "Watch it, Arnon! There's somebody here!" The Ugandan leaning over Bukhris apparently still hadn't fully grasped what was going on around him. Perhaps he had gone over to Bukhris because he was confused himself by the uniforms and by Bukhris' swarthy skin, the darkest in the Israeli contingent. Arnon heard Bukhris shout, turned, saw the Ugandan with his rifle pointed at Bukhris' head, and shot him.

With that, the contingent of the Unit that had landed in Hercules One had finished securing the old terminal and the area around it. The immediate threat to the hostages and the troops had been eliminated, except for the potential hazard still posed by the control tower. The Unit's second task, assigned to its contingent in the four armored vehicles, was to provide peripheral defenses around the terminal. That force, under Shaul Mofaz's command, landed in the second and third planes, and arrived several minutes after the shooting began, as the assault group was mopping up in the building. Along with it, Shomron also arrived in his command jeep.

When the second plane touched down six minutes after the first, the runway lights were still lit. Mofaz saw them from the flight deck as the plane descended, and could also identify Yoni's vehicles moving toward the old terminal and could see the start of the shooting near the building. Biran was on the same plane, sitting in Shomron's jeep, and as the plane was making its descent, he was also looking out a window. "We're close to landing," Biran recounts. "The strip is nicely lit. I can see the airport over the right wing, and by the lights and other things, I can locate all the landmarks I've planned to look for beforehand. I know, that by the time we land, the force is supposed to be at the objective, and that if I see shooting there while we're coming in, it's a sign that the mission has been accomplished. If our forces are there, I'm not worried — somebody's dealing with the problem. It's right before we touch down, and sure enough, I see out the window that bullets are flying in the old terminal area, and I know this operation's already wrapped up. That is, the guts of the operation have already been carried out before we even got there."

Dan Shomron, along with Lt. Col. Haim Oren and three other officers from his forward command group, had arrived with the first plane, and until the second Hercules landed with their jeep, they waited near the new terminal. They had gotten off the first plane close to where the Unit's Mercedes and two jeeps had been put down. This was also where the main force of paratroops had deplaned to head for the new terminal on foot. The five officers remained alone in the open, near the access strip connecting the main runway to the diagonal one. During those minutes, as they awaited the arrival of their jeep and the first two APCs, the scene seemed surreal — senior Israeli officers standing next to each other in the darkness, in the middle of an airport in Africa, while an operation unfolded to which they were able to contribute virtually nothing. "Dan and I stood on the edge of the runway, with no one around. You had your Uzi, nothing else," says Haim. "I said, 'Dan, what are we doing here? The other planes haven't arrived, the Unit's already cleared out, and we're standing here at the end of the runway. . . .' " The sound of the Unit's run-in with the Ugandan sentries could now be heard in the distance, and Haim suggested to Shomron, "Let's move up landing the other planes." But Hercules Two was already about to touch down.

After the plane landed, Nati taxied it towards the set deplaning point farther down the runway. From inside the hold, Biran could see an airport pickup truck driving on the left. It had left the airport's fire station and begun driving alongside the plane, on a service road parallel to the runway, with the light on its roof flashing. When the plane reached the turn onto the connecting strip where the forces were to deplane, the lights on the Ugandan vehicle suddenly went out. The next moment, perhaps as a result of a message from the vehicle to the control tower, all of the lighting in the area went out in three quick stages — the landing lights on the principal runways, the lights along the access road to the new terminal, and the lights in the parking area for planes — as though someone had flipped three switches. The lights went out just as the third Hercules was making its final approach and preparing to put down. For the pilot, before whose eyes the runway lights abruptly vanished, it was as if the ground had disappeared from under his feet. He skipped about half a mile forward in the air, toward the two short rows of faint lights that had been positioned earlier by the paratroops. Using these, he was able to land safely, albeit with a resounding bang.

Meanwhile, Nati brought Hercules Two to a stop on the connecting strip where Yoni and his men had put down earlier. Shomron's jeep and the two APCs quickly rolled off the plane. Biran hurriedly assembled the antenna for the jeep's radio, and Lt. Col. Moshe Shapira from the Infantry and Paratroops Command, who was serving as driver, picked up Shomron and the other four officers where they were waiting nearby.

The command jeep joined Shaul's two APCs and headed for the old terminal area. Not far behind was the second pair of APCs, under Udi's command, which had landed in the third plane. Shaul moved as fast as possible, having seen from the air that shooting had broken out even before the assault force had reached the terminal and fearing that the operation had run into trouble. When he reached the plaza in front of the old terminal, he saw the hijacked airliner standing there. The presence of the plane here surprised the Unit, since, according to the latest intelligence reports, it was positioned at the end of the diagonal runway. In fact, the gunmen had ordered Captain Baccos to move it earlier that day, possibly in anticipation of the press conference they planned for the next morning to celebrate Israeli capitulation to their demands. Shaul positioned his APC next to the Air France plane, tried to make radio contact with Yoni, and was told Yoni had been wounded. Inside the terminal, the assault force had almost finished mopping up.[18] "There were still some shots here and there," says Biran, who arrived at the same time in Shomron's jeep, which parked under the control tower.

Shaul saw some Ugandans running past but didn't bother shooting, since the plan said his force should not fire at soldiers trying to escape from the area around the building. For the moment there was no fire coming from the tower; soon after, when the shooting from the tower erupted again, Muki ordered Shaul to keep the soldier up in the tower pinned down. Shaul deployed in front of the tower, lit it up with a floodlight on the APC, and poured machine gun and RPG fire on it.

"We fired everything we had," says Danny Dagan. "Even though I was the driver, I grabbed my AK-47 and shot every chance I got, because I felt like I had to do something. I'd get an order: 'Danny, forward!' or 'Back up!' and I'd put my gun down and drive. And in between, I was shooting the whole time." Shaul's fire was directed mainly by Alik, who'd stayed at the position he was meant to take as part of Yoni's command team, in front of the terminal.

The second APC of Shaul's pair passed close to the terminal. Omer, the commander, tried calling Yoni on the radio to see if he needed help; when he got no reply, he continued according to plan toward the Ugandan army base and the Migs.

When the other two APCs, which were responsible for the defenses north of the building, reached the terminal area, they turned left into a compound that had belonged to Shell Oil. From there, they were supposed to find their way into the open stretch on the building's north, which had once been the entrance area for people arriving at the terminal from Entebbe on the old road. When the men in the APCs found a fence blocking their way, they doubled back toward the control tower to look for another way through. They could see the Mercedes in front of them, its doors thrown open and its engine running. They turned left again, and after a few attempts, managed to find their way onto the north side. In the process they fired on some Ugandan soldiers who appeared to them to constitute a threat. They also fired on the generator that supplied electricity to the terminal, knocking out most of the lights in the terminal itself and the area around it. At last they deployed in front of the gate where the road from Entebbe entered the terminal area. As planned, they began calling loudly to anyone who might be in the vicinity to come to them, in case some of the hostages had fled there in panic during the battle. From there they spotted Yiftah and a few of his men, who were combing the area, and the two groups shouted to each other to avoid friendly fire. After that Yiftah cut back through the building to its south side, where the freed hostages and the rest of the assault force were located.

In the meantime, Muki went out to check on Yoni's situation, then returned to the large hall to begin organizing the evacuation of the hostages. Alik asked the doctor about Yoni's condition, and David replied grimly that it looked very bad. Earlier, when David had just begun treating Yoni, Alik had warned him, "If you don't take care of him right, you'll have to settle the score with me." Alik had no idea how David, who was new to the Unit, would perform under fire, and thought that saying this might increase Yoni's chances of getting proper care. Alik now entered the large hall and offered to relieve Muki there, in order to free him to take charge of the rest of the operation. Instead, Muki asked that Alik go to the fourth Hercules plane, which had landed by now, and which was to carry the hostages home. He wanted the plane moved closer to the terminal, perhaps having been told by radio that it had parked farther away than planned.

Alik took Ilan with him, and the two began walking toward the diagonal runway. For a moment fire rained down on them from the control tower, and they pressed themselves against the wall of the building. A few steps farther along, next to the tower, they ran into Shomron and, in response to his agitated questioning, explained where they were going. Then they walked away from the terminal along the access road, only 20 minutes after they'd raced down it in the opposite direction after meeting the Ugandan sentries. They asked over the radio that the Golani contingent guarding the plane be told they were coming so they wouldn't be fired on by accident. The two men walked carefully, guns at ready, on guard in case a Ugandan soldier leapt out at them from the high grass. On the way, Alik told his partner that Yoni had been wounded in the chest.

As they passed the point where they'd clashed with the sentries, they saw the body of one of the Ugandans sprawled on the asphalt. After a short walk, they reached the plane and the Golani troops spread out around it. The job of the 16 Golani officers and men was to serve as a reserve force and to help evacuate the hostages. Alik and Ilan told the pilot to pull closer to the terminal, and headed back to the building.

By the time they got back, Yoni had been evacuated. Before he was moved, Dr. David Hasin had dressed the wounds on his chest with vaseline gauze and bandages, mostly to mark them for the doctors who would treat him on the plane. Without the help of the medic whom Yoni had taken off the mission roster at Lod, there was little more David could do, and he preferred in any case to move Yoni quickly to the plane, where there would at least be some chance, however slight, of saving him.

The blood continued to flow from his veins, and with it Yoni's life was ebbing away. Yet a last spark remained. When David and Arnon were loading him onto the stretcher, "he regained semi-consciousness," David recalls. "Apparently his soldier's reflexes were stirred. There was tremendous shooting at the tower, which made a lot of noise, and he tried to get up."[19]

Shaul walked over from his nearby APC to the entrance plaza to help organize the evacuation and saw Yoni being treated. Danny Dagan, who had asked him to take the first opportunity to check on Yoni's condition, got back a faulty report third-hand via another soldier that Yoni was "moderately" wounded.

David asked Shaul to call over one of the jeeps from the covering-fire team to evacuate Yoni. Hostages had already begun to gather outside, and some of them jumped into the jeep to be taken to the plane. After a brief exchange of words, the hostages got out and Yoni was lifted up on the stretcher and put in their place. Rami, commander of the covering force, drove the jeep to the plane. David couldn't go with Yoni himself since he'd begun treating other wounded. The drive was very short. On the way Rami heard Yoni mumble something he couldn't make out.

The medical team from the fourth Hercules had spread out on the runway about 50 yards from the plane. The doctors and medics had begun preparing to receive the wounded the minute the rear gate of the plane had opened. Now they saw a jeep approach, drive past them, and stop at the plane itself. The members of the resuscitation team — two doctors and a senior medic — ran from their position to the ramp of the plane, and began right there to treat the soldier who'd been brought to them. Acting automatically, they administered CPR, with Yoni's ammo vest still hanging on one shoulder. Dr. Eran Dolev, the head of the plane's medical team, rushed over, and saw that the wounded man was Yoni — and that he'd suffered near-total blood loss.

The central venous line was in place and blood was being pumped in, but to no avail. Yoni had passed the point of no return. After a while the two resuscitation-team doctors looked at each other, knowing there was no hope.

"There's nothing we can do here. . . ." one said to Eran.

"Keep working! It's Yoni!" he answered.

As the hostages had begun emerging from the hall, another burst of fire had come from the tower. Shaul's APC had responded with heavy fire once more and silenced the tower again. The evacuation resumed, with Shomron pushing the men to work as quickly as possible and wrap up the mission. Most of the hostages were still in shock and had not so much as uttered a word. Muki instructed them to leave their belongings and begin to evacuate the hall. Most did as they were told and hurried outside through the two doors. But some refused to part with their luggage and carried it with them. One even went back inside the hall to collect his duty-free bags. From where Rani was crouching at the doorway of the customs hall, he could see the freed hostages pass on their way to the plane. Most of the lights in the area had gone out when the generator was hit, but the huge flames leaping from the Migs at the nearby air base, along with the light from mattresses set afire by bullets, allowed everyone to see what was happening. Rani could not help but be amazed by the way hostages doggedly insisted on bringing their bags with them. Amos Ben-Avraham, who was assigned to counting the hostages, told Muki that there was no way he could provide an accurate number.

The hostages were shuttled to the plane on the jeeps. Occasionally they quarreled over spots on the Land Rovers, but for the most part they remained orderly. Despite the terrible crowding, though, some insisted on pulling their suitcases onto the jeeps. "Muki shouted at them to leave the bags, but when he turned his head they picked them up again," recounts one soldier. "What mattered to them most at that moment was the bags."[20] Amitzur remembers driving a "pile of people" to the Hercules. His gun had been shoved somewhere under them, so that he wouldn't have been able to use it even if he had needed to.

Inside the hall, Amnon called Amir over to explain something in English to a pair of hostages — in fact, the pilot of the Air France plane, Capt. Michel Baccos, and the French flight engineer. Amir told them the procedure to follow, as set in the briefings before the operation: Leave everything, put on your shoes, and go to one of the exits, from which you'll be taken to the plane.

But the flight engineer couldn't find his shoes. "He looked around, lifted the mattresses, picked up the blankets, and just couldn't find them. It was dark, there was noise and shooting, and the poor guy was sure we were going to leave him behind," recalls Amir. "Then somebody told me they were bringing the plane closer . . . so I said to him: 'Forget the shoes, just go to the door.' "

He did — but a soldier standing at the doorway saw him approach barefoot and told him to go back and put his shoes on. The flight engineer went over to Amir again.

"Even at the time I could see how funny the whole thing was. I was just 22, and he was a flight engineer on an airliner, responsible for 300 people. And he says to me, like a kid talking to his kindergarten teacher, 'But he told me to put on my shoes!' "

Finally the farce ended. The flight engineer found his shoes somewhere and proceeded to the plane, properly shod.

When only a few hostages remained in the hall, Amnon again called Amir over and asked him to talk to another hostage who didn't speak Hebrew. "She was a young woman, maybe one of the stewardesses, without much clothing on because it was very hot there at night. She said to me in English, 'I'm wounded.' I asked her to show me where she'd been hit, and she showed me a small wound from a ricochet. 'It's nothing,' I told her, 'You can walk.' 'No,' she said, 'I'm wounded somewhere else.' 'Where?' 'Here,' she said. She pointed to her inner thigh, but refused to show me what was wrong. A battle was raging a second before, but what mattered to her was that I wasn't supposed to look. So I looked anyway, without her permission, and said to her, 'It's just another ricochet, and it's nothing. You can walk. We can't carry out everybody who feels like being carried. Please go to the door. It'll be okay.' "

But the woman reacted hysterically, "almost went into a coma," as Amir puts it, and refused to stand. In the end, Amnon ran out of patience. "Come on, just get her out of here," he told Amir.

"I threw her over my shoulder, like in the movies: the heroic soldier carrying the girl out in her slip in the middle of the night. I went outside, and suddenly a bullet flew by my head. It was the only time in my life that I heard one whistle by close like that, and it was really scary. I made a quick calculation: If it was some soldier who ran 300 yards away and was shooting from there, then it was just luck that the first bullet had come so close, and the next one would be ten feet off. But if they were shooting from the tower, 30 yards away, then the next bullet would be in my head. I said to myself, *I'm not going to die because of her stupid stubbornness.* I pulled her around so that, if they shot again, she'd take the bullet. The funny thing was that I saw her later on TV, and she said, 'Everyone had forgotten me, except for one soldier, a hero, who saved me and carried me out.' "

Through all this, Omer and his men had been alone on their APC near the Ugandan military base. When they'd arrived, the area had been absolutely quiet.

Omer had thrown on the APC's floodlight, swept the area with it, and spotted the Migs they'd been told to expect. The planes were lined up in two rows, five Mig-21s to the south, and three Mig-17s to north. When Omer saw that the operation was going as planned and that the evacuation of the hostages was beginning, he asked Shaul's permission to open fire on the Migs, as Yoni had instructed him to do at Sharm al-Sheikh. "Wait," said Shaul, "I'll find out if you can shoot."

Shaul tried to raise Shomron, but the radio link with him was very poor. Just at that time, Yekutiel Adam was informing Shomron from the airborne command center that the Migs should be destroyed. Amnon, who picked up the order on the radio, passed it on to Haim, who conveyed it to Shomron. Shomron, though, told them he was busy with the evacuation, and not to bother him about the Migs right then.

So Omer, ironically, got no answer — and decided by himself to destroy the planes, since he knew from Yoni that there had been a decision in principle to hit them. He strafed the Migs with machine gun fire, one after another, punching holes in them from one end to the other. Two or three exploded, producing gigantic flames that lit up the entire area. Shomron, who saw what was happening from a distance and could not understand why Omer's men were shooting at the planes, succeeded in getting Shaul on the radio and asked him about it. Shaul was at a loss what to answer. But Adam's order had been carried out, even if it had not exactly gone down the proper chain of command.

The first hostages reached the Hercules transport shortly after Yoni did. The medical team was still working on resuscitating Yoni by the ramp of the plane, and the dazed hostages trampled past them on their way into the hold. But that minor disturbance no longer made a difference in Yoni's condition. The two doctors stopped their efforts. Yoni had slipped from life, and there was no way to bring him back. His body was brought up to the front of the plane. There it was laid on a stretcher and covered with an aluminum medic's blanket.

The entire airport had already been secured, including the area of the main runway, from which Hercules Four would take off in a few minutes with the freed hostages.

The new terminal, which dominated the runway, had been taken by the paratroops at the outset of the operation. They had deplaned from Hercules

One on foot, immediately after Yoni's Mercedes and two jeeps had left, and advanced a short way toward the new terminal, coming to a halt in the wet grass some distance from the building. From there they could make out the Unit's three vehicles heading toward the old terminal, until they finally disappeared from sight. The paratroopers spread out facing the building, prepared to respond if they were fired upon, and waiting tensely for the distant shots that would herald the beginning of the action at the old terminal. That would be their signal to charge into the new terminal. The structure was well lit inside and out, and the plaza in front of the entrance appeared completely deserted. Vilna'i, the commander of the force, spotted an external staircase near the entrance and pointed out to one of his officers that he should climb it to the roof when the assault began.

The sound of gunfire, from the Unit's skirmish with the sentries, was heard, and the paratroopers began running toward the new terminal building. Surin didn't bother waiting for his team's commander — the officer to whom Vilna'i had just spoken — but rushed inside the main hall with the other soldiers. Surin's team had been assigned to go up to the roof of the building; not knowing about the order to use the outside staircase, he searched the hall for the stairs leading to the top of the building. Several Ugandan civilians, looking extremely surprised, sat watching silently, without interfering with what was happening around them. Nehemia, Surin's battalion commander, sent several men to the second floor, and Surin went with them.

They found the floor nearly deserted. Through a wide window, Surin saw the members of his own team climbing the external staircase to the roof. There was no way of reaching the stairs from the second floor, and his friends signaled from the other side of the window that he should go outside and come around to join them. When Surin came out the main doors of the building, he saw Matan Vilna'i standing there and heard the distant sound of gunfire from the old terminal. Until now, everything had been quiet in the new terminal; not a shot had been fired. Any civilians who tried to escape were caught and brought inside the main hall where the rest were being held. As per orders, Surin had cocked the Israeli-made Galil rifle slung from his neck, but had left the safety on. The order to leave safeties on had been given because here, in the new terminal, it was expected that the soldiers would run into civilians and probably not encounter any soldiers. Surin rushed to the external stairs at the corner of the building, intending to catch up with the rest of his team, and climbed them at a run. The staircase was built around a square column, so that for someone going up one side, the column partially hid the next side.

As Surin reached the level of the second floor, he suddenly found two Ugandans, a man in police uniform and a woman, coming down the stairs toward him. The man immediately aimed his pistol at Surin and, without hesitating a moment, fired twice at a range of barely three feet. The first bullet missed, but the second hit Surin in the neck. The couple continued fleeing down the stairs as Surin crumpled on the steps. Because the encounter was so sudden and the safety of his Galil was still on — itself a sign that he hadn't expected to use his weapon — Surin never had a real chance of firing first. The Ugandan's two shots were the only ones fired at the new terminal, but for Surin they marked the start of a life sentence.

When he heard the gunshots, Matan Vilna'i rushed up the stairs with the doctor from his command team, apparently after the Ugandans had already escaped. The first thing they saw was the Galil lying on the stairs. A few steps further on they found Surin sprawled on the staircase, blood running from his neck and staining the floor.

Surin was fully conscious but unable to speak. When he realized that he also couldn't move his hands or legs, he understood that the bullet had hit his spinal cord. But he did not yet grasp how severe the injury was, or that it was permanent. Only later would it become clear that the price the operation had exacted from him was higher than almost any that can be paid.

Between the old terminal and the Hercules, the Land Rovers continued shuttling back and forth, carrying hostages to the plane. The Golani force's Peugeot pickup was also pressed into service, and several Golani soldiers came to help out with the evacuation.

Dr. Ephraim Sneh, the chief medical officer of the Infantry and Paratroops Command, and the Golani force's doctor also arrived at the terminal. The Golani doctor joined David in treating the wounded in the entrance plaza. David recalls finding it extremely hard to concentrate on what he was doing — not because of the tension of battle, but because of the deafening bombardment of the control tower by the cover force.

By then, some of the hostages had set off for the plane on foot in several groups, escorted by members of the assault force and Shaul's APC. On the way, Shaul was careful to keep the APC's floodlight trained on the tower, hoping to keep the Ugandan soldier there from lifting his head and shooting at the hostages.

When one of the groups of hostages neared the plane, Amnon, who had led them, pointed at it and said, "There it is." Without another word spoken, they took off and ran toward the plane. Golani troops were fanned out on either side of the rear gate to funnel panicky hostages into the hold and keep them from running into the tall grass.

As the Hercules quickly filled with hostages, the Golani men tried to count them, as they'd been told to do. After Michel Baccos came aboard, he saw Yoni's body, wrapped in the aluminum blanket. "Who's that?" Baccos asked a soldier. "One of the officers," he replied. "He's dead."

The freed hostages, crowded into the belly of the Hercules, stood in silence. Perhaps only now did they grasp that they were leaving the hell they had entered a week before when their plane was seized over the Mediterranean. During that week, many had come to accept that their end might be drawing near. Yitzhak David, who 31 years earlier had been rotting in a Nazi concentration camp, now lay wounded in the hold of the Israeli plane. Freed from his new deathtrap, he would be flying to safety within minutes. At the time he didn't know that only a few feet separated him from the body of the man who had commanded his rescue.

The stretchers were arranged in two tiers, fastened with straps to the walls of the plane. On one lay the body of Jean-Jacques Maimoni, a hostage who had been fatally wounded when he jumped to his feet during the assault, and on another, above him, lay that of Ida Borokovitch, hit by a bullet in the heart. On the upper tier on the left was the soldier from the Unit who'd been lightly wounded in the leg. Another stretcher held Pasco Cohen, who had been hit in the pelvis. When David had treated him outside the large hall, he had still been fully conscious, and after Cohen was transferred to the evacuation plane, the medical team had even succeeded in stabilizing his condition somewhat. But it later deteriorated, and the doctors were unable to save him.

One of the freed hostages, Ilan Har-Tuv, came over to Dr. Dolev and said that he didn't know whether he should fly home or stay at Entebbe. "My mother was taken to Kampala Hospital yesterday after a piece of meat got stuck in her throat," said an extremely worried Har-Tuv. "Maybe I should stay to make sure she's safe."

"If you stay," Dolev told him, "they'll kill you for sure. But an elderly woman like your mother has a good chance of being left alive." Dolev was wrong, at least on the second count. Hours later, on the morning after the raid, Idi Amin's soldiers took Har-Tuv's mother, Dora Bloch, from her hospital room and killed her in cold blood. She was 75 years old.

Freed hostages and casualties filled the plane, and the pilot, Halivni, who wanted to clear out as quickly as possible, asked his load master to report how many of the hostages were on board. The man replied that all the hostages were on the plane, but Halivni insisted that he give him the number on board in writing. The load master wrote on a slip of paper, which was then handed to Halivni, that there were 93 hostages and the bodies of 2 more on board. Halivni asked for a more specific report, including the names of the dead, since, according to the figures he had received, there were supposed to be 106 hostages at Entebbe. Now the man listed, on the other side of the paper, the names of those who had been killed: Ida Borokovitch and Jean-Jacques Maimoni, and at the bottom of the list a third name: Lt. Col. Yoni. Even after repeated counts by the Golani men, the number of those on board didn't line up with the number of known hostages. But the hostages themselves were convinced — correctly — that all 106 hostages, except Dora Bloch, were on the plane.

Halivni stood up from his seat for the first time since leaving Sharm al-Sheikh and went to the rear of the plane to see the hostages and casualties. On the top tier of the stretchers lay the wounded soldier from the Unit — the only member of the Unit's assault force who returned alive on the same plane as the hostages. After the first few minutes of the action, the hostages had not gotten a chance to see the others. Halivni laid his hand on the wounded man's shoulder. The hostages were packed in front of him, most sitting, a few standing, all with eyes staring into space. Amid the hostages were scattered the Golani men, the medical team, and members of the air force crew. Because of the crowding, Halivni could move only a few feet farther along the wall of the plane. The silence was almost complete.

Halivni was immediately able to identify Michel Baccos because of his white uniform and pilot's insignia, and he gestured to Baccos to come over to him.

"You're the Air France pilot?" Halivni asked in broken French.

"Yes."

"Is your whole crew here?"

"Yes. But what about my passengers?"

"They're all here," Halivni told him, "except for Dora Bloch. We have to take off right away."

Halivni spoke briefly with some of the passengers, including Uzi Davidson, who had served with him in the reserves, and then returned to the flight deck and asked permission to take off. From the flight deck, he could still see bursts of gunfire from the exchanges with the control tower, and could only hope that none of the bullets would reach his plane. "We're sitting there, with the engines running, and tracers are flying in all directions," recalls Halivni. "And what's a plane, after all? It's a mass of tubes and wires and cables, and anything can happen to it. And this one thought went through my head: God help Israel — let the plane go without being hit."

Halivni received the go-ahead for takeoff. Twenty-six minutes after he had stopped the plane near the old terminal, minutes that had seemed to him like an eternity, Hercules Four pulled away, leaving the shooting behind. Halivni rolled down the diagonal landing strip to the main runway, turned onto it, and began to speed south. The plane quickly passed the new terminal and rose into the air over Lake Victoria. It was 11:52 p.m., Israel time. Only 51 minutes after the first plane had landed, the hostages were on their way to freedom. Halivni quickly cut east, towards the Kenyan border. Within a short while, the plane was far from Entebbe, and far from any real danger.

After the old terminal had been combed thoroughly, and Muki had verified that there were no more hostages in it, the withdrawal of the Unit's assault force began. One of Shlomo's jobs was to make sure that no one from the force was left behind. In his hand was a list of all the names, written on a piece of cardboard. He stood on one of the jeeps, and began reading the names aloud. When a soldier responded, he put a mark by his name.

"Yoni Netanyahu," called Shlomo when he reached the middle of the list, and waited for an answer.

"He was wounded," someone called out. "They took him to the plane with the hostages."

Only then did Shlomo recall what he had suppressed from his consciousness for the past hour — how he'd seen Yoni sink to the ground in front of him during the assault. Shlomo continued calling out names.

When the roll call was over, the assault force drove to the parking area before the new terminal, where the other three planes waited. There they boarded Hercules One, which had brought them to Entebbe.

Until then, Shani and his crew had remained seated on the flight deck, with flak jackets and helmets on. In the other two planes the crews had also remained sitting. All three planes had arrived at the parking area before the terminal early in the operation, but only after running into some trouble that almost ended in disaster. After landing and letting the force deplane, Shani had rolled down the taxiway toward the parking area. Suddenly, he came to an unexpected turn. According to the diagram in the Jeppesen guide, the taxiway was supposed to lead directly to the parking area at the new terminal, without turns. The lights on the runways had already been turned off, and in the darkness it was extremely hard to make out where the taxiway led. Shani and Einstein stopped the plane for a moment so that they could examine the dark ground before them. Nati, who had landed by then and was taxiing along the same route a short distance behind them, did not know that they had been held up. Suddenly he saw the silhouette of an aircraft fill his windshield, and he quickly jammed on the brakes. When his plane came to a stop, its nose was only a few yards away from the tail of Shani's plane. In the end, Shani and Einstein succeeded in identifying the correct route and continued taxiing to the parking area. Nati followed, as did Aryeh, the pilot of the third plane.

The air crews waited impatiently for any word of how the operation had gone. The ridge of the hill on which the new terminal stood hid the old terminal from view, but through the windows they could see tracers flying at a distance. "My feelings were grim," says Einstein. "Within a very short time, tremendous amounts of fire began spewing from there. I'd never seen anything like it. I'd expected a few bullets at most. Now I was sure a catastrophe was unfolding." In fact, the battle for the control of the building had already been won, and the tracers the pilots saw came from the exchanges with the control tower and from shooting by the Unit's peripheral defense force.

In the meantime, the refueling team had connected the pump to one of the fuel ducts scattered around the parking area. It had taken a while, but in the end the team members reported that they were ready to start pumping fuel into the planes. Just then, though, word arrived from the airborne command headquarters that approval had been received to land in the Kenyan capital of Nairobi and refuel there. So it was decided to do without refueling at Entebbe, especially since filling all four planes' tanks with one pump would take hours.

From the parking area, the crews of the three planes could see the silhouette of Hercules Four lift off the ground with the hostages on board. "That was the climax," says Shani, "because it was clear the operation had succeeded. Of course problems, at least minor ones, could still crop up, but we'd know how to take care of them. The essential thing was that the civilians for whom we'd performed the raid were free."[21]

Nearby, the airmen noticed, another Hercules was parked, not one of theirs. It was Idi Amin's plane. Only a few hours earlier it had brought him back from the Organization of African Unity summit meeting in Mauritius, where Amin had been greeted ceremoniously by U.N. Secretary General Kurt Waldheim. The air force men decided that if one of the Israeli Hercules were hit, they'd take Amin's plane in its place. Between them, they divided up the tasks involved in taking control of the plane and flying it.

The Unit's peripheral defense forces began pulling out. Shaul Mofaz ordered the APCs to leapfrog toward the planes, with one pair covering the other's retreat and tossing smoke grenades behind. As they withdrew, Omer scattered explosives that had been prepared at the Unit's base. They were set to go off about 15 minutes later, to keep the Ugandans from approaching the area by the new terminal where the forces were gathering at the planes.

Now, though, an order came from Yekutiel Adam to Shaul to check the Air France jet parked in front of the old terminal and make sure there were no hostages on it. The Golani soldiers' count of the hostages on the evacuation plane was still less than the number known to have been in the terminal, raising doubts about whether everyone had really been evacuated. Shaul left Udi's APCs standing guard, and headed back with his pair, carefully skirting the explosives already on the asphalt.

To the north Shaul saw the headlights of a pair of vehicles approaching on the old road from Entebbe, apparently carrying the company of reinforcements posted in Entebbe. It's likely that they had no idea what was causing the commotion at the airport. The first vehicle began blinking its lights on and off. Shaul positioned his APC on the access road facing the Ugandan force, switched off his lights, and waited for it to come closer. When the vehicles came within about 200 yards, he opened fire. The lights on the Ugandan vehicles went out, either because they'd been hit or simply because they'd been fired on, and the Ugandans stopped abruptly.

Suddenly, the shooting from the control tower began again. Shaul's men fired back, silencing the tower as they moved toward the Air France plane. When they reached it, Omer climbed up the stairs positioned outside the plane, and shone a light through the windows. It seemed absolutely empty. Shomron passed Shaul an order from Yekutiel Adam not to enter the plane, in case it was booby-trapped. He also ordered him to fall back to where the Hercules were parked after he finished inspecting the airliner.

Hercules One had already taken off, at 12:12 a.m., Israel time. During the withdrawal and the takeoff of the first two planes, the air crews were informed that a Ugandan combat jeep, equipped with a small recoilless artillery piece, had been spotted and destroyed on a hill south of the new terminal. It couldn't be ruled out that other such vehicles were in the area. There wasn't much the air force men could do about this, of course, other than hope that no one tried to shoot at them. The jeep had been discovered by a group of six paratroop commandos, whose assignment had been to seize the new control tower and then secure the surrounding area. After leaving Hercules One, along with the four commandos responsible for putting the back-up lights on the runway, the six had headed for the tower. On their way from the runway to the hill where it stood, they had run into a steep incline, which they'd been forced to climb with a rope. From the top they had spotted the empty combat jeep and tossed a grenade into it. When they'd reached the new control tower, they'd found it dark and deserted.

Hercules Three, carrying Udi's APCs, now stood ready for takeoff on the main runway. Nati, on board Hercules Two, was still waiting in the parking area for Shaul's pair of APCs to arrive. Worried about being left alone at the airport with no way to get his men out if he were hit or a problem developed with the plane, Nati had delayed Hercules Three's departure until he was also ready to take off. Finally, the second pair of APCs arrived and rolled onto Nati's plane. Standing outside, Biran transmitted the final report from Shomron's command jeep, informing the airborne command center that he was cutting off contact, and took down the antenna so the jeep could be loaded onto the plane. The jeep, and with it the last of the Israelis at Entebbe, drove up the ramp and onto the plane.

Now, with everyone on board, Hercules Two left the parking plaza of the new terminal and turned toward the main runway. It was pitch dark outside, and Nati almost drove into a ditch by the side of the taxiway. But the plane managed to reach the runway safely, where it joined Hercules Three. The two planes took off, one after the other. It was 12:40 a.m. when the last Israeli plane rose into the air, an hour and 39 minutes after the first plane had landed at Entebbe. Those who looked back at the ground below could see the flames still leaping from the burning Migs and the two glimmering rows of portable lights, all that testified to the existence of the otherwise darkened airport.

Aboard Hercules One, now flying toward Kenya, the Unit's men and the paratroop commandos were seated again. The men from the Unit knew Yoni had been wounded. Most were not yet aware of how serious the injury had been, and none knew that he was dead.

Surin had been placed in the center of the plane, on a stretcher laid across two seats of a jeep. Both David and the doctor from the paratroops treated him and tried to lift his spirits. One of the doctors told him how successful the operation had been, and about how few casualties there were. It would be several weeks until Surin's ability to speak returned. Unable to respond, he nevertheless understood what he heard and regretted only that he had spoiled the operation's impressive statistics.

It was quiet on the plane. As usual after a successful mission, there was no immediate rejoicing, only a sense of released tension, and perhaps even a kind of emptiness. Here and there soldiers exchanged a few words.

After about an hour, Hercules One landed in Nairobi. The talk on the plane had gradually grown freer as the men began recounting various parts of the operation among themselves. They were ordered not to leave the plane, but when the rear gate opened, several soldiers went outside anyway and stood by the side of the Hercules. Around the planes were posted armed Kenyan soldiers. For the first time since leaving Sharm al-Sheikh about ten hours earlier, Shani shut down the engines of the Hercules.

End of Battle and Evacuation

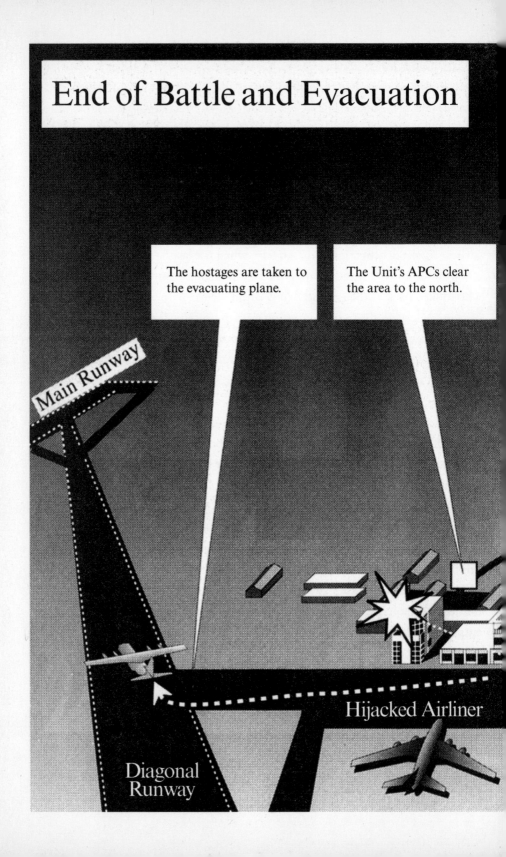

The hostages are taken to the evacuating plane.

The Unit's APCs clear the area to the north.

Main Runway

Diagonal Runway

Hijacked Airliner

Entebbe

e Unit's soldiers finish
ring the building of
andan soldiers and evacuate
hostages to the plane.

An APC of the Unit blocks
the approach from the military
base and destroys the Migs.

Military
Base

An APC of the Unit fires
on the control tower and
on reinforcements
coming from Entebbe.

Military
Runway

After a little while, the Unit's men were joined by Ehud Barak, who had been sent to Kenya on Friday, and Shai Avital, the officer who had fought by Yoni's side on the Golan Heights during the Yom Kippur War and was now stationed in Kenya as an IDF advisor. The two had been waiting in Nairobi and had already been to the hostages' plane, which had landed first, and confirmed what they'd heard earlier — Yoni was dead. "I pulled back the blanket covering his body," says Ehud, "and I saw the white face, pale, strikingly handsome — Yoni's face."[22]

On board Hercules One, Ehud now stood among the men of the Unit, about to tell them of Yoni's death.

"On the plane there'd already been endless chatter, everyone telling his stories about what had happened to him," says one of the soldiers. "It seemed that everything was going great, that we'd succeeded. And then someone came in and said that Yoni had died . . . that he was gone. All at once, it was as if someone had turned off the entire plane. Everybody went silent. . . . We were hit hard, and each of us withdrew into himself."[23]

Danny Dagan sat outside on the wheel of another plane, crying softly.

Amos Goren was sitting with his eyes closed in the front passenger seat of the Mercedes, trying to get some sleep. He didn't know of Yoni's death. When Ehud came and saw him sitting there, he said, "Do you know you're sitting in Yoni's seat?"

"Yes," Amos answered, not knowing why Ehud was asking.

Ehud apparently now noticed the puzzled look in Amos' eyes. "He's dead," he told him.

Matan Vilna'i left Hercules One, and went over to the hostages' plane to see the people for whom the operation had been carried out. "I saw Yoni's body lying in the plane, wrapped in one of those awful aluminum blankets the doctors have. I saw the hostages inside, and they were completely stunned, shadows of men. They were very depressed. And what hit me then was this kind of a feeling that was, for an army man like me, totally illogical — that if Yoni was dead, then the whole thing wasn't worth it."

Surin and the other wounded were transferred to an airborne hospital that had landed in Nairobi during the night. It was an air force Boeing 707, loaded with all the equipment needed to set up a field operating room. Some of the women and children among the hostages were also moved to the Boeing jet to save them the long flight back to Israel aboard the turboprop transports. Pasco Cohen was rushed to the operating room in Nairobi Hospital, but two hours after the operation, he died. Yitzhak David was taken to Nairobi Hospital as well, and after surgery he was out of danger.

The stopover in Nairobi was short. Yekutiel Adam, whose airborne command center had landed at the same time as the hostages' plane, ordered that the stay in Nairobi be kept as brief as possible, and that the planes take off again for Israel the moment they were refueled. Hercules Four, which had been the first to land in Nairobi, was also the first to depart, at 2:00 a.m., Israel time, carrying the freed hostages and the bodies of the dead. The other three planes took off one after another, each making its own way to Israel, without trying to stay in formation.

In Chief of Staff Gur's office in the Kiryah, radio equipment had been set up, and there and in Defense Minister Peres' neighboring office, cabinet members and senior officers tensely followed reports from the airborne command center. When word came through that the hostages had left Entebbe, and then that the entire force was over Kenyan territory, tremendous relief was felt in the two rooms. The gamble — in which the stakes included not only the lives of the hostages and soldiers, but also the future of many of those in the room — had paid off. At midnight, just after the hostages left Entebbe, Gur phoned Peres in the office next door to tell him the operation had succeeded. Everyone in Peres' office went over to Gur's room.

A report also came in that Yoni had been wounded. "They said to me, 'You hear? Yoni's been hit,' " says Ben-Gal. "I knew there was another soldier named Yoni in the Unit, and I said, 'Yes, but it's not the big Yoni, it's probably the little Yoni.' Everyone was running around, worried, very upset. . . . For some reason, I was sure it wasn't the Yoni I knew, and I kept saying, 'It's the little Yoni. It's not our Yoni.' "

When the planes left Kenya, though, there was still no report of any dead among the Israeli forces. "When the last plane took off from Nairobi," says Rachel, Gur's secretary, "there was this wave of rejoicing. The chief of staff's driver brought in a few bottles of champagne from somewhere, and everyone celebrated. In the end, they left. It got quiet, and Motta was left alone in the room with Hagai

Regev. I went to the kitchen to make some coffee. Suddenly, the other secretaries came over, grabbed me and said, 'Yoni's been killed.' It was clear which Yoni they meant. I dropped everything and went to the chief of staff's office. I opened the door of the room I'd left two minutes before, when it had been full of happiness over the success, one that hadn't even involved casualties . . . and I saw the chief of staff sitting, face fallen, terribly sad. Not to mention Hagai, who was just crushed. In one minute, all the joy had been erased. . . . It was as though nothing else mattered. Everything took on different proportions."

It was Ehud who had notified Gur, by phone from Nairobi. Gur went over to Peres' room, where the defense minister had lain down to rest. "He got up to open the door," says Gur. "When he heard, he was in complete shock. First of all, it took him by surprise because we'd already celebrated, not knowing about Yoni's death. Second, I could see he was taking it personally. He said, 'My God,' or something like that, and took it very hard — not like a defense minister hearing about an officer who's been hit."

In his diary, Peres wrote, "At four in the morning, Motta Gur came into my office, and I could tell he was very upset. 'Shimon, Yoni's gone. A bullet hit him in the heart. Apparently, it came from the control tower. . . .'* This is the first time this whole crazy week," Peres wrote, "that I cannot hold back the tears."

Avi was at the Unit's base. During the day, after attending the pressing meeting for which he'd stayed behind, he'd gone to an intelligence base and followed the operation from there until one in the morning, when the news came that the last plane had left Entebbe. Then he drove to the Unit in Yoni's car. Instead of going to sleep in his room, he lay down in his office, to be near the phone. At 4:00 a.m., it rang and woke him. The officer at the other end told him that Yoni had been badly wounded, and that it wasn't clear what condition he was in. A few minutes later, another call came from the same man, saying that Yoni was dead.

Dazed, Avi walked out of the office. Outside, the first faint streaks of dawn showed in the sky; all was silent. Avi crossed the drill area to the switchboard room.

The Unit's secretaries, unable to sleep, had stayed up by the switchboard the entire night. They knew Avi had just been on the phone.

---

* Actually, in all likelihood, Yoni was not hit by fire from the control tower. See endnote 14.

"What's going on, Avi?" they asked when they saw his face.

When he told them Yoni had been killed, they burst into tears.

Instead of driving to the airport himself, as he and Yoni had agreed he would, Avi stayed at the Unit and arranged to have vehicles sent to pick up the returning soldiers. "It was sad. The fact that Yoni wasn't going to come back made the operation — I don't want to say a failure — but turned it into something else, making it very hard to define as either a success or a failure," says Avi. "The objective had certainly been achieved, but even though no one had thought it could be done without casualties, nobody had expected that along with success, the mission would bring us Yoni's death. It was just unacceptable. Everybody's life is precious, but there's no getting around that it's different when the commander of the Unit, the one who led the force, is the one who was killed."

The flight back to Israel lasted many hours. Aboard Hercules Four, the freed hostages sat almost without moving, without getting up, hardly even going to the lavatory. At the front of the plane lay the bodies of the dead, which probably contributed no small amount to the gloom that settled on those who'd just been given back their freedom. Moreover, the shock of everything they'd been through had not yet worn off. After several hours in the air, one of the women raised her hand. Dr. Sneh went over to her. From underneath herself she took something she'd been sitting on until then, and Sneh saw she was handing him a bandolier of mini-grenades. He guessed that the belt had fallen from Yoni's stretcher when it was being moved to the front of the plane. Several of the pockets were open, so that the grenades could be quickly pulled out and used. But none was actually empty.

Michel Baccos sat up front on the flight deck, at Halivni's invitation. Thinking of the dead he'd seen, he felt little happiness over his release.

Halivni had gathered from the few words he'd exchanged with the hostages that they held Baccos in high regard, and during the flight he thanked him for the way he and his crew had related to them.

"I don't understand what you're thanking me for," Baccos responded. "It's my job to take care of the passengers. I don't expect any thanks for that."

Aboard Hercules One, some of the men from the assault force and the paratroop contingent slept. Others sat quietly, absorbed in their thoughts, and a few talked among themselves from time to time, mostly about what had happened during the action. There were those, too, who freely expressed their happiness to have succeeded and to be on their way home, safe and sound. Dr. Hasin sat by himself, his face filled with sadness over what he'd seen, and over his own failure to defeat death despite all his efforts. His mind refused to rest even for a moment, refused to put everything behind him. Again and again, he went over the steps he'd taken to treat the wounded. Had he done everything necessary, everything possible, he asked himself.

During the flight, the crew members turned on the radio to pass the time — and were amazed to hear a report on Israel Army Radio about the raid on Entebbe. They reacted angrily, since they had yet to make the long journey above the narrow band of international water between Egypt and Saudi Arabia, during which they would be completely defenseless against any bid to intercept them. Later, when the soldiers and crew heard Idi Amin's announcement that he had "reconquered" Entebbe airport, they broke out laughing.

Early in the morning, the Israeli Phantom jets that were to escort the transports home appeared before them. It was a welcome sight for the members of the squadron, to all intents and purposes marking the end of the operation for them.

Only after they reached Israeli airspace did the hostages begin to show any signs of recovery and rejoicing. At 9:43 a.m., their plane landed at Tel Nof Air Force Base. Dr. Dolev disembarked holding Yoni's ammo vest, which he had stashed behind Yoni's stretcher while still at Entebbe. He looked for someone from the Unit to whom he could hand it, and found Amiram Levine who, it would turn out, would replace Yoni as commander of the Unit. Later, when Amiram reached the Unit, he would extract from the vest a flattened AK-47 round from the burst that had taken Yoni's life.

The hostages were taken to a briefing, at which they were asked not to tell the media anything about how the rescue had been executed. Afterwards, they returned to the Hercules and flew to Lod, where a huge reception awaited them. As the crowd sang, danced, and waved flags, the hostages descended from the plane, surrounded on all sides by reporters and photographers. Halivni waited with his crew on the plane until the hostages dispersed, and with them the cameras. Then they too emerged from the plane. Outside, Halivni ran into Foreign Minister Yigal Allon.

"The sun is shining, the flowers are blooming," Halivni began to recite from Hayyim Nahman Bialik's classic Hebrew poem, "In the City of Carnage," about the helplessness of Jews during the brutal 1903 Kishinev pogrom and the world's indifference to their plight. But instead of reciting the next line, "And the butcher has slaughtered," Halivni pointed and said, "And the flag of Israel flies above."

Allon began to weep.

The other planes landed at Tel Nof. Shani came back from the flight deck and walked toward the door on the side of the plane. "We had more or less the same people on board, sitting the same way as when we'd set out, except reversed, with the Mercedes facing forward. The first person to come aboard the plane when we landed was Rabin, looking very agitated. I was the first person Rabin talked to, and the first question he asked me was, 'Where's Yoni?' He wanted to see the body for himself."

The Unit's men left the plane. When Muki came out, Peres turned to him and asked, "How was Yoni killed?"

"He went first, he fell first," Muki answered, without elaborating.[24]

There was a great commotion outside, and Danny Dagan said to Amitzur, "Come on, let's get out of here. Let's take the Mercedes and go." Amitzur drove, with others from the Unit crowded in the back. When he reached the base, Amitzur parked the Mercedes and turned off the engine. Later, when they would try to start it again, the starter would not respond, despite repeated efforts. Danny got out of the car, and saw Brig. Gen. Avraham Arnan, the Unit's founder, who had been waiting at the base for them. Arnan asked Danny to tell him how it happened that Yoni had been killed. Danny related what little he knew: that at Entebbe he had received a report, passed on from Shaul, that Yoni had been moderately wounded, whereas later he heard that he died on the plane. "The two facts just don't fit," said Danny. Just at that moment Dr. Hasin arrived and passed by them, crestfallen. Avraham and Danny went over to the infirmary, where they found the doctor unpacking his equipment and putting it away. As though unable to accept that Yoni, whom he'd loved, was dead, Arnan began interrogating David, thinking that perhaps he had not done everything he could have to save Yoni, or had made some error. David, grim-faced, explained that he had never reported that Yoni was moderately wounded — that he had understood immediately that his commander's condition was critical and had done what he thought was necessary. After several minutes, Arnan's questions ended. The death of the man he'd fought to have appointed commander of the Unit, and whom he'd seen as continuing his mission, was an incontrovertible fact.

"What Avraham did," Yoni once said of Arnan, "was something absolutely unique. To take the initiative and build a new unit, of a kind that had never existed before, to build it from scratch in spite of all the immense difficulties, is an accomplishment that few things can rival." Now, Arnan left the infirmary with a heavy heart. He walked along the paths of the base, the place where he had chosen, years ago, to build his unit. It had been his pride and joy, and his attachment to it never wavered. That evening he would drive to Jerusalem to meet with me. From my apartment he went to our parents' house. A year earlier, Yoni had offered to let him live in the house, which was empty while our parents were abroad. Arnan had accepted. The street, Haportzim, was named for the battalion that had captured the neighborhood in the 1948 War of Independence. Arnan, then only 17, had served in that battalion. Now 45, Arnan knew he was suffering from an incurable illness and that his own life was drawing to an end.

The officers and men were filled with contradictory feelings — satisfaction over their momentous achievement and their returning home, and sorrow over the loss of the commander who had led them to Entebbe. The event was still fresh, and deeper thoughts would come to most of them only days or years later.

"When we reached the base, I wasn't the slightest bit happy," says Amos Goren. "Those of us at the Unit were completely removed from the whole festival that followed the operation, and removed from all the publicity. . . . What I, and many others, felt was hollowness."

In one of the rooms in the cluster of offices, some of the support staff had gathered. Through the open door, they could see the returning soldiers climbing out of the APCs. Naturally, some of the men were quite happy. Then one of their officers arrived and announced, "The commander's gone." The men were speechless. Among them was Avi R., the mechanic who had repaired the alternator of the Mercedes on Friday. Like many other members of the support staff, he had known Yoni for years.

"Yoni liked me a lot, and I don't really know why," says Avi. "Once when he was deputy commander of the Unit, I came into the mess hall after having stayed up late working. There was this wild group of drivers that we had then, and they were sitting around one of the tables. I sat down at the table behind theirs. Yoni was there in the mess hall, too, at the officers' table. No one else was around. I was eating my supper, and the drivers started throwing olives at me, into my plate. 'Come on, enough,' I said. It didn't help. I warned them, 'Once more, and I'm dumping this plate on you.' They kept it up, so I took the plate, with everything on it, and threw it at them. One of them deflected it, and it fell to the floor and broke.

"I went outside. After a few minutes, Yoni came out, too. He said to me, 'Come here, Avi, I want to talk to you,' and he took me aside. 'You shouldn't behave that way, throwing plates around,' he said. He spoke in a very quiet tone, not scolding at all, but in a way that was meant to teach you something. With Yoni, everything was done with a human touch. 'Go to the supply room,' he said in the end, 'and sign for a 1065.' I went over there, and of course they laughed at me. 'A 1065? You want to sign for a plate? Get out of here.' "

Now, Avi was brokenhearted. Looking outside, he couldn't fathom the joy being shown by some of the men returning from Entebbe. Within the room there was silence. The members of the support staff — the drivers, the cooks, the mechanics — hung their heads. At that moment, an officer passed by the door, and what he said to them as he went by increased Avi's pain tenfold. "What's all the mourning?" he called out. "So what, another one bites the dust." Then he continued on his way.

Toward evening, when the officers and soldiers were about to go home, the Unit's new commander, Amiram Levine, handed Amitzur a pouch from Yoni's ammo vest, full of grenades. One or two had been punctured by bullets from the burst that had hit Yoni at Entebbe, and had to be exploded. Amitzur took a demolition block and went out into an open field. The cloth model of the old terminal that the soldiers had stormed the previous day under Yoni's direction had already been dismantled. The setting summer sun cast its waning light on the nearby buildings, the trees, the asphalt of the base. Amitzur dug a small pit in the hard earth, put the pouch in it, and placed the demolition block next to it. Moving back, he unrolled the detonation wire. He stopped a safe distance away and crouched.

When he squeezed the detonator, the block exploded. A small cloud of smoke arose, and with it came the loud blast of the exploding grenades, which only the night before, during the assault at Entebbe, had hugged Yoni's body as he went into battle.

Endnotes

1. Gur's estimate of possible casualties is from Y. Ben-Porat, E. Haber, and Z. Schiff, *Flight 139* (Jerusalem: Zmora, Bitan, Modan, 1976), p. 291.
2. Lt. Col. Haim Oren, interview.
3. Jonathan Netanyahu, *The Letters of Jonathan Netanyahu* (Jerusalem-New York: Gefen, 2001).
4. IDF Radio, "To Entebbe and Back."
5. Personal interview with Shani, and IDF Radio, "To Entebbe and Back."
6. IDF Radio, "Special Broadcast in Memory of Lt. Col. Jonathan Netanyahu."
7. Among those interviewed who make this point are Rani Cohen, Amitzur Kafri, Eyal Yardemai, Amir Ofer, Ilan Blumer, Yiftah Reicher, Giora Zusman, and Amos Goren. Additionally, almost everyone who was interviewed describes the guard's actions as threatening. There is no basis to claims made that guard did not threaten the convoy, or even saluted it, or that the guards were not standing in the path of the convoy.
8. This is where the vehicles stopped (next to the control tower) according to Amitzur Kafri, Amir Ofer, and others.
9. There is no basis to an assertion made that the planned point of disembarkation from the vehicles was opposite the terminal entrances. Amir Ofer, Shlomo Reiseman, and Amos Goren point to the gap between the control tower and the terminal as the planned stopping point. Others point to a spot slightly nearer (from the direction of travel) either underneath the tower itself or just before it. In any case, according to the diagram Yoni drew Amos on the plane (see picture), it is obvious that the planned point for stopping the vehicles was not opposite the terminal entrances but well before that.
10. Amnon Biran, on the basis of what he heard from the debriefings of the hostages.
11. Nearly all those of the assault force who were interviewed relate how Muki Betser stopped for a reason unknown to them and how Yoni shouted to run forward. Those who point out where he stopped indicate that it occurred at the corner of the building. Nearly all of the men say that Yoni's shouts of "Forward" were directed primarily at Muki. There are also definitive eyewitness accounts (including Yiftah Reicher's written report following the action) that Muki shot bursts *after* he had stopped. Some of the eyewitness accounts describing the delay in the assault were cited in Iddo Netanyahu, "The Battle for the Truth," *Ma'ariv*, July 19, 1991.
12. Arnon Epstein, interview, summing up what was said in the debriefing at the Unit after the operation. His description is similar to that of Shlomo Reisman, who says, "The force stalled and Yoni pulled all of us forward." (*Yoni*, documentary film, Israel, 2001, dir. Semion Vimokur). There are other eyewitness reports of Yoni bypassing Muki, such as Yiftah Reicher's written report following the action (July 1976) and Tamir's interview

with IDF Radio researcher Danny Veseli (July 1976), in which Tamir recounts: "Muki and Yoni were out in front. Muki [then] went aside to take care of something, so Yoni went on forward. I was behind him." See also p. 168 (Goren).

13. Yiftah's written report after the operation.

14. There is little basis to the widely accepted view that Yoni was hit by fire from the control tower — even though the Ugandan soldier who was positioned there was later decorated by Idi Amin for supposedly having killed the Israeli commander. A bullet that lodged in Yoni's ammo vest was from an AK-47; the terrorists and the Unit's men were using such guns, while the Ugandan troops at the airport were seen to have been armed with weapons of a different make. Moreover, the doctors who examined Yoni's body agree that the bullet entered from the front — as is also indicated by Yoni's ammo vest — while the control tower was directly behind him. Those who were at Entebbe concur that Yoni fell while running forward, away from the tower. The direction of the wound could indicate that the fire came from the building — possibly from a terrorist inside the hall who shot out. Moreover, Yoni was opposite the wide windows of the hall at the moment he was hit.

15. This assessment is based on analysis of information provided in interviews by Dr. David Hasin, Bukhris, Amos Goren, and Shlomo Reisman; and Tamir, quoted by IDF Radio, "Special Broadcast in Memory of Lt. Col. Jonathan Netanyahu."

16. There is no apparent basis to the claim that has been made that Muki Betser did not go into his entrance because it was "blocked" or "non-existent." In his written report immediately following the raid, Muki stated that he "bypassed by mistake" his assigned entrance. Furthermore, Amir Ofer says, "That door was there . . . [and] was not blocked. I know that for a fact . . . it was merely closed. [When the fighting was over] people exited through it."

17. The claim that Muki Betser participated in killing the fourth terrorist in the large hall is, in all likelihood, erroneous. Such an action was not witnessed by the other participants, and careful review of Muki's varied and conflicting accounts of the liquidation of the terrorists in the large hall leads one to the conclusion that such an event did not take place. (Similarly unconfirmed are the claims that Muki killed a Ugandan soldier while the force made its way from the vehicles to the building or that he participated in killing other terrorists.) As to the claim made by Muki that Amos, Amir, and Amnon fired, together with Muki, on the hostage Jean Jacques Maimoni and killed him — such a claim is erroneous. Amos, Amir, and Amnon did not participate in this incident.

18. Shaul Mofaz and Ilan Blumer, interviews.

19. IDF Radio, "Special Broadcast in Memory of Lt. Col. Jonathan Netanyahu."

20. Ilan Blumer, interview.

21. IDF Radio, "To Entebbe and Back."

22. Israel Television, "Now Is the Time," May 12, 1986.

23. Shlomo Reisman, interview.

24. Shimon Peres, *Entebbe Diary* (Jerusalem: Eidanim, 1991).

On the Golan Heights, 1974

CHAPTER VIII

We're on board an Air Kenya plane flying westward over Lake Victoria in the early afternoon toward Entebbe Airport. Below, I can make out many small islands, which in the dark of night 13 years earlier were invisible from inside the Hercules transports. Most of the jungle-covered islands are uninhabited; on a few I can see round straw huts thinly scattered along the beaches or in clearings in the woods.

Africa.

I look away from the window, and the same old thought hits me again: Why didn't I go to the Unit's base at the beginning of that week, when they phoned me and said to stay close to home and be ready to be called up? Could I, in spite of everything, have ended up on one of the Hercules? The thought is futile. Yoni would never have taken me. And besides, hadn't I smiled when I heard the message on the phone? Just more nonsense, I thought at the time.

Bibi sits on the left side of the plane, a little farther forward; Noa, his 11-year-old daughter, sits directly across from me on the other side of the aisle. For the moment, each of us is lost in his own thoughts. The plane will land in a few minutes, and I press my face against the window on the right-hand side, expecting at any moment to see the airport.

"There it is," Bibi calls out suddenly. I rush to his side of the plane and take the seat behind him. The plane circles over the town of Entebbe, and instead of landing from the south, as the Hercules did and as I expected us to do, it will come in from the north. Over there is the new terminal, on an elongated hill. And there, further to the east, is the old terminal, below the town. Even though I knew how close the houses of the town were to the old terminal, I'm taken aback for a moment. We identify the landmarks almost automatically, without any connection to the feelings that take hold of us. We approach the main runway. To its left we see the diagonal runway leading toward the military base. Everything is just where it should be, just as it was 13 years before.

The plane lands, and the old terminal disappears from sight. The new terminal and the big white letters reading "Entebbe" on the grassy slope next to it shoot by us. The plane slows down, turns, and taxies northward. It passes below the sharp escarpment that the paratroop commandos had such a hard time climbing. Now I can see why the commandos hit the escarpment here, at the most difficult spot, for the tower stands above it, on the highest point of the ridge. Finally, the plane comes to a stop in the parking area, next to the fuel lines.

We go down the stairs. Bibi is here as the guest of the new president of Uganda, but there doesn't seem to be anyone waiting on the ground to greet us. As we approach the huge entrance to the passenger hall, I spot a Ugandan soldier in camouflage fatigues holding out a white piece of paper. On it, handwritten in big block letters, is the word "Yoni." This is our reception.

The soldier leads us through the terminal to a small office with a large photograph of the president in uniform on one wall. It's the third or fourth such picture that we've seen since entering the terminal, and it's not hard to guess what kind of regime Uganda has. We wait a long time in the stifling heat of the office for the president's aide to rescue us. When the two soldiers responsible for us leave the room for a moment, Bibi takes the piece of paper that greeted us from the table as a souvenir.

When the president's aide finally arrives, he takes us to the VIP lounge. Everyone in Uganda knows the name "Yoni," the aide says when we ask about the piece of paper. I can't tell whether he expects me to take his comment literally. I look through the windows and say to Bibi, "Those are Surin's stairs. . . ." I want to go outside to photograph them, but refrain; it's not the appropriate time. I'll do it later, I tell myself, not knowing that the next day, when I ask permission, I'll be told not to. The Ugandans escorting us notice where we're looking. "Yes, this is where your soldier was wounded, on these stairs," one says. Thirteen years have passed, and yet they know even this detail. They say it matter-of-factly. But why not? They have no idea who Surin is. How would they know how deeply he has suffered, or how remarkable a man he is?

I'm sitting with Noa in the open tent where the president receives guests. The slope, covered with grass and flowers, overlooks Lake Victoria. With us is the president's aide, an affable man who speaks fluent English. Bibi is in the palace at the top of the hill, immersed in a long conversation with the president. It's dusk, and my mind tries to absorb what my eyes have seen in the hours we've been here — especially during the visit to the old terminal. As I chat with the aide and sip my tea, I try to reconstruct what I've seen, while the images are still fresh and still race through my mind: the half-ruined, neglected, filthy terminal, with its shattered windows, partially collapsed roof, and walls pockmarked with bullet holes. It's impossible to say which holes are ours and which the result of the fighting in this country in the years since Operation Jonathan. There's no sign of the foot-high brick wall in the entrance plaza, behind which Yoni was taken after he was wounded.

"I hadn't imagined it was so large," Bibi said as we stood outside. "Thirty men to take control of a building like this, with lots of rooms, and in a few minutes," he was astonished.

"This is the place," I told Bibi, pointing out where Yoni was hit. Bibi responded only by looking down, as if he were trying to carve the look of the spot of asphalt into his memory. I asked him to stay where he was, on the spot where Yoni was wounded, while I stood in the large hall, close to the second entrance.

Yes, a burst of fire from here could easily have hit him.

But when we climbed to the top of the tower, and saw how completely it dominated the plaza, we said to each other, "But maybe he was shot from here after all. . . ." But no, that seems impossible. A bullet coming from here could not have hit him where it did.

Operation Jonathan has become a legend here, almost a tourist attraction. Driving to the old terminal, our Ugandan escorts tried to tell us the story of "Entebbe" and describe the operation as though we were regular tourists. After we had gotten into their Mercedes, they had trouble finding the way out of the new terminal parking area to the runways leading to the old terminal, and I gave them directions. After all, I've studied the diagrams well. Yet a couple of minutes later, one of our hosts, who was sitting in the front of the Mercedes, asked us genially, "Do you know the story?" The car had just turned left from the diagonal runway. "We'll go from here," he said as he drove us east along the access road, straight towards the control tower, "but the Israelis came from over there, from the south." It was obvious that he did not believe us when we explained that the Israeli force had come exactly the same way we were driving. He already knew what happened. As always, what's told first takes on a power of its own, whether it's true or not.

A pilot who had served in Idi Amin's air force had come with us. "What does it mean when a sentry lifts his rifle and points it at you?" we asked him and the president's aide.

"Halt, or I'll shoot," they answered in unison.

"The Russians were very angry with us the morning after your raid, you know," the pilot took the opportunity to tell us. "Their ambassador asked us angrily, 'Why did you hold the hostages at the airport instead of taking them to Kampala?'"

Now we're flying back to Kenya, aboard Uganda's only civilian plane. As on the way to Uganda, each of us is lost in his own thoughts. I think about the beautiful land I've just left and about how ruined it is — in part because of neglect, but mostly because of deliberate inhumanity. And in fact, the barbarity of human beings never stops, and no one has suffered as much from it as have the Jews. How terribly important, how right it is, to stand up to it; how humane and just was the rescue mission to Entebbe, a mission undertaken in the face a hostile, uncaring, destructive world. "What an insane world we live in!" Yoni had cried out on paper in response to the slaughter in Biafra and to the world's indifference. But at Entebbe something had been done. And Yoni, as ever, or perhaps more than ever, understood the purpose toward which his actions and his life had been directed.

I think about the sadness that took hold of Yoni during the last months of his life — no doubt related, at least in part, to what he saw around him, at the Unit and outside it. Sooner or later, that's the fate of anyone like Yoni: the inevitable clash between the extraordinary individual and the surroundings that oppose him and that he cannot accept.

And I can't help thinking about his last moments. Did he know the operation was about to succeed completely, that the hostages were going to be saved? Did he realize that his men indeed understood what needed to be done, and would act in an exemplary way, just as he'd told them they would? Or had he noticed that some things had gone awry, and assumed that the operation might fail? He had surely been able to see, a second before he was hit, that the team assigned to the first door of the large hall was running past it. Maybe at that moment he turned to the left for a split-second, and that was when he was hit, perhaps by one of the terrorists' shots? But he probably also saw that Amir and Amnon were running straight for the second door. Did he understand that within two or three seconds they would be inside the hall?

To these painful questions, I know I'll never have answers. If he had only been wounded ten seconds later, after all the terrorists in the large hall had been eliminated, after the work of his entire adult life had come to a climax, had borne fruit . . . but it wasn't to be.

If there's any consolation in Yoni's death at that time, it's that the dejection of those last months was erased in one stroke by the preparations for the operation, which gave him the opportunity to show his full stature as a leader and soldier.

I think with a sad smile about those who say that at Entebbe Yoni reached the height of his abilities. Who knows better than I what he could have achieved. Entebbe wasn't all of what Yoni had in him. It was just one example.

If there's any other consolation for Yoni's death, anything else that can ease the pain, it's in the realm of ideas. What, I ask myself, will be remembered from all this? I don't know the answer, but I think of what the African-American leader, Bayard Rustin, said on a visit to Israel: "I am certain that for years and years to come, perhaps even a thousand years from now, when people are confused and frightened, and they are dispossessed of their humanity and feel that there is no way to go except to face death and destruction, someone will remember the story of Yoni at Entebbe. That story will be told to those despairing people, and someone will move into a corner and begin to whisper, and that will be the beginning of their liberation."[1]

Uganda is behind me; the plane is approaching Nairobi airport. I think to myself, *Of all the nations in the world, there is no other, at least in this generation, that would have done what we did at Entebbe.* I say "we" because the operation belonged to the whole people — to the government, which came from the people and was chosen by it, and dared to make the decision; to the IDF, a true citizens' army, which gave its all to carry out the mission; and to the boy from Jerusalem named Amir — and others like him — who, to save the innocent people within that hall, charged right into the line of the German terrorist's fire and killed him.

I think about Operation Jonathan, and about the Jewish nation, which has nurtured the world with its ideas and its deeds for thousands of years. And I know: In this people, there is still boundless ability and strength.

Endnotes
1. Benjamin Netanyahu, ed., *International Terrorism: Challenge and Response* (Jerusalem: The Jonathan Institute, 1980), p. 201.

PUBLISHER'S AFTERWORD

*Keep the faculty of effort alive in you by a little
gratuitous exercise every day. Be systematically
ascetic or heroic in little unnecessary points. Do
every day or two something for no other reason than
that you would rather not do it, so that when the
hour of dire needs draws nigh, it may find you not
unnerved and untrained to stand the test.*

— William James (1842-1910)

In the cool shade of Jerusalem pine and cypress, a grave that is indistinguishable from the thousands of others at Israel's Mount Herzl military cemetery is ringed with small stones. They are stones of remembrance, placed there by people stopping to pay their respects at this sacred spot in Israel's capital city.

This is the resting place of a modern man said to be "the greatest fighter Israel has ever had." He fought for his people all his adult life, but his final battle, at a remote African airport called Entebbe, placed him in a rarified pantheon of defenders.

Jonathan (Yoni) Netanyahu, as expressed by the novelist Herman Wouk, "died for his people and for all men, in the full flush of manhood, doing a famous deed." The spectacular raid on Entebbe signaled a paradigm shift in the war on terror, because it took the fight to vicious killers of men, women, and children.

Entebbe is so critical to understanding our own war on terrorism, launched September 11, 2001, by our enemies, that this book must have the widest possible audience. It presents remarkable insight into the minds, emotions, and agendas of men who are willing to lay down their own lives, in order to save others.

In the spring of 2003, at the edges of Saddam Hussein's hometown of Tikrit, an American corporal awaited orders to move in for what commanders thought would be the final major battle in the war with Iraq. Louis Gubitosi thumbed through his Bible and recalled a passage he had read the day before: "Greater love hath no man than this, that a man lay down his life for his friends" (John 15:13).

"I think about that a lot," Gubitosi said.

It is a sentiment that transcends time and battles and wars. It was the thing that sent Yoni to Entebbe.

In a sublime flash-moment of time, determined Israeli commandos exited rescue planes under cover of darkness. Like the heroes of today's Afghanistan and Iraq, they were common boys and men from average homes. They undertook a mission so dangerous — even absurd — that only a Hollywood writer could possibly be optimistic about its outcome. Yet in minutes, the thing was over. A hundred hostages were free, the millennia-old Jewish bond was flush with a victory of biblical proportions, and a terrorist strategy was devastated.

Because terrorism is now part of all our lives, Entebbe is always fresh. There is a repetitive quality about it, for whenever American Marines hunt down religious radicals determined to kill the innocent, members of Sayeret Matkal are emerging from Hercules transports. Whenever Al Quaida and fedayeen "fighters" are rooted out, Yoni is shouting at his men to run, very quickly, to the terminal building housing terrorists and their captives.

Iddo Netanyahu, once also a member of the Unit, who took part in the Yom Kippur War and commando operations himself, is, like all who think about Entebbe, in a state of wonder even as he retells this story for the ages. Iddo, his beloved mother, Cela, his father, Benzion, a champion and pioneer for Zion, and another brother, Benjamin, whose own actions as prime minister and prescient writings about terrorism were validated in the gruesome World Trade Center murders . . . all knew the man, Jonathan.

Through the sacrifice of this family, a grateful audience trying to grapple with the modern evil of terrorism can understand the degree of courage required of civilizations that refuse to bow to terrorism. Once, Americans felt safe and secure, between the oceans. Now, we know what our allies abroad have known for a very long time: vigilance and action are the parents of security. We understand this, just as Yoni and his friends grasped it. Terror has an agenda, and we must be aware.

This *jihad* — an ideology that now everyone from Pentagon chiefs to soccer moms struggle to understand — targets the innocent. It is a fight to the death. From Entebbe to now, during America's new policy of preemptive strikes, this fight is in process.

Terrorists die so that other people can die. Yoni died so that other people could live.

* * *

Jonathan Netanyahu was tired the last week of his life. There are hints of this in his last letters. In fact, he was in a state close to exhaustion. Indeed, this exhaustion made his last, Samson-like burst of strength all the more remarkable.

For a handful of days in the summer of 1976, "Yoni" became a flesh-and-blood definition of perseverance. He pushed on and pushed himself relentlessly because he knew his people were in danger. Yet when people read Yoni's story, invariably the question of "why" takes center stage. Intellectually, we understand it. The citizens of the Jewish state were fighting, and continue to fight, against people determined to blot out the name of Israel. Yoni and his men were intimately aware of this.

This, then, at least in part explains the perseverance. Yoni would not let Entebbe go. Because he refused to loosen his grip, one hundred people had much longer lives. The person who lays down his life for a noble purpose is, can we say, from a higher root. His belief in the possibility of this rescue, and his own willingness to sacrifice himself for it are at the heart of its success.

Yoni and the men of the rescue force accomplished a great deed through their perseverance. It was big. Epic. They accomplished their goal, but with a tragic personal price. The larger lesson, though, is how the example of Entebbe can show the way to citizens of the modern world.

One of the definitions of perseverance is "The ability and will to keep going when most people would say its okay to quit." To persevere — as Yoni did — is to push on and achieve the seemingly impossible. This is a lifestyle that Israelis have had to live with for over 50 years. Since 9/11, Americans are beginning to understand this lifestyle as well.

The world is a dangerous place. Some credible commentators even speculate that civilization itself is at risk, because, of course, there are those evil men and women whose ideology is rooted in death and destruction.

It is not an exaggeration to say that now, even suburban Americans have to be concerned with contingency plans for terror attacks on schools. Beat cops in cities must now be on the lookout for criminals of a different sort. In short, we are all in this together. In a real sense, the lessons from this book teach us many things, not the least of which is fortitude for a long haul — and the recognition that sometimes victory will come at a personal cost. The terrorists have shown a willingness to wait a long time, years if necessary.

Surviving such a set of circumstances requires steady nerves and, above all, long-term commitment. America understands this, post-9/11. But what about us as individuals? How do we endure the daily trials that bombard us on a smaller, more personal scale?

Again, it is the example of the "citizen army" of Israel that is the key to endurance.

The small story of Shimon Peres calling Yoni into his office for one purpose: to look in his eyes and see any glint of resolve . . . not only made Entebbe possible, it tells us that in the real world (and not just in the world of ideas), men make life-and-death decisions with no regard to their personal safety.

What did Peres see in Yoni's expression? He saw an opportunity, as the author has already stated, that "a deed might be done that would be remembered for generations." He saw that Yoni was willing to expose himself to danger, for a greater good. He embodied the motto of the officers of the Israel Defense Forces: "After me!" The leader is always out front.

While Yoni's eyes were clear and alive with determination, in some mysterious way, it was determined that the "eyes of the wicked shall fail, and they shall not escape" (Job 11:20), and indeed, twilight and the element of surprise closed the eyes of the hijackers at the fateful moment.

For the secular reader, the story in this book is stirring, fascinating. For readers of the Book, the tale of Entebbe throbs with the pulse of ancient glories; it is biblical.

A quarter-century after Entebbe, American and other Western democracies push on in the battle against terrorists. When it would have been easier in the short term to let policy and strategy drift, leaders have taken decisive action. We draw strength from those who have gone before us.

What do we do then, with this, this memory of boundless courage and stirring self-sacrifice?

Well, we contrast the differences between those who give all to preserve life, and those bent on taking it. At a time when Israel is criticized by the international community for fighting terror, we are glad to illuminate the character and valor of the Jewish spirit. Read for yourself and decide who is committed to the ideals of freedom. Israel: this small nation that was willing to take on an impossibly dangerous mission.

It is our privilege to publish the story of the brave men who went to Entebbe. To Yiftah, Amir, Joshua (yes, Joshua!), Amos, and the rest of your fellow soldiers . . . thank you. We salute you all.

— The Publisher